D1055334

A NOVEL

13-digit ISBN: 978-0-8054-3293-0
10-digit ISBN: 0-8054-3293-0

Published by Broadman & Holman Publishers,
Nashville, Tennessee

Dewey Decimal Classification: F
Subject Headings: MYSTERY FICTION \ JOURNALISM—FICTION

1 2 3 4 5 6 7 8 9 10 09 08 07 06 05

Qi

A NOVEL

BEST-SELLING AUTHOR
DAVID AIKMAN

BROADMAN & HOLMAN
PUBLISHERS

NASHVILLE, TENNESSEE

This book is affectionately dedicated, with permission,
to the memory of Murray J. Gart (1924–2004),
chief of correspondents of *TIME* Magazine 1969–1978,
outstanding journalist, mentor, and the best boss I ever had.

Chapter One

*I*t can't be. Not at this hour."

But it was. Twittering maddeningly just beyond my grasp—I'd left it on the dresser instead of on the bedside table before turning off the light only a few hours ago—the latest in fashionably slim cell phones was demanding my attention.

"Oh, stop. Please be a wrong number," I muttered, burrowing my head deeper into the pillow.

But it wasn't. Somehow a shred of the instincts of professionalism—or was it just plain old fear?—triumphed over my irritation. I propped myself up on one arm and lunged toward the maddening noise.

"Richard Ireton," I said as I tried to clear my head of the cottony stupor of jet-lagged sleep.

The voice on the other end was level, confident, almost drawling. "Look, I'm sorry to get you up after your long plane trip, Richard, but this is important."

"Go ahead, Burt." It was the faintly Bostonian twang of my foreign editor, Burton Lasch.

My mind was slowly starting to engage again, and now troubling questions besieged me. Middle-of-the-night phone calls were never good news. Had I totally blown it during the lunch with the senior editors in New York? I had passionately defended the principle of human rights in China, though I probably should have stopped when I noticed the lukewarm response. Or was the call to tell me they were going to close down my bureau in Hong Kong? They'd talked darkly about bureau closings, all part of the relentless cost-cutting going on everywhere in the corporate world. Profits were up, the fat-cat top corporate bosses were now earning nearly two hundred times the average of what the magazine employees were taking home, but—guess what—they had to cut costs. Hong Kong seemed a likely target.

After all, with China reeling from natural disasters and labor unrest and with an economy that had become a major engine of global economic growth and growing more powerful all the time, who needed reporters close to the scene? One reporter in the Chinese capital and one in Shanghai were surely enough to do the job of reporting the activities of one-fifth of the human race. My natural cynicism was keeping pace with my growing wakefulness, but I managed to hold my tongue.

Lasch was drawling on. "The reason I'm calling you now is that you may be able to get on a plane first thing tomorrow morning—no, I mean this morning."

"What? Get on a plane? Where to?" I asked, cringing at how dim-witted I sounded even as the words left my mouth. Well, at least he wasn't summoning me back to New York.

"To Canton, or how do they say it, Gwangjoe?"

"Guangzhou," I corrected him, emphasizing the correct tones for the Mandarin pronunciation of South China's largest city: third, dipping tone for the *guang* part and the high even first tone for the *zhou* (well, it did sound rather like Joe). It was a small act of assertion, a symbolic resistance to the siege my brain and body were under. I was gradually waking up.

"What's going on?" I asked as casually as I could.

"A disappearance. Maybe a kidnapping, maybe a murder, maybe who knows what," Lasch said, as matter-of-factly as though he were recalling a boring movie he'd seen last month. "There's nothing on the wires or CNN yet, and I think we're ahead of everyone else. If it's what I think it might be, there's a nasty but very important story in front of us."

"What kind of story, Burt?"

"How familiar are you with the Chinese Triad gangs?" He wanted to play with me a bit, it seemed.

"Not very. You get involved with them at your own risk. Why do you ask?" For that matter, why was he beating around the bush? Was he showing off or something?

"Well it's not just idle curiosity." There was a hint of warning in the tone, his voice half an octave lower. In other words: Listen up, buddy, I'm the guy who sent you to Hong Kong, and in case you've forgotten, I'm the guy who can recall you.

Time to pay very close attention, I thought, and gave him a straight answer.

"I've met Hong Kong police experts who know a lot about them. They say there's strong evidence that Beijing has unofficially recruited the Triads to do the Public Security Bureau's dirty work. You know, don't have the PSB arrest those smarty-pants dissidents or else half the Hong Kong Foreign Correspondents' Club will be trumpeting on about China's trampling of democracy in Hong Kong. Easier to just get some thugs from Mongkok to firebomb their apartment or poison the dog. To encourage the others, you know."

"I know about Hong Kong," Lasch cut in, a hint of impatience seeping into his voice. "It's the situation in China I want to know about." Another warning signal.

"You probably know, Burt," I continued, "that some of the Triads have established major bases inside China, in Guangzhou. One big-shot under investigation in Hong Kong claimed to have thousands of armed followers under his control in Zhuhai."

"Where's Zhuhai?" Lasch wasn't any better at getting out the correct pronunciation of yet another oddly spelled Chinese city name.

"It's one of these special economic zones not far from Shenzhen, on Guangdong Province's border with Macau."

"Does this guy have contact with the police and the military in China?"

"Yes, corruption in the Chinese military in the south has reached epidemic proportions. The central government in Beijing isn't even sure whether it can count on the Guangzhou Military Region if the country went on a war footing."

Lasch said nothing. I continued quickly. It wasn't a good idea to lob too many slow balls to Lasch; it was well known that he enjoyed intimidating people with his occasional abrasiveness. "I take it you're saying that the disappearance you're talking about might have been a Triad job," I went on. "Was the guy"—I just assumed it was a man—"important?"

"He could be," Lasch went on, his tone a little less frosty now. "He's an old college friend, same class as me at Princeton, who's been in Hong Kong for about six years doing some consulting. He's quite a business whiz, but I've always suspected that his clients included Uncle Sam and that it wasn't necessarily his business skills they were paying him for. They obviously liked his network of contacts in China and around the world. He travels to

China a lot, maybe two or three times a month, yet he seems to get back to the States at least three or four times a year. He occasionally drops in to New York, and we always have lunch together."

Lasch paused. I jumped in.

"Does he have his own company, or does he work for a corporation?"

"He used to be a big wheel in Thorndike-Henderson, the big Hong Kong outfit. I think they call them 'hongs' or something. But he fell out with them for reasons I've never quite fathomed and started his own consulting business called McHale and Associates."

"Burt, if it's not a dumb question," I interrupted, "how do you know he's disappeared? I mean, suppose he just changed his itinerary, decided to stay on a few extra days in China without letting anyone in his company know."

"I got a call from a mutual friend of ours, a Swiss businessman from Canton—sorry, Gwangjoe—a few hours ago. He said he'd been trying to reach me all morning. Of course, it's nighttime over there." I was glad he'd figured that out. "It seems our friend—his name is Chuck McHale, by the way—was unusually nervous the last time the Swiss guy saw him, which was in a bar in a Guangzhou hotel. Chuck apparently had muttered something about 'too many bad guys in town these days,' without elaborating. They'd arranged to have lunch the next day in the same hotel, but Chuck never showed up. He wasn't in the hotel either, but he hadn't checked out. At least the front desk said he hadn't.

"The Swiss guy said he worried all night about who the 'bad guys' might be, and he phoned Chuck's Hong Kong office when Chuck was a no-show for lunch. They said they hadn't heard anything about any change of travel plans. Anyway, Chuck was always meticulous about his movements. Whenever he showed up in New York to see me, he'd call the day before. He was never late. Chuck's Hong Kong assistant was alarmed that this Swiss guy had called her. So on a hunch that I might have heard from her boss, she told him to get in touch with me."

I was wide awake now. Lasch was not his usual calm self as he narrated all this. He must have been a lot closer friends with McHale than he let on. And he wanted to continue talking about him.

"He's, he's,—" I thought Lasch might be unsure whether to say "he was"—"a curious kind of fellow, Chuck. He was always very eager to ask my opinions on things going on in the world, especially in China, and his range of interests was enormous: history, politics, religion, especially Asian religion, literature, the theater. Besides all that, he was actually a pretty good musician, a better-than-average pianist and a great aficionado of opera."

"Sounds like you were a good friend of his, Burt," I volunteered.

"Well, I was," he said, a bit indignantly. "We'd visited each other's families when we were at Princeton. We just hadn't been in the same part of the world much of the time afterward. Chuck was always cagey about his activities. I learned after awhile not to play the nosey hack too much about what he was up to because he would drop some clear hints that there were things he just didn't want me to know. Or maybe they were things he simply couldn't let me know. And that's where it all gets very murky." For the first time, Lasch's voice faltered a little.

"Two or three times when we met over the past year, he'd talked about the Triads, how they were becoming bolder and bolder in Hong Kong and apparently operated almost with impunity in South China. The last thing he said to me really stuck in my mind. I wondered at the time whether I should have passed it on to you, but Chuck wouldn't give me any names or concrete facts. Now I realize what he said may have been part of a puzzle even more disturbing than his disappearance."

Lasch paused for a moment, but this time I didn't say anything. "God knows what's happened to him," he finally said. "It would be one thing if it was just the authorities after his blood, and they'd just arrested him on some trumped-up charge. They would hold him for a few days, then expel him from the country after fining him or something. The State Department deals with those cases regularly. But what really worries me is that the bad guys may have captured him and are even now attaching electrodes to him—or whatever they do over there to extract information from someone."

"Burt, I don't want to be pushy about this, but couldn't McHale just be in the middle of a romantic weekend? It's not that uncommon in South China, you know."

"Perhaps," Lasch said after appearing to give this idea some consideration. "But I don't think so. He's been divorced quite a few years but has been discreet about his private life. He never talks about it."

"Then what is it that he knows that you think the Triads might want to extract from him?"

"I don't know." There was a pause on the other end of the line, as though Lasch was weighing his words carefully. "But I want you to go to Guangzhou right away and find out."

This was awkward. Granted, Lasch was upset about the disappearance of a close friend, someone he had known at least on and off since his college days. But was McHale's possible disappearance "news"? Sure, if McHale really had been kidnapped, not to mention murdered, and we knew that for sure, that would definitely be a story. But all we knew right now was that a Hong Kong-based American businessman had failed to show up for lunch with a Swiss businessman in a Guangzhou hotel. Whether McHale had been mugged or kidnapped, fallen in love with a Cantonese bar girl, taken French leave from his creditors, or gotten into the car-smuggling business might not become clear for days, if at all. Who could ever say for sure when the term *disappearance* would apply to him?

I was uncomfortable with what Lasch was telling me and not just because I had been jolted out of my sleep when I was already jet lagged. Maybe McHale was a spook. He sounded almost caricature CIA to me: Ivy League, jackknife wits, eclectic interests, lots of foreign travel, and "consulting" as a phony cover. Was that reason enough for *Epoch* magazine, leading newsweekly in America and the world, to send a reporter to Guangzhou to investigate this apparent—only apparent—disappearance?

I said none of this to Lasch—not that it mattered. He was shrewd enough to realize that I had misgivings about the whole thing. As usual, he'd jumped ahead of me.

"I know what you're thinking, Richard," he said. "You're asking yourself what kind of news judgment this is to go careening around South China after an unknown American businessman who failed to show up for a lunch meeting just because it's possible something bad might have happened to him. Well, I don't have a good answer to that, but I think you might after a few days of poking around in Guangzhou. One thing you need to know. Chuck told me the last time we met that he was on to something really strange about China's military. He said it bothered him. Something about some meditation program all wrapped up in Buddhism, Daoism, and what have you. Oh yes, something about 'cheegoong,' whatever that is. I couldn't make much sense of what he was saying, but I wasn't going to offend him by saying so.

"Oh, and one other thing that just might convince you this isn't just sentimentality on my part. Chuck said he'd come across something of a fad among history buffs in China, especially in the south, about Chinese peasant rebellions of the past. He said *Epoch*'s reporters would be amazed if they could untangle what the officers corps of China's army in the south was playing around with. I couldn't draw him out on this, but I think it had something to do with this meditation stuff too."

So that was it. Although Lasch was genuinely worried about the odd behavior of his friend and obviously thought he might have come to some harm, his nose for news was as sharp as ever. Lasch had never been especially interested in China, but he had an uncanny ability to spot stories before anyone else did. It had served him brilliantly in his career despite his abrasive disdain for editorial bureaucracies and his impatience with colleagues he didn't respect. I was thinking, of course, of Reddaway, the managing editor.

"Well," I said, at a loss how to respond to this, and not wanting to appear skeptical of my boss's judgment, "I don't think there's a correspondent in the entire foreign news system who wouldn't want to be in on that."

"I thought you'd get the point," Lasch said. I could almost see him licking his upper lip, as he did when something really excited him. Most of the time he was cold in a way that one had to almost admire as an art form. His gestures—the disdainfully slow movements, his way of speaking with annoying deliberateness, his ability to listen to a funny conversation without displaying a flicker of amusement—reflected a personality that seemed to have grown up enjoying a chilly independence from peers and superiors. His reporters liked to joke—out of range of his hearing, of course—that Lasch had spent most of the first decades of his life in a meat locker.

"When you get to Guangzhou, give me a call," he said, becoming brisk now, "but e-mail me something generic-sounding about what you find out."

"How many days do you want me to spend on this?" I asked. "We have that regional sport roundup to do, there's an economic takeout in the works, and Indonesia and Burma have got lots of problems."

"I do read the papers, you know," Lasch growled. "I'll tell Reddaway that I've detached you for the time being from the usual bureau stuff. I don't want him poking around with this until it's clear what we have. A speculative piece would ruin the story at this stage." This was as close as Lasch came to expressing openly his animosity toward Clifford Reddaway, *Epoch*'s managing editor and Lasch's long-time rival. The hard feelings were due, in part, to Reddaway getting the job that Lasch thought should have been his.

For his part, Reddaway had told the editor-in-chief he simply couldn't work with Lasch, a journalist who acted like a cowboy half the time and like a sulky teenager the other half. But the editor-in-chief wouldn't play ball with Reddaway on this. He didn't want an editorial nursery spat going on under his nose. After all, as editor-in-chief, he got to appoint the managing editor, and he certainly wasn't going to let the managing editor tell him who the foreign editor and chief of correspondents would be. That was one prerogative he had held on to even though it didn't make a lot of administrative sense.

Besides, the editor-in-chief had a secret admiration for Lasch precisely because Lasch was something of a cowboy in the world of journalism: intelligent, aggressive, a self-made man who was unimpressed by effete Manhattan editors, half of whom he thought couldn't tell one end of a horse from the other. The editor-in-chief didn't mind cowboys at all, which I'd come to realize over the years. In fact, he wouldn't have minded being one himself—but that wasn't possible: he was far too Connecticut for that. But he liked having a couple of cowboys around, and Lasch was as close as he thought he could get to a real Wyatt Earp at *Epoch*.

Technically, Lasch had to report to Reddaway, but Lasch's contempt for "technical" procedures was so well known that not even Reddaway was able to make the system work the way it was supposed to. It was actually Lasch who decided which correspondents were assigned where in *Epoch*'s sprawling foreign bureau system. As long as the reporters beat out their competition—which they did surprisingly often—Lasch was able to justify his independent status at *Epoch*. As usual, Lasch had anticipated the problem of who would keep Hong Kong covered if I was running around South China. "Meitnic has agreed to step in to Hong Kong for a week on his way back to Delhi," he said, answering what he knew would probably be my next question.

But it was still tricky. I hated the idea of being a pawn in a Jurassic brawl between Lasch and Reddaway. Both men were risk takers in the corporate power game. Lasch was quicker on his feet than Reddaway, and when it came to foreign affairs he was way ahead of his rival. But Reddaway's track record, especially on domestic cover stories, was very good. If he really wanted to, he could probably win out over Lasch in a corporate shoot-out by going not just to the editor-in-chief, appointed with the approval of the board of directors, but to the board and the president themselves. In that kind of high-noon drama, plenty of bystanders would hit the dust, and I would probably be among the first.

Most of the time, I found these displays of raw power, of calibrated put-downs and relentless back-stabbing depressing, yet occasionally they could be mesmerizing. There was something serpentile in the way two corporate editorial executives slithered this way and that to keep out of each other's coils. Reddaway, in most instances, came out just slightly ahead. He was, all things considered, one of the best managing editors *Epoch* had ever had, and his ability to conceptualize news events with laconic brilliance was formidable. Lasch recognized this begrudgingly—he would never publicly admit it—and knew that on some terrain, Reddaway could simply outmaneuver him. He was too smart to provoke Reddaway into a power duel.

Yet Lasch had many times been able to influence the magazine's news judgment by placing his stronger correspondents in locations where their reporting would tip the scales in the way the magazine covered a particular story. He loved foreign policy, and he was almost always warm toward reporters who were passionate about human rights issues. On foreign affairs issues, Lasch got his own way editorially more often than not, and everyone knew that this grated on Reddaway. I think Lasch liked me because of my own interest in human rights, which dated back to my college days when I had been active in Amnesty International.

For all that, to be liked by Lasch was a double-edged sword. It could help you find choice assignments, but it could also render you vulnerable in Reddaway's hands. Lasch was fiercely protective of the young men and women he had hired and groomed. He liked to say it always took about ten years to get the best out of a foreign correspondent. As a result, his reporters often did want to stay ten years or more in the field, knowing that it was easier to paddle steadily through Lasch's deep ocean swells than flail around in Reddaway's shallow-water squalls. In the end, the managing editor put up with the foreign editor because the fine performance of Lasch's men and women made the magazine look good. And that, of course, ultimately made Reddaway look good too.

"OK, Burt," I said, reflecting on all this with just a second's pause, "but if New York"—we always said "New York" when we meant Reddaway and the rest of the editorial system—"wants to know what in the world I'm doing storming off without warning or advance word to Guangzhou, what am I supposed to tell them?"

"Just tell them I sent you," Lasch said portentously. "I'll deal with them." He paused briefly. "You'd better get to bed," he said finally. "I think you should get some sleep before heading out."

"I know." As if I needed to be told. "But just one more thing about McHale. What exactly did he say about China that you found so riveting?"

"He said—and I quote—'China will never get to democracy unless it can control its crime and corruption, and it will never do that until its leadership can stare truth in the face.' He said, 'It's the idols that are the problem, Burt, the idols. You know they've gone back to worshiping them.' I hadn't the remotest idea what he was talking about, but I never got to ask him what he meant. We were at a dinner party together about a week ago, and just then someone buttonholed him in conversation."

"And 'truth'?" I prodded. "What do you think that was all about?"

"I haven't the foggiest. Maybe something about telling the Chinese people the truth about Tiananmen Square in 1989? But doesn't every Chinese know someway or another what happened?"

"They sort of know intuitively," I said much too eagerly—I've no idea why I did this—"but like anyone who's been lied to for so long, they want to hear the truth from their leaders."

Lasch chuckled. "Well, Richard," he said condescendingly, "I won't take issue with you in your philosophical mode. In any case, whatever 'idols' are or 'truth' means, these are things I figure you'll find out if you get to the bottom of the McHale story. Good luck and don't forget to e-mail me."

"I won't."

"Good night, Richard."

"Good night, Burt." I hung up, set the alarm on the cell phone, and was asleep again almost before the glow from the phone's LCD display had faded.

The alarm rang at least six times before I dragged myself out of the sleep of death. I'd set it for 5:30 a.m., the latest I thought I could get up, get a cab to the Airport Express station in Central, then catch the twenty-three-minute train to the Chek Lap Kok airport off Lantau Island for the 7:30 flight to Guangzhou. The daily Guangzhou flights were pretty full these days even though the seats and the aisles—ten seats abreast in a plane designed to hold nine Europeans or Americans across—were maddeningly narrow. But the Hong Kong–China border processing was simpler and less noisy by air.

I was doing my last-minute visual check of the apartment while the cab was on its way—cell phone, laptop, tape recorder, camera, carry-on bag already packed, map of Guangzhou, print-out of contacts, travel umbrella—when the thought of something entirely different made me stop dead in my tracks.

Trish. Trish. I'd completely forgotten about her. She was arriving that morning from Manila, and I was supposed to meet her at the airport. How on earth was I going to let her know I wouldn't be there, much less explain what in my life was so important to cause me to stand her up the day she was arriving on a visit that had been in the works for weeks?

How could I have been so stupid? I should have told Lasch on the spot that I couldn't get away from Hong Kong for at least three days because of, well, because of what? Urgent family business? Stories that needed to be written? Social engagements of a pressing nature? What on earth could I have said?

It was infuriating. Obviously because of the upside-down time of Lasch's call, my accursed jet lag, and, let's face it, Lasch's own subtly intimidating manner, poor Trish had vanished from my consciousness and memory at precisely the moment when she should have surfaced like a Trident submarine.

I barged my way in fury out of the apartment and into the elevator, furious with Lasch, furious with *Epoch*, furious with the Triads, furious over being employed by someone who could play dice with my destiny at a whim, all the way down the fifteen floors to the lobby. By the time I charged through the glass front doors toward the red Mercedes taxi—I did like the way Hong Kong taxi companies did things in style—idling close to the doorman's office, I had vented at least the worst of my anger and frustration. I gave the driver a weak smile and slumped quickly with my luggage into the backseat.

The driver, thankfully, was not the talkative type, and we were both silent as the car roared up Repulse Bay Road, down the Mid-Levels, and into the cross-harbor tunnel. I was left alone to my self-pity and irritation.

The vastness of Hong Kong's Chek Lap Kok airport, literally rising from the ocean off Lantau Island, always amazed me. I'd read somewhere that it was the largest enclosed space in the world. It certainly felt that way. Tour groups that would have seemed massive in any other space shrank to insignificance as soon as their buses disgorged them outside the gleaming, silent glass doors of the Arrivals Hall. The stores inside looked petite beneath the cathedral-high and curved-glass ceiling that made the cavernous interior airy and bright with sunlight.

The original Hong Kong airport, Kai Tak, always felt overcrowded and confined. Landing there was an adventure. The final approach to the single runway had terrified generations of arriving passengers as their 747s banked sharply to the right before lumbering past the open windows of crammed apartments below. Kai Tak's ceilings were low, and the corridors to the departure jetways were always clogged with tired and overloaded travelers anxious to escape the elbow-to-elbow crowds. Kai Tak offered a sense of worn familiarity—but comfortable it definitely was not.

Chek Lap Kok, by contrast, was huge, designed and constructed in haste in the 1990s, in the nervous countdown to Chinese sovereignty, to demonstrate both the British commitment to the colony they were about to leave and the organizational and financial wizardry of this big Asian metropolis. I thought there was a grandiose vision behind the twenty-billion-dollar complex, as if the parting Brits were thumbing their noses at the incoming Communists. How's this, the building seemed to say, for the rule of law, modern capitalism, brilliant engineering, and a laissez-faire labor market? Can you people do this? We don't think so. Look what really made Hong Kong great. Hong Kong, Hong Kong: all about efficiency, vulgarity, luxury, and pretentiousness. How I loved it.

I checked in quickly at the nearly empty airline counter; then, making my way to the gate, I took out my cell phone to try to get hold of the people I needed to contact. It was important that I reach Trish in Manila before she left her apartment.

A maid answered, with the sweet, slow speech of so many Filipinas.

"What do you mean she's already left?" I snapped. "Her flight isn't until 10:20."

The voice at the other end twittered; I found it maddening. "I'm very sorry, sir. She didn't say where she was going, sir. Would you like me to leave a message for her, sir?"

"No, no thanks. Just—if she by any chance calls you before her plane takes off, please tell her that Richard is desperately trying to reach her because of a . . . a sudden work crisis." Should I tell Trish's maid that I wouldn't be at the airport? Better not. Maids have a way of getting things wrong.

OK, I'd started making progress covering my foul-up, and I still had about twenty minutes before my flight would start boarding to make some more phone calls. Maybe I could reach someone at the Manila airport who could get the message to her. But who? I could spend the twenty minutes just trying to track down the right phone number.

Then, as I found a seat in the spacious lounge by my gate, it came to me. Clarissa. Clarissa Jones. If I could just reach Clarissa and if she were free—she often was—she would surely agree to help. She could come to the airport, meet Trish, and make the right excuses for me. Trish was sure to be furious. I'd stood her up. I hadn't warned her about this. Was this any way to welcome your new girlfriend on her first visit to your city? Clarissa at least would forestall one possible problem: Trish's thinking that I was two-timing her.

I realized with a pang of guilt how early it was, not even 7:00 yet, and I wondered if it would be OK to call. That was one of the curses—and attractions—of the hack's life: there was never a routine and we certainly didn't keep bankers' hours. But thank God, Clarissa was a missionary. Weren't they always getting up at unearthly hours and praying for all kinds of things? I wished fervently she would start praying for me at this moment.

Clarissa was unique in a totally eccentric way. She had grown up in Richmond, Virginia, and could remember well the indignity as a child of being forced to sit in the back of a public bus because she was, as they said then, "colored." She'd become devoutly religious—she hated that term herself—as a child and most of her life had been associated with what she described as one of those noisy, foot-stomping, tambourine-shaking Pentecostal churches, a term I'd never even heard before. She married, raised three kids—who all attended excellent colleges, on scholarships—and when her husband, a schoolteacher, died five years earlier, she finally felt herself free to do what she'd wanted to do all her life: be a missionary.

She was in her sixties now, a retired federal government manager with what she said was a "calling"—whatever that meant—to speak about God to the Chinese. She told me all this when we'd met at the home of the U.S. consul-general on the Peak, and I was incredulous. How could a black American woman with absolutely no knowledge of China or the Chinese and with about as much command of the language as I had of Albanian ever imagine that the Chinese would want to hear what she had to say?

It had been one of those Hong Kong evenings when the setting sun seems to throw a golden mellowness upon everything below—cityscape, green hillsides, and the relentlessly kinetic harbor. Maybe it was that the mellowness had invaded me as well because I seemed to set aside the typical reporter's cynicism that would have been my usual reaction and found myself disarmed by her warmth, even her naiveté.

"Oh my, you must have an interesting job!" she had almost bubbled to me immediately upon learning I was *Epoch*'s Hong Kong bureau chief. "Now be honest, honey, don't you ever get just a teeny bit lonely with all that traveling?" In a hardened city like Hong Kong, where everyone was always trying to prove himself, Clarissa's comment seemed strangely out of place but also strangely warming. And after the cynical, bored conversation I usually encountered at most receptions in Hong Kong—a city that was a constant whirlwind of social activity—Clarissa was truly different. My respect for the consul-general went up several notches for having invited her, even if it was only at the urging of the wife of some corporate bigwig who had heard her speak at the International School.

The week after, I took Clarissa to afternoon tea at the swanky Mandarin Hotel. She had been in the city just three weeks and still hardly knew Hong Kong from Kowloon, much less the Mandarin from the YMCA, where she was staying initially. Afternoon tea at the Mandarin was still one of the delights of Hong Kong, conveying the self-assurance of an imperial era that never contemplated its own demise; and for some reason that eluded even me, I wanted Clarissa to experience this last vestige of a more genteel time.

I still don't know why I did it. I certainly didn't want any sermons from her though I was pretty sure she wouldn't unload any on me—at least not right away, anyway. She seemed too polite for that. She just as politely refrained from asking me any searching questions about myself, but just before we parted, she had looked at me very meaningfully and said, in a low, slow voice, "Now if you need any help for anything at anytime, honey, don't you hesitate to call me. I'm pretty good in emergencies, or just a plain ol' ordinary crisis." She had laughed boisterously then at her own corny humor.

I'd wondered at the time how she thought she could possibly be a help to me. After all, she was new to the city, didn't speak the language, and hardly knew a soul. I, on the other hand, had made Hong Kong my home for three years, had a graduate degree in Chinese history, and had been fluent in Mandarin Chinese even before I arrived in Hong Kong (and my Cantonese now wasn't bad either). Furthermore, I was as enterprising and self-sufficient as my chosen profession suggested and necessitated, which is to say that I could find a way to do just about anything.

But now, here I was about to "eat crow." Uncharacteristically thanking God for the second time this morning, I found to my relief that I had written Clarissa's number in my date book and quickly punched in her number. She had said she lived in Mongkok, and I could imagine a tiny, noisy, fourth-floor walk-up off the perpetual daylight of the Cameron Street night market.

The phone rang just twice before Clarissa's cheerful, lilting, unmistakably African-American voice answered.

"Well, hello, Rick." Clarissa sounded as if she had expected me to call. "How nice to hear from you." There was a quaint, almost otherworldly air about her manners.

"Clarissa, I'm really sorry to do this to you, but it's kind of an emergency. I've got to go into China on an extremely short-notice assignment, but my girlfriend from the Philippines is arriving in Hong Kong for the first time this morning. She's never been here before, and what's worse is that she'll be expecting me to meet her. I couldn't reach her before I left for the airport, and she'd already left her own place in Manila to catch the flight here when I called just now."

"Honey, think nothing of it. I've got the morning free, and I'd be delighted to help out."

"Clarissa, are you sure? I know it's really short notice."

"Well, isn't that what makes life interesting?" A giggle followed at the other end of the phone. Was I hearing right? I had hoped, desperately, that she would come through, but I couldn't believe she was being so pleasant about it.

"Are you sure, Clarissa?" I asked again, not quite sure how to ease my own embarrassment.

"Why, of course. I told you I was good at plain ol' ordinary crises." And she giggled infectiously once more. It helped relieve the tension, and for the first time that morning I laughed too. "Can you tell me her name, Rick?" she added.

"Trish, or rather, Tricia. Tricia de los Santos."

"Why, that's beautiful. I'll bet she's just as easy on the eyes too. When does she get in, Rick?"

"The Philippine Airlines flight is at 12:15. From Manila."

"OK, and what would you like me to do when I've met her?"

I had been prepared for this. The plan had been for Trish to stay with me, but for two nights she would officially be at the Hong Kong branch of the Manila-based international hotel chain where she worked in public relations. But of course, I couldn't have asked Clarissa to drop Trish off at my apartment. Even I knew about missionaries and their sense of morals. Whatever I privately thought about this, I wasn't going to open myself up to any old-fashioned lectures from Clarissa about boyfriend-girlfriend sleeping arrangements.

A large gaggle of Americans in a tour group seated in the next row was starting to gather up their belongings. They apparently had gotten some unseen signal that our flight was ready for boarding.

"Clarissa, I'm sorry, but I think they're about to call my flight," I said hastily. "Listen, you don't need to take Trish anywhere. Her hotel chain has already arranged to pick her up at the airport. All I need you to do is . . . well, tell her that I'm really sorry about this change in plans and that I'll call her from the Golden Panda Hotel in Guangzhou. And . . . um, tell her I miss her too. Clarissa, are you sure this is OK?"

"Honey, I told you it was absolutely fine, so don't even think twice about it. I know that Trish and I will get on like two sweet cousins." How could she possibly know anything of the kind? "But you haven't told me how I'm supposed to recognize her." Another giggle. The tourists around me were talking animatedly now and shuffling in a group toward the gate.

"Well, she's about five foot six, slim, with long hair and . . . er . . . long legs." I faltered. I was certainly very attracted to Trish's good looks and great figure, but I didn't really want that to be so obvious to Clarissa. I tried again: "Maybe you could just hold up a sign with her name on it. Do you remember it?"

"Yes, Trish Delli something or other." That high-pitched giggle again. The airline staff was announcing my flight in English now, and the departure area was emptying quickly. With an effort, I reined in my impatience.

"De los Santos, Clarissa, S-A-N-T-O-S, and de los is spelled D-E space L-O-S."

"OK, honey. Got it. Delli Santos. Now you run along and don't miss that flight. Bye."

"Thanks, Clarissa. You're a great help."

"Yeah, yeah, I know." She giggled again. "Now go on, honey, and don't you worry about a thing."

"Thanks. Bye. See you in a few days."

How did I know that it would be "a few days"? It was nothing but a hunch. It was always like this on a breaking story. You went out without much of an idea of what you would uncover, and you only began to see a pattern to things when you were already two-thirds of the way into the reporting. I was always excited about a new story, but in all my twelve years of being a journalist, I had never really gotten over being a bit scared too. What if I couldn't find a decent lead? What if I was led on a wild goose chase by some smart aleck who acted like he knew the scene but who in fact knew nothing?

Then there was the deadline always hanging over you the whole time like a dark cloud. The editors and the deadline don't wait. You have to produce: details, color, quotes, anecdotes, analysis, some sort of balance and perspective, all in three or four days at most, and preferably with something that no other news organization has. Could I really get everything I needed to do a halfway decent job? I was never really sure at first. But I guess it was that unknown but exciting element that kept me in the business despite the lousy hours, the havoc it wreaked on personal life, and the mediocre pay (well, *Epoch* did pay better than most other news organizations).

Sometimes there was yet another nuisance: editors who got too interested in the story for their own good—or yours. "We'd like you to stay the weekend in Plonkville in case the story moves significantly over the next few days." Never mind that this was the weekend with your girlfriend that you promised her back in February—and it's now June—or that it was your parents' fortieth wedding anniversary. Forget it. If these were the sorts of things that are really important to you, you would have become an accountant or a professor at some state university.

So here I was with Trish, not really a bona fide girlfriend yet despite my referring to her that way to Clarissa, more a prospective girlfriend, showing up for what should have been a fabulous few days of mutual discovery. But now I was at Lasch's beck and call again, traipsing out of the Hong Kong Special Administrative Region like a well-trained spaniel on what might turn out to be a wild goose chase. It suddenly felt like a big disaster, and I didn't even have time to cheer up with a fat-free latte because we were being herded toward the boarding gate.

But the rush I had anticipated turned out to be no rush at all. A large group of loud and boisterous "mainlanders" was taking their time shuffling forward in front of me, their progress hindered by the electronic gear and other Hong Kong goodies they were trying to drag on the plane. I should have felt annoyed, but usually I just felt sorry for these clueless mainlanders: bad teeth, baggy pale gray suits with that strange fashion statement of leaving the label on the sleeve of the suit jacket, hair inevitably brushed forward over the forehead or around the temples. "Country bumpkin"—or the equally descriptive equivalent in Chinese, *tu baozi*—always came to mind whenever I observed this strange mix of innocence and boorishness.

Most Hong Kong Chinese looked down on the mainlanders with a mixture of irritation and wry contempt. There was the language difference—the mainlanders speaking their Mandarin just loudly enough to ensure that the locals knew the visitors hailed from the motherland. There was sometimes an abrasiveness too: Listen, you not-quite-Chinese, we—not the British—run this place now. Get it? Of course, this was never actually said, but it was conveyed in many unspoken ways. Hong Kongers used to get their revenge by commenting snidely—never to a mainlander's face, of course—that having a Beijing bureaucrat try to tell Hong Kong how to run its affairs was like expecting a truck driver to service a Rolex watch. And not just that—a truck driver who didn't really like Rolex watches.

I was lost in thoughts like these, standing close to the end of the line slowly moving forward, when the last man in the mainland delegation suddenly turned around and faced me with a broad grin, a gold tooth glinting in his mouth. I was taken aback. Mainland Chinese, especially in groups, almost never talked to westerners, or *gweilos*, "foreign devils" as the Hong Kong Chinese termed us. But this fellow turned out to be positively garrulous. He looked to be in his late forties or early fifties, possibly older, and he had that gaunt, pinched face of many educated urban Chinese who had grown up during the great nationwide famine of 1958–1961 that had resulted from Chairman Mao Tse-tung's misguided utopian experiment, the Great Leap Forward.

"'Cuse me, is this your faahst visit to China?" he asked. Chinese-accented English is just as distinctive as any other accented English, and this guy was having the usual trouble with the *x* and *r* sounds.

"No, no," I answered, perhaps a little too emphatically. I just wasn't in the mood for camaraderie in the Hong Kong airport so early in the morning. But he did seem to be trying to be nice and no doubt just wanted to practice his English. Maybe it was because Clarissa had just done me a good turn, and it would be bad karma now to be rude. So I didn't brush him off the way I normally would have.

"Do you often go to China?" This seemed like a well-practiced follow-up. We shuffled in tandem a few more yards closer to the gate, he carrying under each arm a large cardboard box that looked to be purchases from some electronics store. How he had gotten them past the Chek Lap Kok dragon ladies who decide what can and cannot be carried on the aircraft I couldn't imagine. But he'd obviously succeeded. I nudged just a little bit closer to him before I replied.

"I go occasionally on business," I said.

"What is your business?" he asked, his gold tooth glinting.

Then it occurred to me he might be one of those I-want-to-know-everything-about-you bored travelers. I'd been tempted a few times to write a snide newspaper piece on how to cope with this global phenomenon. I'd even thought up the perfect headline: "How To Deal With Terminal Curiosity." But Clarissa seemed to have a lingering effect, and I decided to be nice.

"I'm a journalist," I said with a sigh. If I'd said "businessman," within twenty seconds he'd have been asking me for the Fortune 500 rank of my corporation. If I'd said "teacher," he would have demanded sooner or later the name of the school's principal. It just seemed easiest to tell the truth at this point.

Now he shut up abruptly. He stopped smiling. I assumed he had the same allergy all Chinese Communist officials have to journalists and that I had effectively shut him out of my universe forever. Not a bad thing, perhaps.

But if I'd succeeded in shutting him up, it didn't last long. I'd started to doze off soon after the plane had taken off on its thirty-seven-minute flight to Guangzhou, and I'd forgotten about him. Then, as I pulled myself together just before the approach to White Cloud airport and had started to catch up with life by skimming the latest issue of *The Economist*, I suddenly noticed a presence close to my aisle seat. It was him again. He was bending over, close to me, asking, "Do you have a business card?" even as he placed his own atop my magazine. He'd used the customary polite Asian way of offering the card with both hands, but the move had been just a bit more brusque than it might have been.

"Yes, I do," I replied instinctively and reached inside the folder of my notebook. I handed it to him Chinese side up. Still leaning over, his face registered surprise as he read my Chinese name. But he ought to have known that just about every westerner in Hong Kong, every gweilo, had one.

"Do you speak Chinese, Mr. Ai Erdun?" he asked, saying out loud the name my first-year Chinese teacher at Berkeley had given me years earlier.

Now, he was smiling pleasantly rather than grinning his earlier foolish grin as he perused the rest of my card. "Wo hui jiang yi dianr," I replied in

Mandarin. "Wo de zhongwen shi zai jiazhou da xue xuede (Yes, I speak a little. I learned my Chinese at the University of California)."

"Very good," he said in English, his I'm-a-simple-traveler grin back on his face. "I hope we can meet again."

"I hope so too," I answered automatically, not at all sure that I meant it. We shook hands, and he went back to his seat just as a flight attendant came to shoo him out of the aisle. It wasn't until the wheels had set down that I glanced at the card, which like mine was in Chinese and English. I was astonished that he had introduced himself to me. "Yao Fanmei," it read, "Foreign Affairs Department, Guangzhou Municipal Public Security Bureau"—the police. Perhaps because of the unsettling middle-of-the-night conversation with Lasch about suspected dark doings in China, my mind immediately made a leap: was my grinning acquaintance a spy, or even a counter-espionage secret policeman? And why would he want me not only to know this fact, but also suggest that we meet again? Had he known in advance who I was? My mind returned to the disturbing news from Lasch. Did this have anything to do with the McHale case?

Oddly, I didn't see him once we got off the plane. His luggage was probably all carry-on, like mine. I wondered if he was watching me from some cranny of China's immigration operation at the airport. Well, if he was, there was nothing I could do about it and, without bothering to look around, I hopped a cab for Guangzhou's city center.

Chapter Two

I took a cab directly downtown from the White Cloud airport to the Pearl River and the Golden Panda Hotel. The handsome, thirty-story streamlined tower commanded a magnificent view of both the river and Shamian Island, the former sandbank on the Pearl River where the Western trading "hongs," or corporations, had set up their warehouses in the mid-eighteenth century.

I was in graduate school when I first read the history of this place. The sandbank, gradually transformed into an island with elegant stone embankments, had come into its own over a century-long domination by wealthy foreign traders. In the course of time, China succumbed to a series of humiliating "unequal" treaties with Western nations, starting with the forfeiture of Hong Kong after the Opium War of 1839–1842. Guangzhou was one of five "treaty ports," navigable harbors that were ceded to direct Western control when the war ended with the catastrophic defeat of the Chinese and the humiliating 1842 Treaty of Nanking.

Conveniently separated by the tributary of the Pearl River from Guangzhou proper, Shamian Island became something of a quarantined compound for foreigners. Governed by European laws and regulations and separated administratively from the miasma of the rest of Guangzhou, it was a comfortable location for British, French, and eventually American businessmen late in the nineteenth century. They and their ladies lived genteel and sequestered lives, protected from the toil and harsh realities of life in China by stern foreign police and liberal supplies of maids who were called amahs, cooks, gardeners, drivers, house guards, and errand boys. The dinner parties, the ice-cold lemonade, the fresh lychees, the mosquito nets—all helped to neutralize the local discomforts, even when the subtropical sun hovered over Cancer for unbearable weeks of steamy, enervating heat from June through August.

The westerners might have stayed far longer in China had the country's great unraveling in the twentieth century not finally driven them out. The imperial system had imploded after the 1911 revolution, ostensibly into a republican democracy but in reality into warlordism. The ill-fated successors of revolutionary leader and statesman Sun Yat-sen and his coterie of Soviet advisors who had helped push forward the republic succumbed to corruption, more warlordism, the Japanese invasion, and finally full-scale civil war.

Nearly four decades after the empire fell, its decrepit democratic heir, the Republic of China, collapsed, exhausted, into the arms of the Communists in 1949, a remnant of it retreating to lick its wounds—and learn well from all of its past mistakes—on the island of Taiwan. Most of the westerners had already gone well before then, leaving Canton, later to be known internationally as Guangzhou, which was a closer transliteration than Canton of the city's Chinese name in Mandarin, to settle down puckishly to Communist rule.

Like a berouged and powdered old actress who stopped getting offers of new roles long ago, Guangzhou had faded slowly but steadily beneath the heat and the rains of South China and the wild gyrations of Chairman Mao's unpredictable utopian experimenting. Despite years of privatization, free enterprise, foreign tourism, and foreign investment, Shamian Island nonetheless still exuded the sadness of a once-raucous but forever lost past. Apart from the luxurious, high-rise Golden Panda Hotel, the island, less than one thousand yards long from east to west and about three hundred yards wide from north to south, had declined from its former vigor to a gently decaying repository of nineteenth-century Asian colonial architecture. After establishing diplomatic relations with China in 1979, the Americans, almost wryly, had found a good site, next to the hotel, for their new consulate-general. At least their diplomats could eat well, swim, and play tennis at lunchtime without having to venture into the cacophony of an economically and meteorologically overheated Guangzhou.

There were more expensive hotels in Guangzhou, and more luxurious ones, most of them close to the site of the city's twice-yearly mammoth international Canton Trade Fair. A surplus of cheap, well-educated labor provided the larger hotels with everything from shoeshine boys to full-scale string orchestras that resonated in the marble lobbies with extensive repertoires that ranged from popular movie sound tracks to Vivaldi.

But I, for one, had a special liking for the Golden Panda. It had been the first of the major Western-standard hotels in Guangzhou, and it remained impressively well run. Its luxuriant lobby and waterfall-thronged gardens filled on weekends with gaggles of Chinese grandparents, parents, and children of the rising Guangzhou bourgeoisie, cameras and all. For serious businesspeople, especially those from Hong Kong, who had no particular need to camp out at the trade fair end of town and who wanted an almost nineteenth-century-style view of the muddy, heavily-trafficked waters of the Pearl River, the Golden Panda was a favorite.

I checked in, got to my room on the twentieth floor, then flopped down for a few minutes on the king-size bed. I really had no clue how to proceed. Where was I even to begin looking for McHale? Of course, the obvious place to start was the hotel itself, but even this needed some careful thought. What if McHale had been kidnapped—or worse—by Guangzhou-based Triads, perhaps in league with officials of the city? It hardly seemed to matter whether they were technically gangsters or just corrupt customs officials. The result was the same, and I wasn't exactly planning to end my days in a barrel of cement subsiding into the Pearl River mud.

Then there was the Trish issue. I was unnerved by the fact that I had completely forgotten about her in the rush to get into China after Lasch's phone call. Had I become so slavish to every whim of *Epoch* that my personal life leaped out the window every time professional demands banged on the front door? It raised disturbing questions.

Marcia, for one. She had betrayed me in Brussels less than three years into our marriage after running around with all those wacko and anarchist art students. Actually, it was simpler than that. She'd started an affair with Jean-Luc while I was away on assignment in Bosnia. He was the sort of man—well, I thought "boy" was more accurate—for whom I'm sure I would have developed contempt fairly quickly even if Marcia hadn't thought he was the most fascinating artist since Leonardo da Vinci. He was stringy, short, and had poor muscle development. He wore only faded blue jeans, a black T-shirt, and a stained cotton vest that was once probably purple but had now settled, after numerous careless washes, into something of a faded lavender. With a pungent French cigarette, usually a Gitane, permanently dangling from one side of his mouth, and a flop of long straight hair constantly obscuring half of his face, he had an ability to convey simultaneously both intensity and a laid-back *je m'en fous* (I could care less) approach to life. I thought at the time he was a caricature—no, a parody—of an alienated French student of the 1960s.

At first, I hadn't paid much attention to him. I even thought him mildly entertaining in small doses. He obviously had charm or Marcia wouldn't have fallen for him, and he could actually be funny, especially when mimicking some of the more pompous of Brussels' overabundance of foreign diplomats. But it wasn't long before I took his sardonic fatigue with life as nothing more than a pose that had gone on too long. I began to detest him. I think I really would have fought hard to keep Marcia if she had strayed with just about anyone else. If it had been a Belgian bureaucrat or an Argentine polo player, I probably would have gone down on my knees and tried to get her to stay. But what was I to make of this self-parody of a French student, this intellectual poseur who helped himself to the liquor cabinet and, when I was away working a real job, to my marriage bed as well?

It was this contempt I felt for him that quickly transferred itself to Marcia too. Of course there was rage, but that was rapidly subsumed in a withering contempt. If she had lowered herself so much to fall for such a slimeball, to be angry with her was surely a waste of energy. Besides, it was easier to feel contempt. It didn't take much effort to display it. Old-fashioned anger was a clumsier emotion; it required action.

But now, suddenly, it bothered me that I hadn't fought for Marcia. It was odd, too, because I hadn't thought about her for months. I had let her go, just like that. I had sensed ever since the break-up four years earlier that her betrayal was really an act of extreme anger, but I had never had the guts to ask myself—much less her—why she had been in such a rage. We'd certainly loved each other passionately. I was twenty-six when we tied the knot, an age when compatibility between the sheets is still pretty much the most important factor in a relationship. That, plus the fact that everyone told us we made a great-looking couple and we were about the right age to get married were essentially the reasons why we did.

Marcia was a brunette with a riot of curls, a very pretty face that a generation earlier would have been described as pixie-like, a small, trim figure, and excellent legs. By contrast, I was tall and lanky, but that was part of the appeal. I looked and felt like the manly man when I was with Marcia, whose head just barely reached my shoulders. I was the type that mothers always liked their daughters to bring home—a pleasant, good-looking guy in a nondescript sort of way. Brown hair, physically fit, good manners, middle America.

At first, that had been enough for Marcia too. But when we got to Brussels, I guess she started to see what a really ordinary guy I was. Thinking back later, I realized that the first sign of trouble was when she stopped being funny with me. Marcia had a great wit and a great sense of humor, one of the reasons I first fell for her. And it had puzzled me when she started to display her wit only with company, almost never alone with me.

And then there was the politics. She was much more politically liberal than I was—though, for crying out loud, I had usually voted Democrat— and we had some heated arguments over politics. But it had never occurred to me that these disagreements might in any way have contributed to the betrayal. But perhaps they had. What I had always assumed to be a genuine mutual acceptance, in spite of sometimes-noisy debates on everything from euthanasia to the death penalty, might on her part have been a jaded tolerance barely sustained by the mutual enjoyment of making love. But the sex, in the end, had failed to keep the marriage together. I now realized that we had actually been profoundly different people.

But why in heaven's name was all of this coming back to torment me now?

Well, I didn't need a two-hundred-dollars-an-hour shrink to tell me that Trish might have something to do with it. Trish, utterly gorgeous, utterly charming—Trish, herself barely recovering from a one-year romance with a married Swiss businessman in Manila. I had met her just two months earlier, hadn't even kissed her yet, even though she conveyed sexuality as though it was a birthright. Simply put, she was ravishingly attractive. That, in and of itself, would have been enough to have me almost panting to be in her company. But she was far more than just a pretty face and an exquisite, slim body.

Our meeting was complete happenstance. I had finished a story on the latest episode in Philippine celebrity politics and had planned to head back to Hong Kong on an evening flight. But the flight was overbooked, and I was forced to stay one more night in the Hyatt. With nothing to do for the evening, I contacted the hotel's public relations department and was told there was going to be a reception for hotel PR chiefs from all over the Philippines. To be honest, the only reason I considered going was that the food would be gratis, there would probably be a halfway decent band, and maybe I'd meet one or two good-looking women.

I was right on all three counts. In fact, the women were even prettier than I'd anticipated, and it was hard choosing which group to chat with. But I wasn't in any hurry, and I certainly wasn't planning on actually finding a date at the reception. As I surveyed the room, however, I noticed a very boisterous group of young executives, men and women, who seemed to be having much more fun with one another than any other knot of people in the room. I immediately caught sight of Trish in the middle of the group, not for the obvious reason that she was strikingly beautiful but because it was clear she was very funny.

I'd often heard the old cliché that good-looking men are seldom witty (because growing up they had learned to use their looks and not their brains to get attention), and I assumed that this was true of beautiful women too. But Trish was unlike any other attractive woman I had ever met. She was genuinely funny and had the group captivated with some engaging story.

I'd hung around her group for awhile, enjoying her humor. But then something unexpected happened. One of the men in the group was laughing so hard that he began to have what looked like a heart attack. The others quickly saw this and made him lie down. It was in the middle of this crisis that Trish showed extraordinary presence of mind. She turned instantly from the life and soul of the party to the expert emergency medical responder. She was the first to call the hotel front desk and get them to send for paramedics; she knew the only physician who was attending the party and quickly found him, and she had the good sense to ensure that the apparent heart attack victim had plenty of space and plenty of air in the corner of the room to which he was taken.

The crisis put a damper on the party, and most of the crowd drifted away. But I hung around because I was intrigued. I had watched Trish's astonishing switch from Bette Midler to Florence Nightingale, and I now thought she was an even more interesting person than when I had first spotted her in full comedic flight. She obviously had several dimensions of personality and I wanted to find out more, less as a typical male in wolfish mode than as a detached observer interested in something he'd never encountered before.

We found a spot away from the main reception area and talked for almost two hours. She must have sensed my fascination, and I think she was struck by the fact that my interest went beyond physical attraction. I learned that she had grown up with four younger sisters, two of them even more beautiful than she (I found this hard to believe). Her father had been a surgeon who had worked in several different countries, taking his family with him. Trish's mother had been—surprisingly, in my view, since I assumed all good-looking women acquired their looks primarily from their mother—not especially attractive, but she was extremely well-read and the family comic.

Both mother and father had encouraged all the girls into witty conversational styles; by the time they were teenagers, each could hold her own in mixed company, by turns extremely funny and, when necessary, quite serious. Yet even among her talented sisters, Trish had shone as a wit and conversationalist.

From her father, Trish had acquired what amounted to medical take-charge instincts. She had hung around enough emergency room facilities with him to know how to handle many medical emergencies.

Not surprisingly, the combination of brains and beauty had intimidated most men she met. Ludwig, the Swiss businessman periodically passing through Manila, had been the only person who could out-joke Trish. He was a self-confidant man and fifteen years older. But he had been attentive, thoughtful, and persistent. The fact that he was married had at first really alienated her, but he had on one occasion brought his wife to the Philippines. Trish had met her and become convinced that Helga was a true shrew, an opinionated, selfish person who showed no interest in her husband's hard work putting together property deals across Asia and who spent a lot of her time in Switzerland pouring out her woes as an under-appreciated hausfrau to a succession of psychoanalysts.

Trish had felt sorry for Ludwig, and her sympathy for him had led first to a genuine friendship, later to a full-blown affair. But Ludwig, though obviously in love with Trish, was also something of a prisoner to his reputation among his Swiss friends. They were conservative and straight-laced, heirs perhaps of the reign in Switzerland of Protestant reformer John Calvin, and they made it clear that they would not consider him a true friend if he dumped Helga for Trish. Trish lived with this dilemma for awhile, but was finally confronted by her father and sisters with the truth: Ludwig was always going to be a married man, and Trish would continue to be, at best, only the love of his life, safely hidden away in Asia.

Trish had painfully ended the affair with Ludwig six months before I met her, and she told me about the relationship that very first night. In turn, I found myself being far more open than I would have been with anyone else about Marcia. We connected effortlessly. But the whole thing didn't make much sense for either of us. Why on earth would we drag into each other's lives the emotional baggage that still lay cluttered about us from the debris of earlier liaisons, mine a marriage, hers a cohabitation, especially when we lived eight hundred miles—a ninety-minute flight—apart? And now, on the brink of getting to know Trish better by having her in Hong Kong with me, here I was stuck 147 miles away in Guangzhou, chasing a story that might lead nowhere at all and could actually keep me here for days.

The phone rang. It was Lasch again.

"Hello, Richard." That Bostonian clip. "Did you get my e-mail yet?"

"No, Burt, I'm sorry. I only just checked into the hotel. I haven't even gotten out my laptop."

"Well, get it out. It may help you in the next phase of this."

Next phase? What on earth did he have in mind?

"OK, Burt, I won't ask you on the phone what that is."

"No, it's all in my message. Get back to me when you've had a chance to look at it. I think e-mail is better for this than the phone."

Right. And guess who didn't want to be called at 3:00 a.m.?

We hung up and I dragged myself off the bed. All I really wanted to do right now was to lie down for a nap, but that wasn't an option. Still, in a small triumph of independence, I carefully and methodically unpacked my bag, ordered a room-service hamburger and coffee, and glanced at the government newspaper, the *China Daily*, before doing anything about my laptop.

When I got to my e-mails, there was Lasch's message, along with a handful of others from friends and contacts in different places. "There's a man called Giuseppe Petrolucci researching Chinese history at Zhongshan University. He may have known our friend and something of the background to all this. His home phone is 8418-8863. Don't mention me, our friend, or anyone when you call. Just tell him you're from Hong Kong. Avoid identifying yourself more than that. Good luck."

That was rich—"good luck." Was the next message going to tell me where to find a bulletproof vest in Guangzhou?

I dug my heels in again. I knew with that certainty that often defies logic that I simply had to get hold of Trish. For one thing, I knew that if I didn't reach her as soon as possible, I would be completely ineffective in my reporting for the rest of the day. For another, I feared she would never even talk to me again if she thought I had casually forgotten about her arrival and been carried away to China by the latest excitement in journalism.

I called her hotel on Nathan Road in Kowloon. They said she had checked in, but she wasn't in her room. I tried paging her in the coffee shop, but she wasn't there either, so I was left with her hotel voice mail.

"Trish, it's Richard. Welcome to Hong Kong. I'm so sorry I couldn't be at the airport this morning, but I think Clarissa must have told you what happened. What I want to say is that—"

"Thank you. Your message has been recorded," the voice mail system interrupted. "If you wish to change the message, press two. If you wish to speak to a hotel operator, press zero."

Madness, sheer madness. I hung up, then immediately dialed again.

"Trish, me again. I'm at the Golden Panda in Guangzhou, room 2014." I succeeded in leaving the phone number this time, with the correct dialing prefix from Hong Kong, then hung up. Would she call soon? I hoped so. I believed so. I mean, would she still be angry at me for standing her up at the airport? Surely Clarissa would have soaked her in a dose of old-fashioned missionary friendliness and cheer?

But then a nagging thought intruded. What if Trish had been put off by Clarissa? It wasn't a question of Catholicism versus Protestantism. Trish's Catholicism was about as active as my commitment to the Flat Earth Society. Nor was it race. In the long conversation at the Manila reception and in subsequent and equally long phone calls, I had never detected any hint of prejudice, though many Asians are strongly prejudiced against blacks.

No, it was something much simpler: culture and class. Trish was born into that social elite in the Philippines, the three hundred or so families who proudly—and in a way, perversely—traced their ancestry back to the earlier Spanish conquerors of their land. It was a curious behavior I'd seen exhibited by others in that elite. They didn't exactly look down on any social group, Filipino or foreign. They were simply oddly disengaged when they were with people whose background they knew nothing about, or if they perceived a lack of interest in them on the part of those they were with. I realized, almost with a cold sweat, that Trish would open up to Clarissa in direct proportion to how confident she felt that Clarissa wouldn't need explanations about her background and her upbringing.

I tried calling Clarissa but got her voice mail too. What to tell her? "Clarissa, this is Richard. I just can't thank you enough for helping me out with Trish. I'm guessing that you did in fact meet up. Wondering how you are getting along."

I wanted to say something like, "I'm sure you brought out the best in her," but I realized just in time that it would sound both condescending and trite, so I changed it. "Someday," I added, with more conviction than I had anticipated, "I need to ask you the secret of your generosity and your sense of humor."

I wasn't sure why I had said this, but at least it was true. I sat for half a minute just trying to allow the various thoughts to filter themselves into appropriate mental pigeonholes. Then, as I scribbled down Petrolucci's name from Lasch's e-mail with a certain deliberate slowness, I remembered with a jolt an altogether different name I had first seen that morning. The business card was still in my coat pocket. I pulled it out and looked at it again. This time, I studied the side in Chinese; earlier, I had glanced only at the English name: "Yao Fanmei, Foreign Affairs Department, Guangzhou Municipal Public Security Bureau." The English side had an official-looking address and phone number, but the Chinese side, which I hadn't noticed before, had a completely different phone number in handwriting. It also had, in parenthesis and beside the phone number, the letters "p.m.," presumably indicating the time of day I should call.

Of course. If Yao genuinely wanted to talk to me about anything on an unofficial basis, he probably wouldn't want me to come strolling like some idiot tourist into the headquarters of the city's police department and asking for him. Officials in any security function in China, almost by definition, stayed as far away from foreigners, and above all foreign journalists, as China's crowded geography permitted. At least, that's what they did unless they had been ordered to keep someone under close surveillance, even to persuade him to reveal what bad things he was assumed to be plotting against China.

Foreigners, according to the line followed by China's security authorities, could not be trusted. Either they were spies, or they were plotting to break down China's social order with decadent and politically subversive ideas. Or, they were just a nuisance: barbarian simpletons who would never understand that a proud and sophisticated civilization had been kind enough to accommodate them as guests, despite their bungling ways. Foreigners, it was known, almost always needed to be watched carefully, handled with cunning, and above all told almost nothing about China. Naturally, under no circumstances should security officers attempt to befriend them.

I considered the most immediately obvious explanation for Yao Fanmei's behavior. This was that Yao was waiting for me at the Hong Kong airport with instructions to inveigle me into a clever entrapment scenario, one perhaps dreamed up by the real counter-espionage heavies, the people at the Ministry of State Security. They were normally the ones who kept watch on all suspicious foreigners and sought to break up a foreign intelligence connection. If it were an entrapment scenario, it would go something like this:

We meet at his suggestion, perhaps in some dark Guangzhou alley, where he would "hand over" to me some dirty manila envelope purportedly filled with secrets of China's national security. Then, as I slunk off with a guilty but triumphant grin, thinking I'd gotten a "scoop" for *Epoch*, heroic uniformed Chinese security officers would leap out of the shadows and seize me before I could "damage" beyond repair China's national interest. Naturally, a camera crew with lights and sound would be on hand to capture for Chinese TV all of these nefarious doings. I imagined the heartwarming *New York Times* headlines:

U.S. Journalist Arrested in Guangzhou

Chinese Accuse Him of Spying

President Interrupts Vacation for NSC Meeting

Experts Fear New Chill in U.S.–China Relations, etc. etc.

Yao's given name actually reinforced this scenario in my mind. I had thought it a little strange when he'd given me his card on the plane, and now, reading the Chinese side, I realized that his name in fact meant "oppose America." I remembered reading that in the 1950s, zealous Chinese Communists saddled their offspring at birth with these revolutionary monikers in the hope that, as they grew up, their names would indicate the socialist fervor of their parents, or perhaps—in some cases—actually add socialist zeal to their career path.

At any rate, "Oppose America" was certainly a more politically vigorous given name than "Brilliant Tiger" or "Spring Peony." I guessed that Yao was probably born in 1952 or 1953, which would mean he was now rather senior in China's security services. That, of course, argued against his use of entrapment, a ruse normally used by relatively junior officers.

Adding to my skepticism about this possibility was the fact that the Public Security Bureau usually wasn't so efficient that they could have known on short notice that I was about to leave Hong Kong on a particular flight. Of course, if they really wanted to "get" me on a China trip, they had full authority to take their time setting it all up; Hong Kong, after all, was "theirs." They were thorough and patient in counter-espionage work, but could they have been bugging my Hong Kong phone and just waiting for me to take the next trip to China?

I doubted it. It just didn't seem very likely because I really hadn't spent a lot of time digging up in China the sort of stories that tended to annoy them. It's true that I had paid special attention to human rights issues, perhaps more so than had other Hong Kong-based foreign correspondents, many of them with much greater malice toward China. Although my passion for human rights dated back to my college days, I was scrupulously fair when reporting these sensitive topics. It was easy to take cheap shots at China on this score, but I considered myself a journalist of a higher caliber than that.

I dismissed quickly another wild thought, that the PSB was simply trolling the Hong Kong airport for some potential big gweilo fish to swim into their net. Maybe they thought I was a bureaucrat from the U.S. Department of Agriculture on a grain-selling expedition, and I might spill all at a maotai-lubricated banquet and tell them the latest secrets of America's negotiating positions on foreign exports. Surely not even the PSB was that inept.

That left the final, the most enticing, yet at the same time, the scarcely credible possibility. And that was that Yao Fanmei was nothing less than a closet dissident, someone who really did have something important he wanted the outside world to know about China. On this line of reasoning, I was as likely to be a shirt buyer for Bloomingdale's or a student of Chinese Buddhism as a journalist when he saw me chugging up to the tail end of the line of passengers about to board the Guangzhou flight. If this explanation were remotely true, he had simply wanted to convey some information to the West and had happened upon me.

Or perhaps he was planning to get access to the CIA, or some other Western intelligence agency, in the hope of "buying" a ticket to America, courtesy of his helpful insider's information on the PSB's operations in China. The sheer, histrionic complexity of all this finally struck me as ludicrous. I burst out laughing as I flopped down on the bed again and stared at the ceiling. The tension drained away. I could finally turn my attention with a clear mind to one priority that I had barely coped with just before boarding the flight. It was moving into early afternoon, and I still hadn't eaten. Nor had I even started to do any work on the McHale business.

I called room service again to prod them about the hamburger I had ordered. Next, I called the bureau in Hong Kong to let them know where I was. Lucinda, the quietly efficient and always unflappable bureau secretary, had already picked up the phone message I had left on her voice mail letting her know Lasch had sent me to China. But as far as she was concerned, it was inconsequential whether I was on a reporting trip. I might just as easily have been on a rescue mission of a different sort. *Epoch* advertising executives sometimes got pickled in regional bars and nightclubs and needed rescuing from hotels after their pockets had been picked and their credit cards stolen.

"How long do you think you'll be there?" she asked, just a hint of amusement in her voice. Over the twenty-five years that she had worked for *Epoch* in Hong Kong, she'd seen bureau chiefs come and go, corporate executives from New York try to flirt with her, and foreign editors touch down forever in search of the Holy Grail of the ultimate Asian news story. China always seemed to beguile them from afar, then infuriate and disillusion them on closer examination. But sooner or later, she would entice them back, hinting at some exotic new angle lurking in a hitherto hidden valley of the country's lush, storied landscape. Lucinda must have thought that Lasch had yanked me into a new adventure to prove some thesis or other of his about what made China tick. I wanted to humor her on the phone, but I wasn't quite sure how.

"I don't know," I said feebly in response to her question. " At this point, I haven't a clue. If it turns out I need to be here for longer than four days, I'll let you know."

"Well, you don't need to worry. Lasch called to say that Meitnic is going to drop by and hold the fort for a few days. Should I bring him up to date on the sports section story on Asian water polo?"

Oh no. I had completely forgotten about this too.

"When's it due?"

"Not till Monday, but I don't think the stringers know about it yet. Shall I send it on to them?"

"Yes, thanks, Lucinda. And apologize to Steve that he's going to be left with a half-started story."

"Oh, don't worry about him. He always loves coming here. You may have trouble convincing him it's time to get back to Delhi."

I laughed. "You're great, as always, Lucinda. I'll call as soon as I know when I can get back."

Lucinda. Hong Kong Chinese, calm, amused, in her fifties now, still stylish and attractive, and still unmarried. This was because she had felt obligated to look after her sick mother, and few men wanted a bride encumbered with a medical case on the side. She used to joke that it was her mother who had prevented her from ruining some man's life, but I always thought that secretly she longed to have a family of her own.

Over the years, she had certainly accumulated many entertaining tales to tell, but she was unfailingly discreet. She went the extra mile to help the bureau chiefs and correspondents look good with New York, reminding them of story deadlines, filling in gaps by organizing the stringers. Often, she came up with some good story ideas herself. People confided in Lucinda; she was so kind. She never contradicted a person to his face, but she managed to convey her opinions in a way that only a blockhead would fail to understand.

And Trish? Should I mention the Trish problem to Lucinda? I thought better of it. It wouldn't be fair to dump on Lucinda the details of my bungled dating life. "Just one thing, Lucinda," I added as an afterthought, "if anyone calls me, please give them my phone and room number here in Guangzhou. I'm expecting some calls, and I thought I would be in Hong Kong to take them." It was true. I had been expecting to hear from a niece who was planning to come through Hong Kong in a few weeks. But of course it wasn't Jenny, the niece, I was thinking of. It was Trish.

"No problem, Richard, I'll take care of that. Anything else?"

"No, that's all. Thanks." We both hung up.

When the room service order finally showed up, I ate the hamburger slowly, then went through the list of people I could contact in Guangzhou. I would get to Petrolucci in due course. There were also some expatriate businessmen, a couple of low-level Chinese journalists, and two American teachers of English. Then there was one man who, if he was in the country, worked just a short walk away from my hotel. He was Michael Young, a witty and intelligent young American consular officer I'd met at a Hong Kong dinner party. Despite the spelling of his name, he was actually a Chinese-American. His last name had been anglicized a couple of generations earlier from its original Cantonese form of Yung. Just talking to him on the phone, you wouldn't guess his ancestry. He spoke like a classic Foreign Service preppie from Westchester County.

I quite casually assumed Michael was CIA because his Cantonese, unusually, was as flawless as his Mandarin, and because he spoke and acted with far more panache than the average consular officer. But consular officers, I'd discovered, seemed to have a larger number of CIA agents within their ranks than any other part of the diplomatic missions. There was logic to this too. It would be unlikely that, given his skills, the real reason he was in Guangzhou was to turn down applications from pedicab drivers to visit alleged cousins in San Jose.

I walked down the spiral stairs to the basement level to use a pay phone. My own room phone was probably bugged, but the word was that pay phones in most parts of China were pretty safe. Even if they were bugged at this time, it might take the listeners awhile to figure out who was calling the U.S. consulate. Still, it was a long shot contacting Young. He was affable enough, which wasn't often the case of Foreign Service officers toward reporters, but I didn't think it likely he would know anything about McHale, or if he did, would pass any of that knowledge on to me. But it was worth a try.

By a miracle, I got straight through to Young.

"Michael, it's Richard Ireton—of *Epoch*. Remember we met at Rebecca Chao's place in Discovery Bay a few weeks ago?"

I'd mentally prepared myself for a long pause as he searched his memory bank for some hack or other he'd bumped into. I was ready to launch into a quick reprise of the memorable part of that dinner when a rich Hong Kong Chinese businessman among the guests—someone who spent several weeks a year chumming around in Beijing—had denied that more than a handful of people had been killed in the Tiananmen Square massacre on June 4. Michael, somewhat to my surprise, had torn into the guy, citing chapter and verse from official New China News Agency dispatches of that fateful week in June 1989 to refute him. I'd backed him up with some strong evidence.

"Yeah, Rick, of course I remember you. That was quite a lively evening. What brings you into town? There a revolution going on or something?" And he laughed the easy laugh of someone who has always been at the top of his class, and without much effort.

"No, but some other interesting stuff. You free for a drink later on?"

"A drink? Well, now, *Epoch* magazine must be on to something if it's inviting consular officers out for a drink." And he laughed again.

I took a chance. "How about six o'clock at the Dong Fang? Or have you got a cable to write?"

"Nothing that's got to be sent tonight." Another laugh. Then a pause. "All right, let's meet at six, but I've got a better idea. Where are you staying?"

"The Golden Panda."

"Tell you what, why don't you get yourself here around 6:30, and we'll decide where to go from here?"

"Great. See you then."

This was promising. He wasn't going to brush me off with some cocktail chitchat at someplace crawling with PSB guys trying to protect China from the sinister machinations of American plotters. He might even tell me something useful. I had the impression he thought I might have something of interest for him. That was always the case with Foreign Service officers. If you showed up to see them on short notice, you had better not waste their time.

I used the time between the phone call and the meeting to try and see who else I could get to. I arranged to see Petrolucci for dinner—a major plus. Banking on the fact that Young probably wasn't going to unburden himself for more than a Tsingdao or two's worth of information about China, I would have enough time to talk to him and then get over to Petrolucci's place. I hadn't done anything about Yao Fanmei yet, partly because I wasn't sure what exactly I wanted to talk to him about. It wasn't a good idea to tell a source the names of the other people you were going to see, or had already met.

Lasch, meanwhile, had been e-mailing material on McHale all afternoon—the early morning hours, New York time. His occasional frenzies of energy at times when most other, more civilized human beings would have been asleep were well known, but this was the first time I'd seen him in action. There was a McHale résumé from his prep school Web site, an urbane article about life in Hong Kong he had written for the *Princeton Alumni Weekly*, a *Wall Street Journal* piece quoting McHale on investment opportunities in South China, a Princeton yearbook page from McHale's senior class, and an e-mail McHale had sent Lasch six months ago describing some of his most recent impressions of conversations with Chinese officials.

These items didn't tell me much about McHale except that he loved Chinese food, wasn't averse to Chinese women (Lasch had said he was divorced, but I couldn't figure out whether he had remarried or not), and had enough charm to talk to anyone he wanted to. So much for his personality. I had no idea what he did with his time in Hong Kong and China. It was all a bit much. I wasn't sure I wanted to know as much about McHale as Lasch seemed to want me to know. It wasn't that I wasn't eager to find out whatever I could about his whereabouts. It was just that being deluged

with myriad details about every recorded aspect of his career wasn't helping me figure out how to find him.

I finished reading the last of Lasch's research on McHale shortly before
it was time to meet Young. As I took my time wandering through the lobby
and next door to the consulate, I looked idly at some of the displays in the
hotel shops, wondering if there was something I could pick up as a peace
offering for Trish.

At the consulate, there were no Marines on duty, as is the case at U.S.
embassies around the world. But a security officer asked me for my passport
and what my business was. He then dialed Young's extension, and it wasn't
long before Young showed up. He wore a perfectly tailored tan suit, obviously from Hong Kong, a cream shirt with thin blue stripes, and a brilliant
gold and blue silk tie. Yet the one item that would have fixed him in my mind
as a dandy was missing; there was no matching silk handkerchief dangling
from the breast pocket. He was strikingly elegant but succeeded in avoiding
the impression of being vain—a delicate line to tread. I wondered what the
rest of the Foreign Service thought of him. He smiled a brilliant smile and
extended his hand before he was even at the bottom of the stairs.

"Good to see you again," he said. "I thought you would agree it made
more sense for you to come here so we can get a drink someplace that's
not quite in the Ministry of State Security repertoire. They like to think
everyone here is a spook or something. It must go with their full-employ-
ment program. Layoffs are fine if you subcontract for K-Mart but not if you
are keeping tabs on those wicked hegemons." He laughed an easy laugh.
"The really thuggish ones practically hang over your shoulder as you order
a drink. Bad breath, you know." Another laugh.

He was level with me now, a few inches shorter than my five feet
eleven, of well-trimmed physique but not bulging out of his shirt with
health club pecs. He had a good-natured twinkle in his eye, but he also
conveyed alertness. I had the impression he could become snappish quite
quickly if he thought the circumstances warranted it. He surely knew that
I assumed he was one of Langley's boys, so he made a point of not playing
games with me about what the Chinese security services assumed him to
be. I imagined that he gave their counter-espionage people a run for their
money: fluent in both Mandarin and Cantonese, disarmingly skillful in personal relations, and unquestionably energetic.

We were on our way out of the lobby, within the security area policed
through bulletproof glass by the guards, when an American woman in her

late fifties came out of a side door and spoke to Young. "Michael," she said crisply, "Josh would like a quick word with you before you head out."

"Right," he said, winking at me before following her back through the door from which she had emerged. "Josh" was Joshua Ehrenfold, "the CG" in embassy-speak, short for consul-general. I had met him only once at a reception in Guangzhou, and I hadn't liked him much. He was aloof, not especially bright, and seemed to speak to all first-time acquaintances as if they could hardly find China on a map, much less grasp what was happening there. I groaned inwardly. A "quick word" between him and Young could turn into a thirty-minute meeting.

But it didn't. Young came out in less than ten minutes. He offered no explanation for the interruption, but I didn't think anything of it. These little bumps in the road were par for the course in the hack's life.

"Let's catch up over a drink," he said, his words not quite as hearty as they had been earlier. "I'm going to take you to a place that's a little unusual, but I think you will find it entertaining. Let's not talk about anything on the way. Just stay close to me and try not to give the impression that you haven't a clue where I am going." With those words, we headed out into the steamy Guangzhou evening.

Chapter Three

*I*t had rained during the afternoon, and a dampness, a hot sticky dampness, close to the skin, lingered in the air. The storm drains were still disgorging the runoff into pipes that led into the Pearl River. On Shamian Island, the old tile roofs dripped on the courtyards and alleyways, and puddles collected on the uneven pavement of the streets. I liked these furious summer downpours of South China; they were restful, restorative. The leaves and the grass soaked up the water greedily and repaid the sky with a welcome freshness. Dust and the muck of a restless city's thoroughfares were washed away in minutes. Even the offensive exhaust from the city's great hordes of motorbikes and taxis was momentarily tamed by the cleansing stream.

We walked slowly, I on Young's right, closer to the curb at first, chatting loudly in an attempt to appear non-conspiratorial.

Young wasted no time in getting us headed toward our destination. But he made sure that if we had any police tails, we weren't making life easy for them. We stopped in a couple of tourist shops close to the hotel, poked around among the tacky souvenirs as if I were the greenhorn visitor and he the jaded veteran of a thousand rummaging visits. I knew what he was doing. If we were under surveillance and Young wanted to slow down his tail, this was a good way of doing it.

It was in the third store that Young made his move. He warmly greeted the owner, who seemed to know him. He was an older, rather distinguished-looking Chinese man who looked as though he'd been born into comfortable circumstances in a different era and was now trying to climb back to gentility after years of threadbare living.

The store was larger than most tourist dives, with American Express and Visa signs stuck prominently on the windows. It was also better stocked, with some elegant Qing dynasty reproduction porcelain of recent manufacture attractively displayed—a vast improvement over the usual dusty bowls full of cheap, pseudo-jade bracelets and knickknacks of questionable taste.

Near the back of the store, out of the line of sight of the front window, were several rows of well-made imperial-style Chinese formal jackets and gowns, along with two changing cubicles. I imagined well-heeled women lawyers from Manhattan's upper east side eagerly trying to recreate the Ci Xi-look, that is, the style of the Qing dynasty Empress Dowager Ci Xi.

Behind the changing cubicles was a narrow corridor that seemed to lead to an area of the store off-limits to the public. But then I noticed what Young obviously already knew. The passageway actually opened onto a side door. I followed him as briskly as I could, without running, as he negotiated the racks of pseudo-imperial robes and gowns and left the store.

We found ourselves stumbling out into a narrow alley strewn with charred pieces of multi-colored paper, probably the remnants of some folk religion ritual. Several small children were clamoring over possession of a battered soccer ball, splashing through the dirty water in the alley. An old Chinese grandma sat impassively on a stool a few yards from the store's doorway. Her blue pant-clad legs seemed anchored to the ground as though, after a lifetime of political meetings, they had finally taken root in the soil of her neighborhood. As we strode by, we nearly knocked her over, but she betrayed not the slightest interest in us. Foreigners, she must have thought, can be expected to do strange things much of the time. That sentiment on her part was reassuring.

Young was walking briskly, avoiding the trash, the puddles, and the slop and—to my surprise—was actually heading farther into the alley and away from the street with all the shops. I stumbled along after him, trying to dodge low-hanging wet laundry and an occasional bird cage while also watching for the puddles and trash. With a quick, dodging motion, Young swung right into an even narrower alley, more like a passage to someone's backyard than anything else, and then suddenly we were out on the main tourist and traffic street near the Golden Panda, exactly perpendicular to the street with the tourist shops that we had started out on.

Hundreds of bicyclists were heading home from work, bells tinkling, faces impassive, and the traffic was barely creeping along behind city buses. Without hesitating or looking back, Young darted nimbly across the street with me close behind, then ducked into the doorway of a building whose second floor seemed to be a bar or restaurant known as the Sunny Times.

It was typical of the spread of bars, discos, and karaoke dives that were sprinkled throughout China's commercial urban gateways close to the hotels where foreigners, and especially foreign businessmen, stayed. There was no elevator, so we mounted the stairs with our heads down, trying to avoid the flow of customers leaving the place by the same route. A T-shirted and slightly drunk German, speaking loudly to a young Western woman as he descended, lurched into us and nearly knocked us over as we neared the second-floor landing. He looked like a vacationing backpacker, but I suspected he was a student on a German government education grant.

I wondered now at Young's judgment in choosing this place. It was neither quiet nor inconspicuous. We could hear the jukebox rattling the thin walls well before we had found the entrance to the bar at the top of the stairs. The sound of the Hong Kong and Taiwan pop tunes being pumped out was so deafening that I couldn't imagine how Young thought we would be able to communicate even the time of day to each other here, much less anything subtle or significant about China.

But Young wasn't a CIA operative—if that was what he was—in a sensitive Chinese city for nothing. He swung confidently past the tables of sallow Western businessmen and fidgety, cell phone-waving Chinese entrepreneurs for a back corner, matter-of-factly handing a bill to a passing waitress as he headed for an unoccupied table, about the only one in the place. The money exchange was done so deftly that I had no idea what denomination it was, or even what currency—U.S. dollar, Hong Kong dollar, or Chinese yuan? But whatever it was, it was clearly enough because the girl stopped in her tracks, followed him to his seat and smiled at him as she handed us a beverages list.

"Perfect," Young said, looking at me with a smile. For some odd acoustic reason, the jukebox music was somewhat muffled in this cranny of the bar, and we could talk without shouting. "I think," said Young, "we can talk here without either the PSB thugs or under-employed chicks leaning over our shoulders." At this, he nodded to the waitress, and she left without a word.

"Or listening table lamps," I added as I took a seat facing him.

"When were you last here?" he asked, wasting no time.

"About six months ago. Some fellow from Georgia had just run from Beijing to Guangzhou. The whole idea struck me as so crazy I thought it worth suggesting a story, and the editors agreed."

"Well, and what brings you here now?" The smile was pleasant, but the eyes were all business, attentive, probing.

"A disappearance," I said. "An American businessman by the name of Chuck McHale, based in Hong Kong, with years of experience trading and consulting in China and a contacts list large enough to make the phone company jealous. He vanished into thin air a couple of days ago."

Young smiled, but there was a twitch of impatience around his temples. "Rick," he said, "you and I both know of people who enjoy disappearing from Hong Kong from time to time. Nine out of ten times, it's a weekend sex expedition to Bangkok or Manila. The tenth time, it's a genuine family emergency, and the guy has to attend a funeral in Minneapolis. Come on now, what's the big deal about this one?"

I looked at him steadily. "I don't know the man at all," I said, "but my boss, who is a pretty sober fellow, has been a buddy of his since college. I can tell you, Michael, I wouldn't have gotten a phone call at three o'clock this morning from a very senior person at *Epoch* magazine if this was just about some errant lothario carousing through the night spots of Guangzhou."

"OK, then, help me out a little. Aside from the fact that your boss is nostalgic about his friends from college"—I thought this was a bit harsh—"what's so special about this *desparecido?*" He had used, brutally, I thought, the term that referred to leftists who had been kidnapped and murdered during the dictatorship of the Argentine military junta in the 1970s.

"First off, they're buddies from college days. Lasch—my boss—never sticks his neck out for someone he doesn't know implicitly who he can trust with his life. Second, the guy who's disappeared is really savvy about China. Third, Lasch says he thinks the man knows something about the regime that he's not supposed to know, or at least something that some people will do virtually anything to keep secret."

"Like what?" Young asked, not looking up from the table.

"If I knew, I wouldn't be about to buy you a Tsingdao," I said as quietly as I could. I had the sense that Young could be brusque to the point of nastiness when he wanted to be, but I suspected he would probably only get this way if he thought someone was trying to put something over on him. As a journalist, I had occasionally gotten sources to reveal things by hinting that I knew something really important even if I hadn't a clue what was going on. But I would only try it with a mid-level bureaucrat who was frustrated about his job, genuinely vain, and not especially bright. Young was none of these.

Another slim waitress hurried past our table. Without thinking, I put my arm out to stop her to take our order. She was a bit surprised but skidded to a halt. She took my hand in both of hers and asked, in perfect English, "So you want to order, do you?"

Young and I both laughed. It was so un-Chinese it was both funny and charming. But I quickly extracted my hand. "My friend here would like a—"

"Tsingdao," Young said quickly, referring to the thoroughbred, German-style brew from North China.

"And I'll have the same," I added.

"OK, coming right up." She hurried off with a giggle.

But none of this distracted Young from our conversation. "Well, first off, let me say that if I had any idea of what has happened to the friend of your boss, the Privacy Act would prohibit me from giving you any information about the individual or the case."

I had to bite my tongue. Of course, I knew that. And surely he knew that I knew that. Neither of us was new to this game, after all. So why was he unloading this bureaucratese on me? And why would he bother to take me to this hole-in-the-wall if all he was going to do was play Mr. Foreign-Service-Goody-Two-Shoes? But then, this was a tack that the better Foreign Service types used with annoying frequency. It was intended to throw journalists and other interlocutors just a little off balance. They were so smooth that they liked to do a verbal soft shoe shuffle in and out of their official (diplomatic) jobs and their real (espionage) jobs. Watching this performance was a little like watching a surgeon mimic his craft while at home carving Thursday evening's roast chicken. I decided to punch back a little.

"Would it make a difference if he were a high-flying consultant for a major Hong Kong red chip 'hong' with deep-throat Beijing connections as opposed to a soap salesman?"

He sat back with a half smile. He knew I wasn't going to kowtow to him. Perhaps, he may have thought, he might actually learn something from me.

"Deep throat, huh? How sure are you of those connections?" It was his way of saying, OK, I'll concede that he's someone I'd be happy to talk to you about.

"To tell you the truth," I continued, "I don't know what they were. I only know that my boss was certain, after various conversations with him, that McHale had entered that twilight world surrounding China's leadership where the right relationship can deliver the moon and the wrong one a disappearing act in a Beijing *hutong*—or Guangzhou alley, for that matter. I haven't a clue what he knew. In fact, I'm just a little surprised that you haven't come across him yourself." This was as close as I could come to hinting that Lasch more or less assumed McHale was CIA, and that I assumed the same thing myself.

"I've never met the man," Young said coldly. I thought it was an interesting statement. After all, it was entirely possible for him to know all about McHale without ever having met him, and therefore to be perfectly honest in saying that he'd never met him. Young paused before asking, "What do you think he may have known that would have caused someone in the Chinese leadership enough irritation to make him disappear?"

I took a gamble. "Michael," I said with a touch of exasperation, "you know as well as I do that anti-foreignism has been on the rise in China, especially here in Guangzhou. If McHale was getting too close for comfort to Chinese who other Chinese didn't want him to meet, he'd certainly be in trouble. And what do you guys think is behind this rise in anti-foreignism?"

"Things have changed a lot since you and I first started coming to China," he said thoughtfully. "Organized crime is really serious now, and the Communist Party at some levels is so compromised by its own involvement in it that it doesn't know how to cope. So it's doing something that Chinese regimes have done from time immemorial with top criminal elements. It's started to co-opt them for its own political purposes.

"The jockeying for political power is intense," he went on, "far beyond the usual Xinhua narration"—he was referring to the dispatches of the New China News Agency, which China-hands always referred to by its Mandarin name because it rolled off the tongue far more easily than the cumbersome English ("of who's in which position at the Beidaihe summer vacation swimming stakes")—now he was talking about the annual gathering each August of party big shots at the seaside resort on the coast of the Bohai Sea in northeastern China. "Our guys in Beijing say they don't detect anything special going on, but we're sensing something very odd happening down here in Guangzhou."

"Like what?"

"People who used to talk to us a lot—just general stuff, cultural developments, the occasional bureaucratic cross-talk in the city government and party lineup—well, they've virtually stopped seeing us at all. Some foreign businessmen have reported that the usual bribe routine to get licensing permits for manufacturing and other commercial activity has gotten completely out of hand. There have been open threats against some foreigners if they don't pay up for all sorts of specious services. Of course, it's against American law for American businessmen to bribe overseas, and though it obviously happens to a degree, it's unusual. But what used to be a bribe, a sweetener for a business deal, has now become, in some areas of commerce, a requirement. It's protection money pure and simple. We've heard of similar developments in other Chinese cities, but nothing to the extent we're seeing here."

"How do you account for this?"

"Hard to say. Other foreign businessmen have gotten creamed by the new breed of protection capitalist, but it's the Americans who've been hit hardest. It's as though the anti-Americanism in China that came out of our accidental bombing back in the nineties of the Chinese embassy in Belgrade has crystallized into something with a harsh, personal edge to it. People in the city government we've had great relations with for years are hard to reach now, even on the phone. Some of my long-time friends around town don't want to be seen with me. Someone seems to have waved a wand over this place, or at least over Guangzhou, and said, 'OK, the time for being nice to foreigners is over. We're bolting the doors again.'" Under the streaky light from the ceiling illumination of the restaurant, Young looked suddenly weary, older.

The same long-legged waitress now showed up with the Tsingdaos. She had obviously been hired for the job because customers liked watching her flit among the tables, chatter coquettishly, and—in the case of the occasional foreigners—speak remarkably good English. And if she liked them, she would hold their hands. Now she seemed to notice Young for the first time. "I like the tie you are wearing," she said, stroking the top of his tie, close to his face, with both hands. She was flirting shamelessly and with the confidence typical of pretty women whose advances men usually find hard to resist.

But Young was having none of it. Perhaps his last comments had sobered even himself. He said nothing, looking at her with such a steady, expressionless gaze that she backed off, startled. She put the tie down and stalked off, flushing and pouting at the same time.

"Look, Rick, this is really sensitive," he said in a low voice. "I know we're on the same side here, and I wouldn't even have said hello if I didn't think you'd play it straight with me. But frankly, even if you wrote about this with no attribution whatsoever, the bad guys in this town would track it back to the consulate whether I'd seen you or not. Then some nasty things—some really nasty things—might start coming down around here."

"Demonstrations against the consulate, rude treatment of Americans, that sort of thing?"

"Oh no. Worse than that. More disappearances. Maybe a murder here and there."

"So you are on track with McHale's disappearance?"

"On track? I'd never heard of McHale—and that's the truth, whatever you think that says about my expertise—until you mentioned his name a few minutes ago. But there have been some rough muggings of foreigners, especially of westerners recently. A Swedish guy was actually murdered, and we are pretty sure it wasn't a botched robbery. He wasn't a tourist, and like McHale, he knew this town pretty well. It never made it into the *South China Morning Post* or Hong Kong's Chinese press, and of course as far as the local papers are concerned, the thing never happened."

"Why didn't anyone report it?" I asked, wondering why this was the first I'd heard about this and fearing I'd missed a story.

"Because every Hong Kong and foreign news agency in town was sent a fax explaining that the unfortunate demise of Mr. Larsen was the consequence of his failure to respect Chinese traditions and his interest in matters that were none of his business. It was politely suggested that foreign reporters leave full investigation of the case to the appropriate Chinese authorities and not jump to their own conclusions."

"Who sent the fax?"

"A group calling itself 'Defend the Motherland.' No names, no address, not even a return fax number. If any reporter were able to trace the source number of the fax, he hasn't told anyone around town that I know."

There was a finality to the last phrase—"that I know"—that said more about Young's obvious power and influence in the twilight world of Guangzhou espionage than anything else he could have said.

"When did the murder happen?"

"I can't say precisely, for several reasons, but put it in the framework of the last six months."

So McHale's disappearance was not an isolated event. It might be part of a growing pattern of Chinese anti-foreign actions. McHale might very well have been murdered, his body dumped, Capone-style, in a concrete casing at the bottom of the Pearl River. We might never find out what happened to him, or whether his disappearance had anything to do with "Defend the Motherland."

But if the U.S. consulate in Guangzhou, or at least one part of it, had been aware of a burgeoning anti-foreignism in China for several months, no one in Washington or New York or London seemed very attentive. There was just too much happening in too many places. North Korea, the Middle East, Iraq, Afghanistan, Sudan. How could anyone keep track of slow-moving events in China? The lazy explanation in Washington about the outraged Beijing demonstrations against NATO after the Belgrade bombing was that the Chinese leadership had orchestrated it all. Translation: it didn't merit serious thought. China, to use a phrase often bandied about in Washington, simply was "not on the front burner of America's national security concerns." I wondered about that.

Young was now scrutinizing me closely. I returned his gaze.

"What do you think this McHale was on to?" he asked after a pause, looking down at his Tsingdao before sipping it.

"That's one of the things I'm here to find out," I replied. "I thought you might have some ideas."

"No ideas. They don't pay me to have ideas. But some surmises."

I took a stab. "Let's start with the anti-foreignism."

"Not bad, Rick, not bad."

The waitress came back again, and this time she was not flirting at all. In fact, she looked very serious. "Where are you from?" she asked us both with surprising directness.

"Oh, just passing through," Young replied with a laugh. "And you are probably from Meixian, right?" I'd heard from several people that Young's ability to identify regional Cantonese accents was uncanny. This time, though, he'd actually figured out that this waitress was from the part of northeastern Guangdong Province called Plum County—just from her spoken English.

But Young's bantering had been a mistake. Now she looked not just startled but angry. "How did you know?" she asked. Young simply shrugged. "Would you like something else?" she asked, attempting to sound matter-of-fact. We declined, and she quickly darted away. The flirtation was definitely gone now.

"Do you remember the Boxer Rebellion?" he asked, turning back to me and posing the question in the same tone he might have used to ask if I remembered an evening of chamber music with the consul-general. I didn't know where he was going with this.

"About as well as I remember the Taiping Rebellion or the Nian Rebellion or the White Lotus Uprising, for that matter," I said, playing along. "Or are you asking me about David Niven and Charlton Heston in *Fifty-five Days at Peking?* Not a bad movie, in my view, considering they could only get extras to play Boxer rebels by raiding half the Chinese restaurants and Filipino dance bands of Western Europe."

"I'm not asking you about David Niven," Young said levelly, "but maybe the White Lotus Society or maybe, in today's language, the secret societies and even"—and here his voice got very quiet—"the Triads."

There it was again, the Triads. It had been less than twenty-four hours since Lasch had first raised it in connection with McHale.

"Of course there's a possible Triad connection to McHale's disappearance," I said carefully. "You can't spend much time doing business in South China without bumping into them sooner or later."

"The Triad connection in McHale's disappearance is obvious," Young interrupted impatiently, for the first time indicating that he certainly knew something about it. "What's far more important is, which Triads? Most of them are thugs and gangsters. But some are a lot more sinister. That's why I asked you about the Boxers."

He paused again. I poured some Tsingdao and took a slow sip. No point in getting excited just yet.

"Come on, Richard," he said, sounding like a college professor patiently trying to get through to a slow student, and using my full given name to emphasize the point. "I remember at that Discovery Bay dinner when you told me you were fascinated by China's efforts in the late nineteenth century to modernize. You said the reformers advocated 'Western learning for practicality, Chinese learning for the essence' but were perplexed that when the really vicious anti-Western grassroots revolt kicked in during the Boxer Rebellion in the year 1900, even the Qing dynasty got caught up in the mumbo jumbo of Chinese folk religion. The politically correct name for that, of course, is religious Daoism. Now let me ask you: What was it about the Boxers that both seduced the Qing dynasty authorities and nearly led to a horrific massacre of foreigners in the Chinese capital?"

I racked my brain. If Young knew far more about McHale than he had first let on, I wished he would just get straight to the point. But it just wasn't his style—or the spook style in general.

"Well, the most startling thing about the Boxers," I said, thinking hard back to my graduate school studies, "was that the movement grew out of an occult-based secret society in Shandong Province in the late 1890s, something called the Spirit Boxers. The movement's followers believed they had been endowed with supernatural power to save China from the foreigners. They thought they would be protected from bullets, even foreign bullets. They were fanatical and ruthless. As far as I can recall, the first people they picked on in their rampage through North China were Chinese Christians and then any Western missionaries they could find. I think they killed more than a hundred missionaries altogether."

"Not bad. Actually 146. And what they really wanted to do was to establish a new dynasty in China that would forever be protected from foreign incursion and Western religion. And that protection was supposed to come from powers endowed by a legion of sympathetic gods and goddesses."

"OK, so we're in tune on the substance of one of the most intriguing episodes of Chinese history in the past century or so. What's that got to do with McHale?"

"Richard," Young said in a voice so low I wasn't sure I was hearing him properly—but he was using my full name again, so I knew what was coming next was serious—"the Boxers never went out of business."

"What?"

"I said, 'The Boxers never went out of business.' The Boxers are back."

"What's that supposed to mean?" I was the one taking the offensive now. I didn't have a clue what he was getting at. What he said just didn't make sense.

But instead of answering me right away, Young leaned back slowly and smiled slightly. Then he scratched the back of his neck and moved his head slowly back and forth. I knew what he was doing—"clearing the room" with his eyes just in case the PSB had showed up and were observing us from across the room or somewhere. I was nervous, too, particularly after the abrupt change in the demeanor of our waitress.

"I don't mean literally, Rick," he said with a quiet laugh, now looking down. "I mean that the obsession with occult magic, the belief that China could somehow acquire power over the foreigners by setting up a whole new dynasty entirely subservient to, and protected by, various local gods— entirely Chinese gods, of course—was not stamped out when the Boxers were defeated in 1900. It never disappeared. It simply went underground.

The Communists persecuted the grassroots expressions of Daoism, China's folk religion, wherever they found them, just as they tried to stamp out all religions, particularly Christianity, which they feared because it had come from the West and they thought it was an instrument of Western imperialist control.

"But you know what?" he continued. "Not even the Communists could get rid of Christianity, and they failed miserably to stamp out religious Daoism. In fact, you might be surprised to know that virtually every major branch of the Chinese government, and especially some parts of the military, has been totally penetrated by Qigong practitioners and Qigong masters." Curiously he pronounced Qigong not in the light, Chinese manner but as a westerner would who didn't know any Chinese at all—Chee-gung.

I was tempted to interrupt him, but I bit my tongue. I wasn't the least bit interested in Chinese folk religion. It had always irritated rather than intrigued me: the smoky incense in squalid temples, the grubby bits of scorched paper covered with prayers to local gods, everything as meaningless and discordant as the screeching and cymbal clashing of Chinese opera. Besides, what did any of this have to do with McHale?

Young sensed my impatience but ignored it completely. He went on. "You think the Triads are simply Mafia East? Oh, most of them are just typical mob rackets, prostitution, drugs, protection stuff, the usual, albeit on a big scale. Hong Kong's infamous 14K Triad outfit has actually cleared out rival gangs pretty impressively, while keeping the police guessing the whole time. But I'm not talking about them. There's something else going on that's way beyond old-fashioned crime. You know what Qigong is, don't you?"

"An ancient Chinese breathing and exercise routine that's supposed to give its practitioners some kind of super health and super strength?"

Young nodded. "Well, we've noticed a pattern. By the way, everything I am saying now is open-source stuff. But for your purposes, I want it to be kept total deep background. Not even 'Western diplomatic sources.' You do understand me, don't you?"

He was suddenly all steel and U.S. government bureaucrat again, no doubt another behavioral trick they were taught at Langley.

"Gotcha," I said.

"The pattern we've noticed—sightings around the city, name references in local newspapers, appearances at semi-official receptions—has been of a striking number of Qigong practitioners from all over China converging on Guangzhou in the past eighteen months.

"Now why should that be a big deal?" Young asked rhetorically, setting up the question I was about to interrupt him with. "Can't Qigong masters, just like generals, shoe salesmen, or tennis players, drop into granny's hometown for a visit whenever they want? Why shouldn't people who are interested in breathing, exercise, and health techniques wander around China as and when they choose? Well, three things make this travel pattern noteworthy. First, while these same Qigong fellows have built a cottage industry doing Qigong performances in literally dozens of Chinese cities, not one of these guys has performed in Guangzhou in all this time. Not one.

"Second, for people who are supposed to model a healthy lifestyle for just ordinary folks, they've spent an amazing amount of time in the company of the local military. And not just any old foot soldiers, either."

I interrupted him. "You mean the senior commanders of the Guangzhou Military Region?"

"Yes, why do you ask?"

"Just a hunch. Go on."

"Frankly, it's odd. The population of Guangzhou is a lot richer than the people in almost any other Chinese city except Shanghai, and people will pay big bucks to watch a Qigong master lie down on a bed of sharp knives without drawing a single drop of blood. You ever seen one of those performances?"

"Yes," I said. "A couple of years back some monks from the Shaolin Temple performed in Hong Kong. I paid thirty Hong Kong dollars to watch a dozen bald guys get whacked over the head with telephone poles and smash bricks with their foreheads, all with no evident sign of getting hurt. It was quite a trick. They even had one guy standing on a table with nothing under each table leg but a raw egg. Some skeptic from the audience insisted on inspecting one of the eggs after the Qigong expert got off the table. This guy grabbed the egg and got the shock of his life when it shattered in his hand. The audience roared as the egg dribbled down his girlfriend's blouse—boy, was she ticked off. The showmanship was corny, but the head-bashing stuff was weird and pretty amazing stuff. Frankly, though, I would have rather spent the money to watch nubile blondes getting sawn in half by some fellow in a top hat and cape."

Young didn't laugh. "It wasn't a trick, Rick," he said quietly.

I was stunned. "Come on, Michael, you don't believe all that mumbo jumbo about Qigong people having supernatural powers, physical, spiritual, or whatever, do you?"

Young looked offended. Oops, maybe he did, I thought.

"I'm not paid to believe anything," he said coldly, "anymore, I'm sure, than you are. I'm paid to observe and to analyze. Let's drop the word powers. That's already loaded. What we do know from both Western and Chinese scientific studies is that some of these Qigong people have abilities at mental projection—if that's a sufficiently neutral phrase—that researchers have traditionally characterized as 'paranormal.'"

"You mean telepathy, hypnotism stuff, that sort of thing?"

"Yes, these things, and more. Do you know anything about any of them?"

"Just a bit about hypnotism that a reporter friend doing a story on the faith-healers of the Philippines told me. He'd seen an American who was a true believer actually snuff out a burning cigarette on his arm without a trace of pain or any burn mark showing. The guy with the cigarette said he'd hypnotized his arm. I'd have laughed at the story if it had been anyone else, but Carlos—my friend—is your absolute skeptic about most things. He certainly had no reason to make it all up."

Madam Butterfly now floated back into our vicinity to ask how we were doing. She'd recovered her poise and smiled coyly at Young. He finally allowed himself a sly grin in response. She giggled and disappeared again. But something about her bothered me.

"Let's get back to those visits to Guangzhou by Qigong masters," I said, not wanting to interrupt Young's flow. "Why do you find it odd that there was no public performance involved?"

"Because, ever since these particular people became famous, virtually all of their travels have involved public Qigong demonstrations, for which they are well paid. A couple of them have done stage tours in Europe, so they are not averse to publicity and handsome payment, by Chinese standards. But in Guangzhou, only one of these guys has ever done anything in public, and that was three years ago. As it happens, it was at a variety show for officers from the Guangzhou Military Region. We know because the consul-general, along with other foreign diplomats, was invited. Since then, people we talk to have told us that there is hardly a military reception in town where one of the Qigong guys doesn't show up.

"And there's one fellow among them who seems to be the big enchilada though he virtually never shows up in public. He's got quite a following all over China and even some outside. He is always introduced as 'Great Master Wu.' I met him once very briefly at some official function, and he even said 'hello' in English, but that's all he said before some aide steered him away. We are pretty sure he's in Guangzhou."

Young was now watching me steadily, perhaps sizing me up to see whether he should say anymore. I returned his gaze, careful not to look too skeptical. Then a thought struck me. I remembered Lasch had said McHale made some comment when they last met about China's leaders "worshipping old idols." An odd phrase. What had McHale meant?

"So you think this Wu guy is up to something in connection with China's leadership that reminds you of what the Boxers were trying to do a century ago?" I asked.

"To be honest, we are not sure what his long-term objective is. We don't know whether he's dangerous or just a flash in the pan. I think it would certainly be journalistically interesting to get to him if you could." He looked at me meaningfully.

"And if I did, you think that might put me on the track of what happened to McHale?"

"It could. You got any better leads? Could be a good story," he added unnecessarily.

"Fine," I said and laughed openly. "What makes you think if I tried to interview this 'Great Master' and even his Guangzhou Triad pals I wouldn't stub my own toe rather badly?"

"I think the worst that could happen is that Wu would simply say no to the interview request and you might be under closer than usual surveillance for a time. Nothing beyond that though."

"Do you know where this Wu is?"

"Not exactly, but you might try the Guangzhou Qigong Scientific Research Association, or a handful of so-called experts on traditional Chinese martial arts. If you do this, though, I suggest you simply show up, say you are a journalist, and most importantly, play dumb. Foreigners, especially Americans and Australians, do knock on their doors from time to time eager to become Qigong experts. These folk are easily flattered by all the attention and wouldn't find your visit so strange. But remember, play dumb. If they suspect for a moment you have any agenda beyond studying Qigong, they may not be so nice."

"That's very helpful," I said, with genuine gratitude. I hadn't expected half as much help at this stage of my reporting. Then I remembered again what Lasch had said in his early-morning call. "Does the notion of China going back to 'worshipping idols' make any sense to you?"

"Who came up with that term?"

"My boss Lasch said that in the last conversation he had had with McHale—and that was only a few days ago—McHale had added something about the danger of China's leadership 'worshipping old idols.' But Lasch didn't know what McHale meant, and I certainly don't. And just what did you mean by saying earlier, 'The Boxers are back'?"

"I think they are," Young said simply.

"You can't be serious, Michael," I protested. "We're in a different universe today from what China was like in 1900. There's been a century of political revolution, half a century of brutal industrialization, and two full decades of China's economic waltzing around with the rest of the world. What kind of place do you think we're sitting in now? It's a bar, for crying out loud, not exactly an example of traditional Chinese culture. It serves beer, German-style beer, to be precise, with waitresses who'd feel at home if you parachuted them into Malibu, or Milwaukee or Mainz-on-the-Rhine, for that matter.

"And in case you hadn't noticed," I continued, "that jukebox piece we just heard was Eminem, though I might be mistaken. Our waitress would know, though. See if she's even heard of the Boxers! There's no incense burner at the door or big fat Buddha anywhere. Listen, there's probably not a single small town in all of China that doesn't have a karaoke bar and a rock group that plays the latest *Billboard* hits. You think anyone here thinks that bullets won't kill them?"

Young laughed slightly and looked down at his beer. Perhaps my skepticism had offended him. Then he looked up with a kindly smile. "Does the name Von Ketteler mean anything to you?" he asked.

"No, frankly, it doesn't."

"Well, he was a German diplomat in Peking"—he used the old transliteration of the name of the capital—"who was murdered at the very start of the Boxer siege of the legation quarters in June 1900. He was hacked to death in cold blood almost directly outside his own embassy. He'd insulted a Boxer he'd run into inside the diplomatic quarter. They didn't like that. If he'd known just a little bit more about the Boxers, he'd have steered clear of the guy immediately and gotten back to the safety of his embassy. We think that's what happened to Larsen."

"And you think McHale's gotten into the same kind of trouble?"

"If your boss Lasch is so close to him, I doubt whether he's dumb enough to go around insulting people, but he may have just asked too many questions in the wrong place. Oh, and by the way," he added quietly, changing the subject, "do you mind if we go right away? I've got a dinner engagement I don't want to be late for."

"No problem." But I knew he was lying. Out of the corner of my eye I could see our waitress talking intently to two Chinese men in business suits who were looking in our direction from the cashier's desk. Young put a fifty-yuan note on the table under his glass and said briskly, "Follow me. Let's leave the restaurant by the side entrance. When we're out the door, do you mind if I just take off? I've got some things to do on the way."

"No problem," I said. "This is your city."

"Well, it's about to become yours," he said. "Just remember, act dumb."

Young was being brutally honest. Just about every diplomat I had ever met thought journalists were dumb.

Chapter Four

The Boxers are back." It was such a jarring, strange statement from a savvy American Foreign Service officer, even if he was CIA, that it kept ricocheting around my mind as we made our way swiftly out of the Sunny Times Restaurant and back into the steamy atmosphere of Guangzhou. Young had disappeared within seconds of leaving the door at street level. I moved about ten yards from the door, took out a map of Guangzhou, began to peruse it as if I wasn't sure where I was, and waited. Sure enough, the two men in business suits quickly came out, followed by the waitress who had served us. They all glanced briefly my way, though the waitress looked embarrassed when she saw that I'd seen her in their company. The men then darted off to the right, perhaps thinking they knew where Young was headed.

I found it all disturbing. If Young, an experienced operative, could slip up like that and get himself fingered by a suspicious waitress, what chance did I have in this intrigue-filled city? I put my map carefully back in my coat pocket, looked around to make sure no one was lurking in the shadows watching me, and walked back to the Golden Panda Hotel. I had Petrolucci's address in my notebook, so I went straight to the line of taxis at the hotel entrance.

When I got into my cab, Canto-pop was playing so loudly on the car radio that I had to ask the driver to turn down the volume. He did so but grumpily. We took off, initially going north along the elevated expressways that festooned Guangzhou before descending to head in the direction of Zhongshan University, the city's premier college, named after that most famous of all Cantonese citizens, Sun Yat-sen, but using the Mandarin version of his name (Zhongshan) instead of the Cantonese version (Yat-sen) more widely recognized in the West.

Giuseppe Petrolucci, it turned out, lived in a small, elegantly decorated apartment a few hundred yards from the university's main campus. The street was a little quieter than the busy thoroughfare on which the campus was located, and the building was less than ten years old. Intended to house foreigners only, it was of far superior quality and design to the typical Chinese apartment building. Even the construction materials were some of the best: teak wood flooring from Thailand, marble from Italy, tiling from Finland. Petrolucci told me the story later.

In the mid-nineties, Zhongshan University had eagerly tried to attract back to China the many talented scientists and technologists who had graduated from mainland universities and then headed off to pleasant sinecures on campuses in California and elsewhere in the United States. Two Hong Kong Chinese businessmen had put up the money to finance a handsome faculty residence, which, it was hoped, would attract these wayward academics back to the motherland.

It was a wonderful idea, except for one thing: there was a three-year limit for returning scholars living in these fancy apartments. The apartment block, in effect, was a kind of bait-and-switch waiting room, an inducement to the scholars to come back to China in the first instance but not a lifetime reward for their decision to do so. Returning scholars, the authorities assumed, would eventually become reconciled to the cramped and harried conditions of Chinese academic life after a halcyon introductory sojourn in American-style comfort.

But that was not what happened. When it became apparent to the would-be returnees that the nice apartments were only a temporary attraction, the stream of homeward-bound scholars dwindled to a trickle, and then to a drip. At which point, the university made available almost all of the unfilled apartments to visiting or transient foreign scholars and faculty, and Petrolucci was one such beneficiary.

When my cab arrived at the address, he was waiting for me at the building's front entrance. It occurred to me that he was simply displaying classic, old-fashioned European courtliness: the host greets his guests at the front door upon their arrival, and sees them out the door and into whatever conveyance they use when they leave. He was dressed in the eponymous style of European breeding: a pink dress shirt open at the neck and a rich, maroon-colored, paisley cravat crisply knotted at the shirt opening. His double-breasted, dark blue blazer was clean, though obviously well worn. He wore stone-colored pants that looked to be of microfiber—a concession to the challenge of good grooming in the pollution of Guangzhou—and his shoes were medium tan loafers with tassels.

But what caught my attention before I noticed this display of fastidious taste was what was above the cravat. He was completely bald on his forehead and crown, but his temples and the sides of his head were a Dionysian riot of great white curls. His face was that of a man still in his early forties. A rather wicked thought entered my mind before I even had time to return his "hello": he seemed to personify the amalgamation of Carlo Ponti, the husband of 1960s–era Italian movie idol Gina Lollobrigida, and Tiny Tim, a strange English pop star whose photo I had once seen. Getting out of the taxi, this all passed through my mind in a split second as Petrolucci bounded forward to shake my hand.

"So glad to see you," he said in perfect English with just the faintest hint of Italian pronunciation. "Thank you for coming out here to my home. We could have met in town, but I find the crowds so tiresome. Besides, I have some things I think you would enjoy seeing. Please come this way."

He led me through the lobby and up the stairs to a second-floor apartment overlooking the road and a park in the distance. The door was already open, and a slim, beautiful European woman was standing in the hallway with a smile as welcoming as Petrolucci's had been. She had almost translucently clear skin, very high cheekbones, and a cascade of brown hair in carefully trained curls. Her mouth was startling: the lips were not only full and velvety looking; they were responsive to every expression of her face. They "talked" as much as her mouth did.

"Meet Francesca," he boomed, striding past her into the apartment, and indeed it was a pleasure to do so. "Francesca, this is Richard Ireton, from *Epoch* magazine in Hong Kong." She shook my hand as I walked past her, following Petrolucci into the living room.

I looked around in amazement. Two walls were completely covered by books standing on rows of glass shelves fitted into a metal frame locked on to the wall. The other two walls were dominated by four gigantic reproductions of elegant eighteenth-century woodcuts of Roman antiquities. I had seen smaller versions of these prints in Roman tourist shops, but these huge versions of the same images dominated the room. The enlarged black lines of the woodcuts had the effect of a new kind of abstract art. The arch of Constantine in one print and Caracalla's baths in another were obvious at first glance, but the swirling black lines and spirals of these enlarged woodcuts became a rhythmic pattern all their own across the enormous prints.

"Please sit down," Petrolucci said as he watched me all but gaping at the prints. "Francesca will bring us some refreshment." I thanked him and tried to focus my thoughts on how to explain the purpose of my visit. He was too well-bred to ask me directly how I had his name and phone number, but the expression on his face made it plain that he wanted to know this before we started talking about anything serious.

"I got an e-mail from my boss"—and I now paused, put a finger across my lips, and pointed questioningly to the light fixture above us—"who said that you were quite an expert on some things that I am looking into. By the way, do you usually talk here?"

"Certainly not," he replied with a laugh, "and since the heat seems to have been drawn off a little by the rain, we could sit on our balcony at the back. I've had it—how to put it delicately?—inspected by acoustically learned people, and it's quite safe." At this, he walked into the spacious living room and out through French doors on the other side. I followed. Comfortable plastic chairs had been set out, and Petrolucci wiped them dry of the rainwater that had collected from the afternoon storm. As he finished, Francesca brought out a well-chilled bottle of white wine and poured for us. "Italian?" I asked as I raised the glass.

"Oh no," another laugh, this time Francesca's. "Australian. It is quite good and in Hong Kong a fraction of the price of Italian wines. New South Wales, you know. A Sauvignon Blanc." As she said "Sauvignon Blanc" her lips seemed to be caressing an imaginary glass. I had never seen such expressive lips.

Petrolucci, sitting down carefully and crossing his legs, said, "That's better," as he cradled his glass. "We honestly don't know if they bother listening all of the time, but we're pretty sure they can eavesdrop inside the house whenever they want. Of course, if they really wanted to, they could listen to our conversations out here with those long-range sound enhancers, or whatever they're called. They're not at all happy about the research I am doing because it's just too close to home for them. But on the other hand, it's not like I'm investigating anti-tank rockets or something, so they don't waste their time hearing me blather about conditions in China in distant dynasties that might remind people of what's going on today."

"On that point, Giuseppe, what is your research field?"

"If you don't mind, Richard, first I'd like to hear how you got my name." I kicked myself inwardly. I'd strayed from what was considered good manners by being too pushy and trying to bypass polite conversation because I was impatient to get the information I sought. It was an occupational hazard to which all journalists occasionally fall victim.

"I'm so sorry. I was starting to say—before we moved out here—that my boss, Burt Lasch, the foreign editor of *Epoch*, e-mailed me this afternoon."

Petrolucci all but guffawed. "Oh Burton! So typical of him. He is a wonderful man and so crazy about his working hours. That doesn't surprise me a bit; it's 2:30 in the morning in Manhattan, and what is Burton Lasch doing? Why, he is sitting at his computer making trouble for his reporters eleven thousand miles away." Now Francesca joined in the laughter in a low but distinctive baritone.

"But you know," Petrolucci went on, "Lasch is a wonderful man. We met in Florence almost ten years ago when I was attending an academic conference and he was doing some reporting in Italy. We got on very well, went through some terrific brandy—*Epoch*'s expense account, no doubt—and sat up late for three nights in a row talking about absolutely everything. And we've kept in touch ever since. I think it's sort of an attraction of opposites. He is this tough New York newsman, and I am this Italian dilettante academic. Actually, I respect his judgment a lot and we agree on a surprising number of things."

"And you represent," I butted in, "the European sophisticate that Burton would love to have been but . . . well . . . isn't."

Francesca now burst out with more of her low laugh, something of a bass counter-point to Petrolucci's tenor guffaw. "Now how is he, and how is his wife?" he asked.

"Well, he was fine when I saw him in New York last week. I didn't see Margie, but I had the impression from others she was back to her ebullient self and in good spirits. I suppose you know a bit about that story." Lasch's wife had been troubled by a series of seemingly mysterious headaches as well as low-level depression, and, despite a lot of time in hospitals and with specialists, hadn't seemed able to find a cure.

"Yes, a lot. Very sad, but I think Burton handled it very well." A pause. Petrolucci's face turned serious.

"McHale. Chuck McHale," I said simply. "Do you know anything about him?"

"Know about Chuck McHale? Of course. He's been quite a landmark around Guangzhou—well a moving landmark, to be honest—for a few years. We often have lunch when he's in town. He's even been to dinner here, was quite taken with Francesca, and got inspired enough to cook us a wonderful sampling of crepes Suzette." The crow's feet had now returned. "Why do you ask about Chuck?"

"Because he's disappeared here in Guangzhou. At least that's what Burt said in a phone call at some ungodly hour this morning. Burt told me just a little about him, but made it clear they were very good friends from Princeton days. He wanted me to come here immediately and see if I could find out what had happened to him. To be perfectly honest, I'm not very comfortable doing this. I don't have anything against McHale, a man I've never met and hadn't even heard of until this morning. But it seems to me just a bit too personal. I mean, I'm as distressed as anyone if an American suddenly vanishes from the radar screen in a foreign city, but in the news business, we usually only report these things if the man is super famous or if there is a chance of foul play afoot. As I told Lasch, what if McHale's just gone on a romantic week with his girlfriend in, well, Shanghai?"

Petrolucci frowned, and Francesca went back into the apartment, whether to give us more privacy or to do something in the kitchen, I wasn't sure.

He said, "Richard, I am not familiar with any of the details of McHale's personal life, but I have every reason to believe something serious has happened. Let me show you something." He got up and went back into the living room where I heard him opening what sounded like a large drawer in a cabinet. When he came back, he had two printed pamphlets with him. I couldn't see at first what they were, but he put them down on the plastic table and spread them out. They were similar in format: three lines of larger printed Chinese characters, each with exclamation marks at the end of the line, then tightly printed Chinese text on the following three pages.

My knowledge of written Chinese wasn't fluent, but I could read the first three lines of the leaflet Petrolucci had handed to me: "Down with the Oppressors of China!" "Down with the Enemies of the Yellow Emperor!" "Down with the Foreign Barbarians!" I turned the pamphlet over and scanned quickly to see who had signed it. There was no name, but in bold characters centered on the bottom of the back page were the Chinese characters for "Defenders of the Motherland."

I frowned involuntarily, and Petrolucci commented, "You are right to be worried. Have you seen anything like this before?"

"No, but I've heard the name of this group."

"You have?" Petrolucci's bushy white eyebrows rose in surprise as he considered this.

"Someone in this town told me recently about the murder of a Swedish businessman not so long ago and the warnings sent out to foreign news organizations based here to back off. Better not investigate, they said. Those faxes were also signed by the Defenders of the Motherland."

Petrolucci was on the point of commenting when he suddenly changed tack. "Francesca, how is dinner coming?"

"It's ready," she said as she approached the balcony, "but where do you want to eat?"

Petrolucci frowned briefly. "I think we should eat inside," he said, "talk about everything except what we have just started discussing, then resume this conversation out here afterward."

With a slight nod, Francesca turned around, went back into the house, and started bringing the food out to the dining room table in a large alcove off the living room. To my surprise, though, after she gestured me to a seat, she also sat down, and it was Petrolucci who actually served the meal. He stuck with the same Sauvignon Blanc from Australia that we had started with, which was fine, because what Francesca had prepared was a delicious fettuccine marinara.

We talked about many things over dinner, but when the conversation turned to Petrolucci's graduate studies at Columbia, it quickly got sidetracked to a retelling of how they met. Francesca had been an intern in New York with an Italian law firm while he was at Columbia probing the arcane world of Chinese secret societies and sects during the late Ming and early Qing dynasties. They had fallen in love, lived together for a few years, quarreled furiously, broken up, made up again. Meanwhile, Francesca, after completing her internship and deciding to interrupt her law studies to stay with Petrolucci, had after a second major breakup in the mid-1990s returned to complete her law studies in Rome. "Poor Giuseppe was like a sick cow," she said with another one of her deep-throated laughs. "He kept sending me these e-mails telling me how heartbroken he was that I wasn't there anymore."

"And you, heartless one," Petrolucci broke in, "were carrying on in our capital city like a Hong Kong movie starlet. What did you care about the love of your life back in New York?"

"Well, it's true that I had many admirers," she responded with a pout, her lips doing more phenomenal acrobatics, "but what did you expect me to do? You were with me for years in New York, and you never asked me to marry you. Was I supposed to mope around like a teenager when I got home?"

"So what happened?" I prompted.

There was a moment of silence, and they looked at each other, then as if on cue burst into laughter. "You tell," she said almost fiercely to Petrolucci.

"No, you were the one surprised by it all. Tell Richard how I swept you off your feet."

She threw her head back in delight now, and they both laughed again at what must have become an oft-told tale.

"Well, I have to say, I was a bit surprised," she said, evidently willing to tell the story. "Of course, I missed Giuseppe, but I assumed he couldn't get his act together to bring an end to his bachelorhood. Perhaps his mother had dominated him. Or something like that. I missed him, but I can tell you, I wasn't going to sit on my hands back in Rome. There were a lot of good-looking and successful men in the city, and many of them seemed to enjoy my company. Of course, I was having a ball. But Giuseppe pulled something off that really got my attention."

"And I had planned it very carefully," Petrolucci chimed in, grinning broadly.

Francesca ignored the comment. "My boss called me one Sunday night. My boss—he's retired now—had a lot of friends prominent in politics. He also knew most of the country's senior policemen. You can't be a lawyer and have anything to do with criminal stuff without knowing policemen. Anyway, one Sunday evening, quite late, around 10:30, I get this call from Rudi—the boss. Could I please come to his home quite early the next day, around 8:30 instead of the usual time of around 10:00 at the office? 'What for?' I asked. 'I can't tell you on the phone,' he said. 'Just come.'

"Very mysterious. Perhaps we had to defend some businessman in a big bribery case. Perhaps one of Rudi's politician friends was in trouble and needed a friendly lawyer but not an actual friend, you understand.

"So I drive over to Rudi's apartment on the Via dei Pastini, ring the doorbell, and am let in by a maid. A maid? Rudi never had a maid. His wife wouldn't have put up with it. Anyway, she takes my coat—it's been raining furiously—and shows me into the living room. There's a man I'd never seen before standing at the window looking out. Not a sign of Rudi. No sign of Rudi's wife either, for that matter. Then Rudi suddenly bounces in from I don't know where. 'Francesca,' he booms out—you know, he's not a quiet sort of person—'thank you so much for coming at short notice. I want you to meet Aldo. Aldo's from Milan.'

"Well, it occurs to me that's about as helpful as telling me the truck blocking my parked car is from Stuttgart. Who cares where Aldo's from? Then I notice that a small table in the living room has been set for breakfast with just three places. So we sit down to breakfast and Aldo starts talking. He's also a lawyer and says his family has had some distant connection with mine. He talks about law, about the academic life, about the challenge of raising children in Rome. The conversation is going nowhere, so I interrupt rather rudely and say to Rudi, 'Rudi, forgive me, but what's this meeting about?'"

Petrolucci was grinning and obviously enjoying the tale. She went on. "'We have a very important case for you,' Rudi says, all straight-faced. 'Aldo will explain.' So now Aldo starts up: 'I have a close friend in the academic world who is facing a decision about his professional future. He has a contract at a university but not a permanent one. It's not what the Americans call "tenure," if you know what I mean. He wants to know if he can argue legally that his teaching position at the university for several years can count as de facto qualification for a permanent position.'

"'Well, I'm sorry,' I say. 'I don't know anything about tenure track or university positions. C'mon, Rudi, you know that's not my field. What's this all about?'

"Aldo and Rudi grin at each other, and Aldo gets up from the table. 'My friend,' Aldo says, 'thought that you might have some wise counsel for him if you looked at this item that he is sending for your inspection.' I tell you, I'm beginning to feel a little confused at this point. So Aldo goes to the coat closet, gets a brown shopping bag, and pulls out a shoebox meticulously wrapped in ornate paper. I realize at this point that a joke is coming and I start to giggle. 'Oh,' I say, 'is this some kind of Cinderella act?' But when I unwrap it and see that there is another, smaller box also beautifully wrapped in the middle of the shoebox, intuition kicks in. Of course, this has Giuseppe's fingerprints all over it. Sure enough, when I open up the last box there is the most exquisite diamond ring inside, together with the simplest, sweetest note, in Giuseppe's handwriting. All it says is 'Will you?'

"I'm sort of gasping with surprise," she went on, "and then Rudi's phone rings. It's Giuseppe, of course. How did he know how to time the call? Because Rudi had quietly text-messaged him on his mobile as soon as I had started to open the last box. And you know, silly though it sounds, I started to cry. I don't think I knew till then how much I wanted to be with Giuseppe. Of course, I didn't stand a chance anyway. Rudi and this red herring Aldo—Giuseppe's second cousin by the way—were just gaping at me, grinning as though they had won the lottery. So when I croaked out 'Yes,' on the phone, they cheered and Rudi went to the kitchen to get champagne."

Petrolucci's tenor chuckle lent a musical counterpoint to Francesca's story as she concluded it. Then, rather surprisingly, he turned to me. "So Richard," he said, his tone serious in contrast to the earlier banter, "can I ask if you have a wife or a girlfriend?"

I sighed involuntarily. "Well, it's a little complicated," I said. "I was divorced a few years ago after being married for three years, and I've just met someone I'm kind of interested in. But she's just arrived in Hong Kong this morning for a visit, and I'm here."

Francesca giggled almost involuntarily. "You do lead an interesting life," was all she said. "Now let's move outside again so you and Giuseppe can discuss those interesting matters. Rick, in this house, we drink real coffee after dinner, but I can locate some of that—what do you call it—'decaf?' if you'd prefer." I was beginning to fade, however, and I was grateful for some brisk Italian espresso.

Back on the balcony, the air was so thick that it seemed to have a flavor of its own. The wetness of South China and the patina of rich vegetation had blended together wondrously this evening. It was so sensual, so tangible, that I was reminded how much I preferred the southern half of China and Guangdong Province in particular, which the northerners had so often considered "barbarian." Many people liked the brisk autumnal temperatures of Beijing but not me. The dust and dryness got to me. I just loved the heat and humidity of the south.

"OK, back to those Motherland Defenders," Petrolucci said once we had settled into the cheap but comfortable balcony chairs again.

"Do you know anything about them?" I asked.

"Not a thing except the name. Of course, I read carefully the smaller text. Some of it is very interesting. Here, let me show you." He reached over to the folder into which he had put the two pamphlets before dinner and pulled them out. Putting on his reading glasses, he looked closely at the text and read the Chinese aloud:

"'The life of China is being suffocated by foreign devils. Unjust demands are being made upon us every month by foreign governments. The sons and grandsons of the Yellow Emperor must jump to attention at the demands of these barbarians. The artistic beauty of our great Han culture is being polluted by exposure to vulgar foreign fashion. And the worst offender in this polluting stream is America.

"'The just demands of the Chinese people for national reunification are being treated with insult and treachery by the foreigners. America is at the forefront of the treacherous foreign mob.

"'No more compromise in the name of diplomacy! No more surrender to foreign pressure! Reunification of the Motherland now! End all foreign naval presence in the South China Sea now! Expel from China all foreigners not serving the Motherland!'"

Petrolucci put the papers back and turned to me, a frown across his face.

He said, "This sort of language hasn't been used since the darkest days of the Cultural Revolution, say 1966–1967, and it goes far beyond that. I don't think we have seen this language from any political group in China since the time of the Boxers."

Immediately, Young's words came to mind: "The Boxers are back."

"Well, I grant you that the rhetoric is extreme, but do you think this movement is really that big?"

"I don't know. Some of the diplomats in this town have told me that their normal official contacts have stopped seeing them, and a few foreign teachers have told me that they don't go into certain parts of town anymore because they've experienced open hostility there. But the mystery to me is where the organizing center of this movement might be. I don't think it's in the universities, or we would have learned about it on campus. I've heard speculation that some units of the military may have been affected by this, but it's so hard to know what's going on in China's military circles. No one I know would be able to check that out."

He paused, then reached for an inside pocket of his blazer and took out a large, sealed cigar. "Do you smoke these?" he asked. I shook my head. "Mind if I do?"

"Of course not."

He took a cigar guillotine cutter from another inside pocket, trimmed the smoking end of the large Havana, and then carefully lit it, puffing languidly as he rotated the tobacco. While he was doing this, Francesca emerged again with a tray. "Coffee, Rick?" she asked, "And Ghirardelli chocolates? I don't think you are from San Francisco, but I'm sure you're familiar with one of its great products." I marveled at their attentiveness to the good life—no, elegant life—here in Guangzhou, a city generally characterized by raucousness, and often by bad taste.

"Richard," Petrolucci continued, "I don't usually spell out the details of what I'm researching here to people I don't really know. But I do know Burton well, and I'm confident he wouldn't have sent just any reporter to see me. Let me tell you what I am doing. The Italian government has several academic exchange programs with China, administered through different universities. I have been teaching in Rome for several years and quietly doing research on Chinese history.

"About a year and a half ago," he went on, "one of our better diplomats in Beijing asked our government if they could send someone to Guangzhou to do something in Chinese history of the past two hundred years or so. I've met him since then. Very bright. Very alert. Without having any concrete evidence of what he thought was taking place in South China, he told me he was beginning to see the repetition of a historical phenomenon that was apparent in China in the nineteenth century: a resurgence of ancient folk religion tied in to a visceral anti-foreign nationalism. He wanted someone with academic credentials to investigate things here on the ground. And I was the one they asked to come.

"Francesca jumped at the opportunity too. Though she's a lawyer by training, she loves to paint, and she thought this would be a rich new location to take it up again. My field, by the way, has been Chinese peasant rebellions in the Qing dynasty, mostly from about 1700 onward. I did some summer research for my Ph.D. dissertation on the Boxer Rebellion, at Berkeley, which, by the way, explains Francesca's taste for Ghirardelli."

Petrolucci went on. "I'm not sure how much you know about Chinese peasant rebellions—"

Francesca now interrupted him with another deep, throaty laugh. "Giuseppe," she admonished, "Think about that: 'I'm not sure how much you know about Chinese rebellions.' You are beginning to sound like some octogenarian Hungarian professor of Altaic linguistics!" I laughed now, too, as did Petrolucci, reddening self-consciously. But it was clear they were really delighted with each other. Even as she was laughing, Francesca was making a mischievous face at Petrolucci.

"Well, I'm sorry if that sounded pompous. But actually it could be connected to the McHale business. I hope that nothing bad has happened to him."

"Giuseppe," I said, "so do I, and so, of course, does Burt Lasch. But I need you to help me. First of all, I want to know what McHale might have been looking into that could have gotten him into trouble. Can you give me any background information that might help me locate him?"

"Well, I can tell you what he was interested in. You know, I have been studying the Chinese Qigong tradition here in Guangzhou, as part of my general interest in peasant rebellions. Actually, North China is where the martial arts played a big role during the Boxer Rebellion of 1900, and there was a group there called the Spirit Boxers. During the Taiping Rebellion there were all sorts of fortune-tellers and diviners, and a big part of the rebellion was motivated by revelations supposedly from God himself. I have made many Chinese friends and developed many contacts who know a lot about that. Chuck's interest, on the other hand, has always been in the Chinese Triad criminal gangs. Of course, there has always been some crossover from mere gang activity into the realm of occult hocus-pocus. It's hard to know where gang initiation ceremonies end and plain old occultism begins.

"When we had dinner in Hong Kong, Chuck told me he was fascinated by how many criminal gangs in Chinese history had been deeply connected to secret societies, with their occult traditions and claims to supernatural powers. We talked about the White Lotus Society and the secret society resistance to the Qing dynasty in South China. Then he asked me about the local Qigong leaders here in Guangzhou. When I realized what he was interested in, I got quite worried. He seemed certain that the Triads had now become linked to one of the fastest-growing Qigong cults here on the Chinese mainland. He was especially interested in the leader of the most prominent cult."

"And that would be?"

"They call him Great Master Wu."

Wu. It was the second time that day I had heard the name. I decided to play dumb again. Petrolucci was open and guileless, but I didn't need to tell him about Young or about Young's suspicions.

"And he is . . . ?" I asked, downing the last of my coffee.

"I don't know much about him, and I've never actually met him. But he has a big following in this town, especially among high army officers. He's a Qigong master who is supposed to be able to do very unusual things like communicate telepathically with people and even cure cancer. After the crackdown on Falungong, he had to lie low for awhile. Falungong was itself a Qigong cult, as I'm sure you know, and its founder, Li Hongzhi, made all kinds of claims about how he was more important than Jesus or Buddha. His followers, you'll recall, made the big mistake of embarrassing China's leaders by surrounding the leadership compound at Zhongnanhai in Beijing back in 1999.

"But this guy Wu is a lot more subtle. He hasn't made any political statements yet, at least not in public. Nor have his followers. What I am curious about is whether he has any connections with the big Triad bosses."

"Why on earth would he have?" I asked.

"Richard, you need to understand a very important fact about Chinese history. In almost every single change of government for the past two thousand years, organized crime has been on one side or the other. The Triads trace their roots to secret societies opposed to the Ming dynasty. The Boxers originally were opposed to the Qing government in Beijing before being co-opted by them to annihilate the foreigners. General Chiang Kai-shek employed Shanghai's underworld, the so-called Green Gang, to help eradicate the Communists in Shanghai in 1927. And before China took back Hong Kong in 1997, Beijing made strange noises about organized crime in the British-run territory, saying mysteriously that it hoped they would be 'patriotic.' Even China's current leadership is ambivalent about organized crime."

"That's because half the senior officers in the People's Liberation Army have criminal connections themselves," I said cynically, recalling the hair-raising stories I had heard of Hong Kong businessmen getting the shake-down from PLA officers while doing business in China.

Petrolucci laughed at this.

"There's another question, Richard, that I'm wondering about. Do the Triads have any connection with the Defend the Motherland group—whoever they are? Does Great Master Wu have any connection with them? I just don't know. I think Chuck may have gotten a little too close to the answers to those questions. I just hope he's not sticking out from a cement block at the bottom of the Pearl River."

I shuddered. This image was coming up for the third time today, and it was a line of speculation I wasn't eager to pursue.

Petrolucci immediately picked up on my quietness. "I'm sorry, I shouldn't have said that. As long as there is a chance someone is alive, it is not good taste to suggest otherwise."

A silence fell on us both as I started to digest all that Petrolucci had just told me. Francesca—who had slipped out during Petrolucci's history lesson—came out on the balcony just then, sat down in an empty chair, and looked inquiringly at me.

"Rick, we don't know anything about you, where you are from in America, or anything at all. You said you were married before and that you have a new girlfriend. But we'd like to know what your hobbies are, where you like to go when you are not doing journalism."

"Francesca!" Petrolucci interrupted, laughing again, "Give the man a chance! Maybe he wants to keep all of that to himself."

"Oh no," I replied, glad that the conversation had taken a new course. "I don't really have all that many secrets. I've told you that I was married and that my new girlfriend is in Hong Kong and that, thanks to Burt Lasch, I am here. I'm originally from Grand Rapids, Michigan, but I haven't been back except for family occasions since I left high school."

Petrolucci interrupted. "I've been to Grand Rapids. Some college or other, Calvin, I think it was called, invited me to speak. Was your father a professor there?"

"Oh no. I'm the classic second-generation breakout case. He was an electrician who liked to go bowling and was totally working class. He thought I was some kind of weird nerdy kid for wanting to read the *Chicago Tribune* when I was in high school. I went first to Northwestern University, near Chicago, and studied journalism there before going on to Berkeley for graduate studies.

"I guess I've wanted to be a journalist ever since high school. You know, people who are journalists are born skeptics. We never believe the first thing anyone tells us. We're always accused of being cynical, but someone's got to rake up the muck.

"I got married soon after getting hired by *Epoch*. We were married for three years, but I guess she didn't find me very interesting or handsome, or something. We got divorced when I was in Belgium."

"Well, people often make serious mistakes when they get married the first time," Francesca said sympathetically, and I was filled with gratitude to her for that. I didn't like to admit it, but I hated saying that I was divorced, though I could not recall anyone ever holding it against me. "What do you really like to do, when you're not uncovering wickedness and corruption in high places?" she continued.

"What do I like to do? I like to sail, that's what, and occasionally I like a round of golf. But you know journalists: basically we're slaves to our editors. I think I've only had one vacation when I wasn't summoned at least to a phone, if not to a nearby airport, by New York. By the way, speaking of being summoned, I think I ought to get back to the hotel. I've got some phoning to do."

Francesca glanced quizzically at Petrolucci, but her husband looked at me quite genially. "Well, we will not keep you, Richard. We'll see you get a taxi." As we said our good-byes, I decided that they were an immensely likable couple: no pretension, old-world courtliness, and a genuine interest in others.

On the way back to the Golden Panda Hotel, the warmth of the domestic cheer I had just left caused great pangs of longing to be with Trish, or at least to talk to her. But there was a slight feeling of unease too. What might Clarissa have told her about me? What if she had suddenly been overcome by maternal protectiveness toward this attractive young woman who was being wooed by a pushy journalist?

I was in such a hurry to get to my room and phone Hong Kong that at first I didn't notice the three young Chinese men in business suits talking to the receptionist. But as I neared the elevator it occurred to me that they didn't look like visiting salesmen, and they certainly weren't from Taiwan. Their hair was brushed forward over the forehead in the style that said, loudly, "Made in the People's Republic of China." One of them noticed me heading across the lobby and motioned to his friends. I walked slightly faster.

I called Trish's hotel as soon as I got into the room. To my surprise and delight, she answered as soon as the operator put the call through to her room. Trish's unusually low-pitched voice always startled me. For her height and slim build, she ought to have been a typical soprano. I'd never heard a woman with such a deep voice before. It made her just that much more intriguing.

"Well, Rick, since you were too busy to meet me, I've had a very good time with your friend Clarissa. I must say, she's quite something. You've never told me about her."

"Told you?" I said, somewhat defensively. "What was there to say? I really don't know Clarissa that well at all. To be honest, I was desperate to find anyone who could meet you at the airport today."

"Well, desperation makes for great inventiveness. I wouldn't have thought of you being friends with such a religious person. Maybe you thought that my soul needed some attention?"

"Hey, I'm not religious, you know that, but you're right, I did have to be inventive at seven in the morning to find anyone who was able and willing to go to the airport and meet you. So, did Clarissa spend time trying to convert you or anything?"

"No, she didn't. But I found I learned a lot from her. I think it's pretty amazing that she's an African American who says God told her to be a missionary to the Chinese."

I felt a little uneasy. What could Clarissa possibly have said to elicit the comment that Trish had "learned from her"?

"Well," I said, changing the subject, "how's the training going? Are they keeping you busy?"

"Yes, of course. They didn't fly us to Hong Kong to play mahjong, you know."

"Didn't they?" I said, happy to be bantering with her. "I thought your hotel chain was educating you on keeping the guests amused."

"Not amused, satisfied. The amusement of the guests usually comes from being with one another. Our job is to make sure that they have full scope for self-entertainment. Listen, tell me, what's happening in Guangzhou that requires such immediate attention?"

"I can't tell you all the details over the phone, but let's just say that there's an American businessman I'm trying to locate. We think he may have gotten too close to the scent of some really bad boys."

"Rick, you're not going to be in danger or anything, are you?" Her solicitous tone made me wish I could hug her. It had been ages since a woman had shown such concern for my safety.

"Don't worry, Trish, I'm not planning any Jean Claude Van Damme heroics on this assignment, but I'm sure I'll have to stay alert. What are you doing tonight?"

"Well, let me see, I had drinks with the beverages manager at six, then dinner with the reservations manager. And I've just had after-dinner drinks with the general manager. I popped into the room to change because now we're going dancing."

My first reaction was a flash of jealousy, but then it occurred to me that she was deliberately teasing me, seeing how I would respond. I laughed out loud and said, "Well, I can see your dance card is pretty full. What's it going to look like when I get back?" And I laughed again. Wouldn't do to give someone as lively as Trish the impression that I was a whiner.

"Well actually, I was hoping to get to know you a little better," she said. "This is the first time we've had a chance to spend any time together since that reception at the Manila Hyatt, and you know, I don't know that much about you. Maybe you're the great-grandson of Jack the Ripper."

I laughed again. I loved her zany, irreverent sense of humor.

"No, great-nephew, actually," I said, returning in kind. "But I've got an English civil war general in my past, and you might find that interesting. Signed King Charles the First's death warrant actually and married Cromwell's daughter."

"Rick, you're too much," Trish said, laughing to herself this time. "Call me tomorrow if you have a moment. I'm going to see Clarissa again, and I'll give you a full report. Gotta go now. Good-bye, General Ireton."

"Bye." We both laughed and hung up. I sat on the armchair, phone still in hand, for a moment longer, savoring the light mood that just talking to Trish had put me in.

But duty beckoned, and, putting the phone down, I went to the desk and opened up the laptop. I could have kept the computer hooked up to the direct cable connection in the room, which would have saved the hassle of constantly shutting it down and booting it back up again. But if there was any chance of avoiding having all of my e-mails read by some Chinese spook that the maid had let in, I wanted to avoid that. They could, of course, ransack my computer with ease at anytime, but accessing my e-mail online would be difficult without knowing my unusual password. I wanted it to continue to be difficult.

When I got to my mailbox, I was relieved that there was nothing from either Lasch or Reddaway. I'd done my best to look into the McHale business, as Lasch had requested, but even he would have been hard-pressed to justify my hanging around Guangzhou much longer. I didn't think my other Guangzhou contacts could add anything to the startling information Young and Petrolucci had told me. I had a hunch, too, that I would learn more about the Triads, and perhaps about Qigong as well, back in Hong Kong. I decided to return in the morning by train.

I could have flown, of course, but there wasn't the need to rush back, now that I had at least digested something about McHale and his difficulties. I thought about it for awhile and then e-mailed Lasch, informing him that I had learned a few things in Guangzhou but needed to return to Hong Kong to check some other things out.

I actually preferred the train for traveling between Guangzhou and Hong Kong, though immigration and customs formalities were sometimes a nuisance. Going first class was clean and comfortable, and fast. The terminus at Hung Hom station in Kowloon was a lot closer to the heart of Hong Kong—the Central District—than Chek Lap Kok airport was out there on Lantau Island. Besides, Kowloon was where Trish was doing her hotel training. And I wanted to see Trish very soon.

Chapter Five

*I*took a cab early in the morning to the Guangzhou East railroad station. I was always relieved that this was the terminal for the Hong Kong trains rather than Guangzhou Central. The city's main train station required careful navigation through throngs of milling, destitute migrants from the countryside trying to make a go of life in the big city. Of course, pickpockets were plentiful in both stations, but somehow Guangzhou East always seemed less crowded and felt a little safer.

Another thunderstorm swept down on the city as the train began to rumble out of the station, and an ominous darkness descended over Guangzhou. It didn't seem to bother the two Hong Kong businessmen sitting across the aisle animatedly going over some contract they had signed in China, but it left me unsettled. Perhaps I was just overwrought. The call from Lasch two nights ago had jolted me from sleep, and yesterday's meeting with Young and the information from Petrolucci had unnerved me.

As the sheets of water lashed against the train's windows and the sky flickered intermittently with lightning, I tried to encourage myself with a pep talk. I had a good job doing what I loved, a stunning new girlfriend, a pleasant apartment in one of Asia's most exciting cities, and friends who seemed to like me whether or not I worked for *Epoch*. Trish was just visiting Hong Kong, but Clarissa had proven to be a true pal ready to lend a hand when I needed help. True, her missionary zeal was a bit much, but whatever unnerving sermons she might have subjected Trish to probably wouldn't stick. At least, I thought it unlikely that they would, knowing Trish.

I bought a box of chocolates on the train as a thank-you gift for Clarissa, and doing this steadied me somehow. She was genuinely kind, Clarissa, whatever her religious enthusiasms. Guiltily, I realized that the gesture might have been motivated by a desire to impress Trish with my thoughtfulness. It had occurred to me before that when I was focused on pleasing a particular woman, my every act was consciously and unconsciously directed at winning her over. It troubled me.

Did this indicate a colossal insecurity, a deep personal need to be appreciated by someone of the opposite sex? Or was it just the way men had always behaved, since long before the advent of commercial florists or boxes of chocolates? Clamoring to be king of the roost, always wanting to get the prettiest girl, thus ensuring a genetically gifted mother for one's offspring—was that the way it had always been? I didn't know. But I was a little alarmed by how much I wanted to please this particular woman.

I was digesting this thought when another came to me: I could hardly present Clarissa with a gift but meet Trish empty handed. Fortunately, a peddler had set up a temporary flower stand at the Hung Hom station close to where all the taxis were pulling up, and I bought a dozen expensive long-stemmed red roses.

Getting a cab took no time at all, and ten minutes later, I was pulling up to the Park Century Hotel on the Kowloon side of Hong Kong's harbor.

Trish was in the hotel lobby when I arrived, leaning across the front desk talking to someone at reception. I snuck behind her, tapped her lightly on the shoulder with the roses, and said in a quiet teasing voice, pretending to be a hotel employee speaking to a guest, "Can I help you?" But she recognized me immediately, spun around and hugged me, nearly knocking the roses out of my hand. I handed the bouquet to her, and she lit up in delight. "Well, you did the right thing, this time," she said with a laugh. "Flowers from the descendant of General Ireton. I think Cromwell would approve." Cromwell? I was amazed that she remembered my passing reference to this distant ancestor of mine.

"Just hang on a minute, Rick," she said, turning back to the counter. I had interrupted Trish as she was checking on meeting-room availabilities for the afternoon training session, but it didn't take long to sort out. "Let's go and have some coffee," she said. "I'm free until 1:30."

Leading the way, she strode off briskly across the lobby toward the coffee shop. I had to walk quickly to keep up with her. I was mesmerized by the way she walked, almost panther-like, with long, loping strides that showed off her long, slender legs. In college in the Philippines, she had been on the track team, and her calves and thighs were still toned and muscular. Out of the corner of my eye, I noticed several men in the lobby turn to watch her as she walked by. The short-skirted, white lightweight business suit and its contrast to her dark skin no doubt had also attracted their attention. Filipinos are generally darker than most Asians except Malaysians and Indonesians, but Trish was darker even than most Filipinos. It was almost startling.

We were in the coffee shop just ahead of the lunchtime crush, and it took no time at all to place our orders: a salad and a milk shake for her, a hamburger for me. Before the food arrived, I took a moment to savor the image in front of me. Her long black hair framed her face prettily and cascaded around her slender neck to lay against the white blouse she was wearing under her jacket. She had large eyes that were more Spanish than Asian, and a nose that was well-proportioned, not flat like that of many Filipinos. Her hand gestures—picking up the glass in front of her or opening the menu—were both supple and stylish.

She looked at me with a friendly smile but also with a slightly quizzical expression. I was lost in my reverie, but she obviously expected me to begin the conversation.

"I'm so sorry about yesterday," I began. "I got this call from my boss in New York at an ungodly hour of the morning. He was really worried about something that had happened in Guangzhou and wanted me to get out there immediately. What I couldn't say on the phone last night was that an American who had been a close friend of his in college had disappeared in Guangzhou. I tried calling your apartment from the airport, but you had already left."

"Well, you would have gotten hold of me if you had called before you left your apartment," she said indignantly, causing me to wince inwardly. But then she smiled winningly to let me know she was only teasing. "Maybe you forgot I was coming."

I had indeed forgotten. I reddened involuntarily. But then I thought, I might be forgiven if I just 'fessed up. So I did. "I'm sorry, Trish. You're right. I should have called before the cab arrived to take me to the airport, but it was six in the morning and I was in a huge rush and sleep-deprived, and jet-lagged from my trip back from New York. What with everything else, I just got discombobulated."

Trish laughed with a deep, throaty laugh, about two octaves lower than that of most women. "Well, that's a funny thing to happen to a person so early in the morning. Were you also addled and befuddled?" she laughed. Boy, she was smart. How many people would be able to come up with two synonyms for discombobulate just like that?

"That's OK, I forgive you, Rick," she continued. "After all, we're still just getting to know each other."

"Thanks," I said with genuine gratitude. I looked at her intently and she smiled back. She was so pretty that I wanted to kiss her on the spot, but even I had the good sense to realize that doing so in the coffee shop, with her hotel colleagues around, would have put her in an awkward spot. So I just said, "And if it's not too late, welcome to Hong Kong."

Her full lips curled charmingly. "Thank you, Rick," she said, as our food arrived.

"What did you think of Clarissa?" I asked. But I realized, as soon as the words were out of my mouth, that the answer would probably not be what I wanted to hear.

"She's a remarkable woman. You know her story, don't you? She told me what it was like in Richmond, Virginia, during segregation. How she had to sit at the back of the bus and all that. She had been a schoolteacher and then a school official for many years, rising to an important position in the system. Now she wants to convert the Chinese in Hong Kong to Christianity. I've never met anyone like her."

"Me neither."

"But you know," she said, her words slowing now. "She has some remarkable insights into almost everyone she meets."

"I suppose she read your palm right away."

"Oh, come on, Rick, reading palms is not what missionaries do."

It had been a silly comment, and I realized it almost as soon as I said it.

"Well, she did have interesting insights into you. Do you want to know what she said?" Trish's eyes twinkled.

"Of course," I said, though I really didn't.

"Well, she's sized you up as very intelligent and ambitious—and she's right about that. And she also thinks you are kind beneath a gruff exterior. She told me that you had gone to the trouble of taking her for tea at the Mandarin Hotel and she thought that was really sweet of you." Trish took my hand now and spoke gently. "You know, it was, Rick."

Again, I just wanted to kiss her. Everything about Trish was becoming dazzlingly attractive. It was all I could do to stay in my chair and not leap up to embrace her. But she was not finished with Clarissa's insights. Her face turned serious, and she looked down at the table. I was reminded that Trish was as lovely to look at when she had something serious to say as when she was smiling. In Manila, I had been as mesmerized by her in her serious mode, attending to the party guest who suffered a physical collapse, as I had been when she had been the source of the reception's heartiest laughter.

"And?" I prompted her.

She sucked on her milk shake. "Now I know that she was not saying this critically," Trish continued, "But she says she thinks"—she paused, seeming to consider whether she should say it—"she thinks you're not yet fully directed."

"Not fully directed!" I shot back. "What does that mean? Trish, I know that Clarissa's a missionary, and I suppose that means she thinks she has inside knowledge on people's personalities, but honestly, how can she make judgments like that when she hardly even knows me?"

She gave me the gentlest of looks, and I realized that I'd probably over-reacted. But I was really irked. "You know," I said, "some people might think of 'not yet fully directed' as pure psycho-babble. C'mon, Trish, I know that Clarissa helped me out by meeting you at the airport, but does that give her the right to say critical things about me?"

"Rick, she wasn't judging you. In just the little time that I've known her I've found her to be very kind, very thoughtful, and very perceptive. You needn't worry; she likes you and respects you. I wouldn't be over-sensitive about this."

Well, perhaps I was being just that. But the people I normally met didn't go around making comments like that about people they hardly knew. What gave missionaries the right? I decided to change my approach.

"Trish, I don't want to make a big deal of this, but I suspect that Clarissa has sort of roped you in a little. Am I right?" Trish didn't say anything, so I went on. "I have the feeling that she has already influenced you a little toward me. Now, when I invited you to come to Hong Kong, we agreed that you'd stay in my apartment. Of course, you couldn't do that yesterday, but what about today? Are you going to come over? Clarissa doesn't need to know."

Trish took my hand again but kept looking down at the table. Then the corners of her mouth turned up again. She was so very pretty.

"Rick, I've been thinking. You know, this is my first trip to Hong Kong, to visit you in your own neighborhood, as you would say. Do you mind if I stay in the hotel tonight? We can discuss tomorrow's arrangements tomorrow."

This wasn't the answer I'd hoped for, but I said, "No, of course I don't mind." After all, what could I say? "You have the right to stay wherever you want. But I hope this won't affect our . . . our getting to know each other."

I knew better than to say that I hoped she wasn't getting cold feet about staying with me, with all that it implied.

"Thanks, Rick." She ignored the second part of my response and changed the subject. "Now, tell me, what did you find in Guangzhou when you went searching for your boss's friend?"

"I think I only scratched the surface of what is going on. There's some sort of strange anti-foreignism taking root, and it seems to be connected to both a magician-like Qigong practitioner called Great Master Wu and secret criminal groups called the Triads. There seems to be a lot of support for him among Guangzhou military circles. The problem is that this businessman—McHale is his name—may have stuck his nose too far into what's been going on. Either the People's Liberation Army in Guangzhou has got his number, or the Triads or both. I just don't know. Or maybe he's simply in hiding out of fear for his life. Either way, I'm going to spend a day or two here trying to get a handle on the story." I slowed down a little and added, "I hope we can see each other."

"Yes, tonight, Rick. Will you be available for dinner?"

"Available" for Trish? What could she be thinking? Of course I would be "available." But I liked the fact that she had taken the initiative. It restored my confidence that, Clarissa or no Clarissa, she still wanted to get to know me. But my resentment toward Clarissa lingered. She'd become—without invitation—too involved in my life and in Trish's.

Trish looked at her watch. It was time for her to get to her afternoon training session, and I needed to show my face at the *Epoch* bureau. I asked for the check since this was my treat and I didn't want to be a freeloader at the hotel on account of Trish.

We kissed, European-style, on the cheek and parted.

Now I had to get to Clarissa's apartment and thank her for meeting Trish at the airport. I was also more than a little curious—and frankly, annoyed—about what she'd said to Trish. I told the cab driver in passable Cantonese Clarissa's address on Fa Yuen Street in Mongkok. He looked at me a little quizzically. Gweilos didn't usually go to Mongkok addresses in broad daylight. This part of Hong Kong was one of the most densely populated urban areas on the planet. At times, you could be pinned to a spot on the sidewalk as the tide of people coursed around you, throngs of Hong Kongers swept up in thousands of life's different priorities.

I had never been to Clarissa's walk-up, and my expectations of the neighborhood were pretty much on the mark. It was truly seedy. In the narrow doorway off the street, an elderly man in a stained undershirt was selling plastic combs and nail clippers from an open suitcase that he was ready to snap shut in an instant if police came by to clear out loiterers and unlicensed peddlers. Glancing at him, I remembered many headlines I had read of violent crime in Mongkok, people with meat cleavers going berserk in butcher shops or jealous wives pouring acid on the faces of their sleeping husbands. This man clearly wasn't a licensed hawker. His chin sprouted gray stubble, and his dark eyes roamed up and down the street. As I negotiated the staircase behind him, I felt him sizing me up through the dark hoods of his eyelids. He was probably wondering why I was carrying a box of chocolates.

Clarissa's apartment was on the fourth floor. There was an elevator, but it was broken so I had to walk up, wondering the whole time what on earth I was doing visiting a missionary's run-down apartment in the middle of a dubious neighborhood in Kowloon. Somewhere between the second and third floors, a beefy Chinese man barged past me, headed down in a great hurry, shoving me rudely out of his way without a word of apology. Perhaps he had just narrowly escaped a cleaver attack in his apartment.

But order seemed to reign outside the door of Clarissa's apartment. The small landing area in front of the elevator separated by the narrowest space two identical apartments. The landing had been swept clean, and the door to number 4A had been repainted recently. "Clarissa Jones" was written neatly on a piece of white paper taped carefully to the door. Just the name, nothing else, handwritten in bold capital letters, as though Clarissa were welcoming first-graders at the start of a new school year.

The doorbell rang with a sharp, alarm-clock-like rattle, and a moment later Clarissa was at the door. When she saw it was me, she beamed with apparent pleasure. "Come in, come in, honey," she said, as though she had been waiting several days for my arrival. "Make yourself at home. Did you come straight from China? No, that was a silly question. You must have gone straight to the Park Century to see Trish. You must be tired. My goodness, what's this?" she exclaimed, as I offered her the box of chocolates in response to her chatter. "Honey, you didn't need to do that. What a treat! Come on in, sit down. I've just put a pot of coffee on."

The apartment was tiny: just a bedroom, a miniscule bathroom, a kitchen too small to do anything other than stand up in, and a living room that was no more than six feet square. But it was clean and freshly painted. Clarissa had festooned the walls with posters announcing the arrival in

Hong Kong of this or that famous American evangelist, and she had set out pictures of her own—framed photos of her college graduating class in South Carolina, another of what I assumed to be her mom and dad arm in arm, and a color print of the Damascus Gate in Jerusalem. I noticed on a small table behind the door a timetable of Bible studies and counseling sessions. I marveled at the naiveté of this woman's uninhibited boldness in believing that she was somehow supposed to be preaching to the Chinese.

I gratefully took the coffee she offered me—I'd been so distracted with Trish that I had forgotten to order coffee—and noticed that the cup was quaintly matched with a saucer and was not the standard mug that most people drank their coffee from.

"You know, Trish is a lovely young woman. Well, that she's lovely is obvious," and Clarissa giggled at the obviousness of what she had said. "After picking her up at the airport, I showed her around a little, and then we got her to her hotel. They seemed surprised that she had arrived so soon. They weren't expecting her yesterday." I almost froze in embarrassment. I wondered if Trish had let on to Clarissa that she had planned to stay in my apartment for the first few days of her week-long visit to Hong Kong. But Clarissa had barely paused to catch breath. "You know, she's such a well-mannered young lady. She kept thanking me, and she insisted on taking me out to dinner last night. A real fancy place, Gabby's or something, in the Peninsula Hotel."

"Gaddi's," I corrected her.

"Yes, that's it! You know, we had quite a talk. She told me all about her family, of her travels all over the place when she was younger, about the job she's doing now. You know, I had no idea that she meets all these important people. She's quite a lady, Rick."

"Yes, I know," I responded.

"So, forgive me if I am being a little nosy," she continued, "but are you two very close?"

What did she mean, "very close"? Was she asking if Trish and I had slept together, which we hadn't—we hadn't even kissed—but I hoped we would kiss and more this week in Hong Kong. Or did she have an altogether more innocent question in mind—like, were we an item? I smiled inwardly at this quaint and outdated concept, which harkened back to junior-high-school–era dating. Not wanting to reveal my true intentions, I decided to assume that the latter was Clarissa's intended line of questioning and replied with mock innocence that we were still getting to know each other.

"Trish hasn't been to Hong Kong before, at least I don't think so, and certainly not since I first met her," I explained. "But then her hotel chain arranged this business training session, and I was glad to be able to play tour guide to her here."

"Yes, of course." She paused. "You know, honey, Trish and I also talked about some pretty deep subjects, like what she wants out of life, what her most important values are. And, you know, we also talked about matters of faith, and I learned that she has a serious side too. She was quite drawn to the things of God as a child, you know. She told me that for awhile she had wanted to be a nun."

A nun! What the . . . ? Trish had never mentioned this to me.

"She also told me about some of the men she had gotten to know earlier on who, perhaps, were not the most suited for her."

I thought I knew what "not the most suited" meant. That would be Ludwig, the married Swiss businessman. I felt increasingly uncomfortable. It seemed that in just one short day, Trish had been inveigled by Clarissa's warmth into something approaching a confession of all her life's doings. I wasn't at all happy about that. I wanted to cut this conversation short and leave.

But Clarissa, no fool, had anticipated this. "Now, you mustn't think I was giving her the third-degree, you know what I mean?" And she laughed so entertainingly as she said this that I laughed with her. "She just seemed to want to talk, and I think she realized that I was absolutely no threat. I am not part of her world at all—or of yours, Rick—and I think she just felt comfortable with me because, you know, I take everyone as she is, I don't have these great expectations"—and here she broke into another of her giggling fits, as though she had just said something hilarious—"not that anyone would expect me to have any."

She laughed a second time at the idea: "great expectations." Then she looked intently at me and said, "Of course, Rick, I know that you will treat her with real respect, like a princess. I know that's what she really appreciates 'cause that's what she told me. Now, run along, I'm sure you've got plenty of things to do now that you're home. You know, we had breakfast together this morning in her hotel. But I expect now that you're back you'll be taking up all her time." She giggled again.

Thus dismissed, like an errant fifth-grader who had been summoned to the principal's office for a talking-to, I said good-bye to Clarissa, thanking her again for meeting Trish for me. As I left, I realized the message Clarissa had just delivered to me: slow down in your pursuit of Trish and treat her right because I'm going to be watching. I swallowed my indignation. I didn't think Clarissa's helping me out yesterday gave her any right to take an interest in what I did in my personal life, and certainly not my love life. Reentering the smelly, noisy universe of Mongkok's streets, I hailed a cab for Hong Kong's main business district on the island side of the harbor.

At the *Epoch* bureau, Lucinda wore a knowing smile as I walked through the door. I grinned back at her. She was intelligent, thoughtful, and most of the time about three jumps ahead of everybody else.

"Well, did you find out what happened to Burton's friend in Guangzhou?"

I was taken aback. "How did you know about that?" I asked, astonished. I had told her nothing about McHale when we'd spoken by phone yesterday.

"Oh, I have my ways." She smiled. Then I remembered: Katie. Lucinda was a good friend of Lasch's personal assistant, Katie Andreas. They talked on the phone for hours, Katie recounting the latest episode in her love life, Lucinda listening patiently and intently. It was safe for Katie with Lucinda, who lived half the world away and was unfailingly discreet. In return, Lucinda was able to winkle out the flotsam and jetsam of corporate and editorial gossip at *Epoch*. It was a useful arrangement for both of them.

I realized that Lucinda probably had information for me that wasn't in any e-mail that had come in. And I was right.

"I think Reddaway's on the warpath at the moment," she said. "He thinks Burton is spending too much of the company's money on journalistic wild goose chases. Katie told me he and Burton had something of a shouting match last night, and it was over Burton's sending you off to Guangzhou. Nothing from Burton has come in, but Katie says she thinks we ought to tread softly for awhile. That means holding off on getting back to Guangzhou for a few days."

On one level I was relieved. It meant that I could spend more time with Trish as well as get up to speed on the background to Great Master Wu and Qigong. But I also had a nagging feeling that time might be running out for McHale. It was difficult to say whether he had been kidnapped in Guangzhou or was on the run trying to stay out of the way of the Triads and Great Master Wu's various friends.

"Oh, and sorry to mention this as well, but that sports section roundup is being brought forward. They want to close the story this week. I've alerted the stringers, but you will probably want to polish up what they write. Meitnic's here already and he's staying at the Intercon. I think he went out to get a suit made or something. What do you want him to do? Maybe you could get him started on the sports section roundup? Oh, and did your friend get in touch with you?"

Lucinda had missed nothing. I'd not even mentioned that there was somebody called Trish or that she was going to be in Hong Kong this week, but Lucinda, both intuitive and relentlessly logical, had figured out that the "anyone" I had anticipated calling me was likely to be female. Now it was my turn to smile. "Yes, she got here just fine," I said with a grin. "And I think that's a good idea to get Steve working on the sports roundup."

Lucinda had smiled for an instant when she had asked the question about my "friend" but now was all poker-faced professionalism again. "Do you want me to stay late tonight?"

"No way. I'll play catch-up with the e-mails before I head out again. You get home to your mom." Lucinda's devotion to her mother was legendary at *Epoch*. It was Chinese filial piety writ large.

I went into my office and surveyed the neat pile of stringers' stories that Lucinda had printed out for me from the morass of e-mails that had piled up. Now that they were in front of me, in paper form, it wouldn't take long for Meitnic to wrestle them into shape for the roundup. But I still had half the day ahead of me, and I wanted to get started educating myself on Qigong.

I'd been to a Qigong demonstration at the Hong Kong Convention Center, when those Shaolin monks had demonstrated hitting each other on the head and standing on a tabletop on eggs. But what was happening in Guangzhou, if Petrolucci and Young were on target, seemed to be more than magicians' tricks. I needed more on the subject from someone with a long-term grasp of trends in China.

I scrolled through the address book on my laptop until I came across Father Radim Malek. Of course. I should have thought of him immediately. The septuagenarian central European Jesuit had been producing a weekly analysis of events in China for more than three decades. It was entirely a one-man publication, a distillation of events and trends relentlessly full of common sense and, like the best of journalism, was always skeptical of overly complicated explanations of what was happening in China. He took the principle of Occam's razor—that one should always prefer the simplest explanation to any other available—to the nth degree.

How Malek got all the stuff together was anyone's guess. A political officer at the U.S. consulate once calculated that Malek would need about twenty hours a week just to digest the newspapers he kept referring to. But his ability to read Chinese was stunning. I figured that he probably knew more than seven thousand Chinese characters, more than twice what is generally regarded as needed to read a mainland newspaper with ease.

But Malek, again more like a good journalist than a traditional "sinologist," enhanced his analysis by looking to sources other than just the official press. He made time to sit down with recent arrivals from the mainland, interviewing them at length: waiters, small business people, and mainland tourists visiting Hong Kong relatives. Just by asking the right questions, about things that real journalists and the overworked cadre of professional China-watchers still in Hong Kong in large numbers often overlooked, he drew attention to what was really happening in China.

His *China Trends Today*, printed every Monday and distributed the next day by old-fashioned mail delivery—rather quaint in this age of e-mail—was often the first thing that I read in trying to make sense of what was going on across the border at Lo Wu, and I was not alone. Malek was both a gentleman and a gentle man. He never begrudged "newbies" in the press corps or the diplomatic corps his time, patiently explaining to them what they should be looking for in analyzing China.

Malek was aided by one flustered assistant, a middle-aged Chinese spinster whose main job, as far as anyone could tell, was watching Guangzhou TV pulled in on a gigantic satellite dish—now hopelessly outdated but still functional—that a rich businessman from Taiwan had, on impulse, bought for Malek long ago. Malek was, quite simply, irreproducible.

To my surprise, Malek said he would have time for me at 3:30 in the afternoon. We agreed to meet in the coffee shop of the YMCA, a place he felt more at home in than someplace like the ritzy Peninsula Hotel across the street. The "Y," part of the Hong Kong scene since 1901, was located in the heart of the tourist center of Tsimshatsui. In the midst of all that upscale glamour and ostentation, it stood out in its no-frills appearance and approach. Unlike Ys back in the United States, this one was more than just a place for neighborhood kids to shoot hoops. Among other services including sports classes, church services, computer training, and camp, it ran a three hundred-plus room hotel that was so popular among budget-minded travelers that getting a reservation required booking weeks, sometimes months ahead. With a harbor-front view and rooms for about one hundred dollars per night (compared with the Peninsula's six hundred dollars per night for a similar view), it was one of the best values in town.

I arrived with plenty of time to spare, but Malek was already seated at a table in the crowded utilitarian coffee shop—more a glorified cafeteria, really—deep into a very pious-looking book. His priest's black cassock, which he always wore when meeting people in public places, was threadbare and stained. Malek was famous for slurping tea noisily and often with scant regard for what it spilled on as he drank. He was a very thin man—I would say almost emaciated—and his gray hair hung thinly over his face. But his eyes were startlingly blue and often had a twinkle in them. I think he took an almost schoolboyish delight in catching the regime in some stupidity or other in its public statements. I always looked forward to my rare meetings with him.

On the phone in arranging the appointment, I had given him just enough information for him to know what I wanted to talk about but not enough for any of the State Security goons surely assigned to listen in on his phone conversations to go on. He wasted no time in broaching the subject.

"So you are interested in learning more about this Qigong phenomenon in southern China, are you?" he began. No polite small talk for Malek.

"I am especially interested in its intersection with political trends in Guangzhou and any possible connections with the Triads."

"Oh, I see. You have got right to the point. Very good. Most people don't see that connection very clearly. And what is the basis for your deduction that the Triads may be involved?"

I decided I had nothing to lose by telling Malek about McHale, whom he might well have met. As he listened to my account of the phone conversation with Lasch and my meetings with Young and Petrolucci, Malek's face wore the most intelligent, attentive look I had ever seen on any man. His thin gray hair inadequately covering his unusually large forehead, his eyes appeared simultaneously to squint and twinkle as he listened.

"Yes, I am almost certain that the Triads, including some of the names associated with organized crime in Hong Kong, have strong political connections with the Guangzhou military leadership. Of course, it's primarily a commercial connection, pure and simple, you know, how can we scratch each other's back most effectively?"—I thought I detected Occam's razor in his comment—"but I think there are some big national political ambitions in Guangzhou also. I think they want to change the direction of China's foreign policy so that it becomes much more nationalistic. I suspect if they could, they would like to provoke military action across the Taiwan Strait."

"Then they are very dangerous?"

"Absolutely. If these people had their way, Beijing would drastically alter its relationship with the rest of the world."

"How so?"

"In almost every area where there is a potential conflict with foreign powers, they would take the offensive. There has always been an element in China's political leadership, even before the Communists came to power, that has been very hostile to foreigners. Of course, they haven't always been visible. Sometimes the leadership has wanted to conceal any signs of anti-foreign sentiment for pragmatic purposes. But it's been hard for China to suppress all non-conformist views in an atmosphere that, for reasons of intellectual creativity in the nation's cause, encourages as much intellectual diversity as possible within a political autocracy.

"For reasons that elude me, the people who harbor strong anti-foreign sentiments have gravitated to South China. It may be because Guangzhou is something of China's 'Wild West'—lots of money, few rules, and the possibility of making connections with high rollers both from the local government and from Hong Kong. For any focused political movement, money is needed, and it's got to come from somewhere, somewhere outside of central government scrutiny.

"Three new think tanks dealing with China's strategic needs have opened up in Guangzhou in the past two years," Malek went on, "and two of them have recruited effectively from Beijing's top military think tanks, for example, the Academy of Military Science. Now, it might simply be that they get paid better down south. But it could also be that they think they will have more political support than they could get in Beijing. China's capital has all sorts of points of view competing for attention, and nationalism is only one of them. In Guangzhou, it is more likely to take hold."

"And what about Qigong?"

Malek took a big slurp of his green tea and seemed to enjoy swilling it around in his mouth before he replied.

"Well, to answer that I must first ask you how much you know about traditional Chinese medicine." He sounded exactly like Petrolucci back in Guangzhou asking about Chinese peasant rebellions.

"Not much. Just the basics." I lied. In fact, I knew next to nothing, being faintly repelled by the musty smell of strange herbs that pervaded every

Chinese pharmacy in Guangzhou and Hong Kong, and not at all persuaded by the mystical, New Age mumbo jumbo with which it is often associated among westerners.

"You know, Qigong is one of the four pillars of Chinese medicine, the others being herbs, acupuncture, and massage. The notion of Qi is a central concept of both traditional Chinese medicine and fashionable modern pseudo-science like *feng shui*. Of course, feng shui is a generally harmless New Age fad, hocus-pocus about which direction your office desk faces or, at a more expensive level, in which direction your corporate office building's windows should look out.

"But I think there is more to the concept of Qi than placating the 'dragons in the hills,' or similar feng shui ideas. In its most central meaning, Qi denotes both the inner energy, the vital life force in all human beings and, in a sense, the very character of events. How should I explain this? The Qi of the French Revolution was not just the murder of the French royal family, God rest their souls, but the overturning of the entire old order in France. Of course, the French revolutionaries themselves may only have been vaguely aware of this at the time, but someone interpreting French history using the concept of Qi might explain it that way.

"Qigong, on the face of it," Malek continued, "is just an effort, through meditation and various exercises, to unblock the flow of personal Qi that courses, supposedly, through everyone, and not only to cure illnesses but to tap into something far bigger than one's personal life energy. But Chinese medical practitioners sometimes refer to what they call 'external Qi,' which is power that they can, in theory, channel toward the illnesses in other people. I suppose it might be analogous to the Christian practice of laying on of hands or healing through prayer."

"You mean faith healing, like what those TV evangelists do in America?

"No, completely different. Faith healing is what they do in the Philippines, and it involves channeling or spiritism. The Filipino faith healers use the paraphernalia of Catholic piety—statues of the Virgin Mary, the Lord's Prayer, rosary beads and what have you—but what they practice is actually spiritism through a medium. The church is totally opposed to that. We"—here the Jesuit self-perception of being the theological honor-guard to the pope himself was surfacing—"oppose that, along with witchcraft and astrology, as being of occult origin and thus forbidden by Moses in the Torah, you know, the first five books of the Hebrew Bible.

"What you see on TV in America is supposed to be healing through God's power," Malek went on, "and the healers sometimes place their hands on sick people. I don't know whether the alleged healings are real or not, but at least what takes place falls within the Christian tradition. Now, in a sense what the manipulators of external Qi do is similar to what Christian healing evangelists claim to do when they lay hands on a person, or point their hands toward a person."

I wanted to set Malek straight at this point, not on American TV evangelists, who usually made me laugh, but on the Catholic Church and faith healing. I knew for a fact that some Catholic priests in the Philippines encouraged visits to faith healers. But I didn't want to distract him from what he was getting at.

"Now, with external Qi," Malek went on, "you are getting into areas I really don't know much about. Some Qigong adepts claim to deploy 'external Qi' in ways that are remarkable. They can supposedly mobilize so powerful a physical force that one man can make ten men fall over on stage. Some of my colleagues who travel extensively inside China report that Qigong masters can exert mind power over people at great distances. I have never seen this done, and I've read that experiments to test this have never duplicated the results that are sometimes carried out on stage. But I have to confess something to you. It disturbs me that what some of these Qigong practitioners may be trying to tap into are real supernatural powers."

"Wait a minute, Father," I protested. "Surely you don't believe those head-bashing exercises with telephone poles or standing on eggs on table tops are supernatural? I've always assumed that it's all a magician's trick."

Malek blinked several times, perhaps in embarrassment. He slurped his tea some more before replying.

"Well, I don't know what your worldview is, so I won't make any assumptions on your attitude. But suppose, for the sake of argument, that there really were forces in the universe, good and bad, that material science couldn't explain, or at the very least, some people believed that such forces existed. Wouldn't various political elements in different societies try to gain access to them?"

I nodded. I had heard how Adolf Hitler had supposedly employed Tibetan monks to pray their incomprehensible prayers in support of Nazi victory. I didn't know whether the story was true or not. But there was another story I'd heard from Lasch. He said that in a cab one night leaving

Epoch's editorial headquarters in New York, the driver, an immigrant from the Soviet Union, had told him that during weapons training in the Soviet army an instructor had demonstrated various paranormal practices for improving their shooting aim. Absurd as it sounded, the cab driver insisted that the accuracy rate of their unit had improved.

Lasch had been skeptical of this story, but I was curious whether it was the cab driver who had invented it or whether, by some chicanery, the weapons instructors had convinced all the trainees that they had improved their weapons skills. I never did come to a conclusion about which it was.

"Take one of the most ruthless and practical of all China's rulers," Malek was saying, "the first Qin dynasty emperor, Qin Shi Huang Di. You know what he devoted the last years of his life to, once he had conquered all six rival kingdoms and unified China?"—he continued without pause—"The search for immortality."

"Didn't he want to destroy all competing historical accounts of China's past?" I suggested. "He started the Great Wall, killed hundreds of thousands of laborers building it, and buried all the Confucian scholars alive."

Malek tossed his head back impatiently. "The story about burying the scholars has been thoroughly discredited by most recent investigations. But it is true"—the Jesuit instinct for balanced argument was coming through in Malek loud and clear—"that Qin Shi Huang Di was in most respects paranoid about his own security, as well he should have been. He feared assassins everywhere. Every day he would conceal his sleeping location from all but a handful of his trusted servants. But he was obsessed by something even more powerful than fear of assassination. He wanted to live forever."

"That's ridiculous!" I blurted, sounding as though I were contradicting Malek rather than expressing my scorn for the Qin emperor.

Malek smiled wryly. "Well, we do agree on something," he said gently. "But I'm sure you know that the search for immortality, often through alchemy, is one of the constant themes of Daoism, China's only indigenous religion. I think, in fact, this is why many Confucian scholars, who were drawn to the sense of spontaneity and wit in such writings as the Daoist philosopher Lao Zi's *Dao De Jing*, couldn't take Daoism very seriously either as a philosophy or as a religion. Educated people were smart enough to know that alchemy was an illusion. But the Qin emperor visited Zhifu Island off Shandong Province three times because it was rumored that the elixir of immortality could be found there. He actually died in the search for immortality, probably from drinking a potion that contained too much mercury."

I found Malek's expositions on Chinese history diverting, but I wasn't getting any closer to Qigong and the Triads. I tried to steer the conversation back to the here and now.

"Well, all well and good," I said. "But what has that got to do with the Triads?"

"I don't know very much about the Triads," Malek said, "only what I have read second hand. But their connection with Chinese secret societies is well documented. The Red Turban Rebellion, which ultimately overthrew the Yuan dynasty in 1368, was a secret society that drew its supporters from among Chinese peasants looking for examples of supernatural power. The Taiping Rebellion of the 1850s started off as a cult based on Christianity—the leader Hong Xiuquan thought he was the younger brother of Jesus—but it degenerated within a few years into a movement whose leaders kept their authority only by constant recourse to supposed new revelations from God on high. The Boxers got their power because ordinary peasants, in trances, believed they had become inhabited by various Chinese gods that would make them resistant to knife thrusts."

"But not to the westerner's Maxim guns," I interjected cynically, referring to the world's first automatic machine gun.

"Well, true enough," Malek responded graciously. "Perhaps their gods hadn't been reading *Popular Science* articles about recent improvements in military technology." And Malek did something I had never seen him do before. He started laughing at his own joke but completely noiselessly, his shoulders jerking up and down as his entire upper body rocked with merriment. Then he resumed his explanation as if there had been no interruption at all. "However," he continued, "don't forget that the Boxers were able to harden their bodies against knife and spear thrusts, which gave the impression to uneducated peasants that joining the movement would render them somehow invulnerable."

I had distracted Malek with my interruption, and now I was anxious for him to return to his explanation of the connection between the Triads and China's historical secret societies.

"So historically, China's secret societies were sort of criminal groups as well as practitioners of magic?" I asked.

"Well, the term used by the various dynasties to refer to them was *xie jiao*, literally, 'evil religion.' It is interesting that today's Chinese authorities use the same term both for genuine occult groups and for underground Christian groups, usually Protestants, who won't register with the authorities.

"A group called the White Lotus Society in the eighteenth and nineteenth centuries united poor peasant communities in southern China who were ideologically opposed to the Qing dynasty," Malek continued. "They became known as 'men of Hong' after the name of the first Qing dynasty emperor. But 'hong' was one of those secret words you weren't supposed to say out loud, so throughout the nineteenth century these groups that were precursors of the Triads became known simply as 'hui' or 'associations.' They had a carefully guarded series of initiation rites, and in their ideology they combined elements of Confucian ethics, Daoist and Buddhist religious teachings, along with China's grassroots popular religion.

"Today," Malek continued, "the Triads are fiercely self-protecting criminal gangs that are utterly ruthless but have a sort of perverse moral code of loyalty, rather like the Mafia, which they impose on all their members, and they have shown signs of wanting to freelance in China's politics. Of course, what they are up to in this area is something that nobody outside the Triads really has much of a clue about. Occasionally, they have surfaced in the Hong Kong media with elaborate plots to spring some of their jailed leaders from prison, in one case supposedly by kidnapping senior officials of the Hong Kong Special Administrative Region. But to be honest, I really don't know very much about them."

I looked at my watch. It was approaching 5:00 p.m. Malek had been talking almost continuously for more than an hour. Though he showed no sign of weariness, I was conscious that his day was normally very busy and that I had monopolized him for much of the afternoon.

"Father," I said during one of his tea-slurping pauses, "I've taken up a lot of your time; I've learned a great deal, but I should probably let you go. I hope you didn't mind all my questions."

"Not at all. Reporters are supposed to ask questions. But I do want to say one thing to you, young man, before we part company. I said earlier that I don't know what your worldview is. I don't know whether you think about spiritual things or not. But I must warn you that there are a couple of things you should keep in mind. First, the Triads do not appreciate outsiders poking around. Second, you would be doubly at risk if, as a foreigner, you showed yourself too interested in the Chinese nationalism that some Triad groups may now be supporting. Third, if you delve too closely into Qigong matters you may give the impression of challenging people who resent being challenged. I've told you about some of the tricks attributed to Qigong masters. I do not know whether they are, as you say, 'magicians'

tricks' or something real. But I think they can be very powerful, and perhaps rather dangerous. Be careful, young man, be careful."

It was a sobering thought. Perhaps I was getting into areas that were
dangerous. But I had promised Lasch that I would do my best to get to the
bottom of the McHale business, and at least, through Young, Petrolucci,
and now Malek, I had gotten a start.

I had arranged to meet my Delhi colleague at the Intercontinental, one
of Hong Kong's leading hotels and just a short walk from the YMCA on the
Kowloon side. I liked Meitnic. A jovial, middle-aged family man, he often
brought his wife, a peppy redhead with a personality to match and a serious shopper, with him on short assignments. She was with Meitnic when
we met, smartly dressed in some new purchases.

We settled down in the amazing Lobby Lounge of the Intercon, which
features a breathtaking view of Hong Kong harbor from its floor-to-ceiling
windows. It is one of the most magnificent places to watch the sun set. We
laughed over stories about bureau chiefs' conferences that Lasch had pre-
sided over in the region, often at opulent resorts, and caught each other up
on the latest *Epoch* talk on who was up, who was down, and who was on
the outs. Meitnic understood that Lasch wanted me detached from normal
Epoch activities for a few days and was happy to take over the bureau for
awhile. Unlike some *Epoch* correspondents, he was not into scoring points
in the perpetual competitive wrangle among bureau chiefs, but was content to carry on until retirement in whatever bureau Lasch assigned him.
Though no workaholic, he steadily produced what was needed to keep the
foreign section happy.

Around 6:30 p.m., I left Meitnic and his wife, already well into their
second gin and tonic, and hopped a cab to the Park Century Hotel. I'd
agreed to meet Trish there and then go out somewhere for dinner, probably
on the Hong Kong side. I was in a very good mood.

Chapter Six

When I arrived at the Park Century, I expected to have to use the house phone in the lobby to call Trish's room, and because I'd forgotten to get her room number, I would have to go through the operator. But to my surprise and delight, she was already waiting for me, looking radiant in a filmy ankle-length summer dress, pale pink and nipped flatteringly at the waist, that showed off her figure beautifully. She was standing to one side of the ornate, marble-floored lobby, half concealed in an alcove, causing guests getting off the elevator to do a double-take on catching sight of this attractive, tall, bronzed Asian woman waiting almost immobile next to a large potted palm tree, her eyes fixed on the hotel entrance. In fact, she saw me before I noticed her.

"I wanted to see what your expression would be as you came into the hotel," she explained with a smile. "You can tell a lot about people by observing their faces when they don't know you are looking."

"I'll say. And I suppose mine showed gloom and despair?"

She laughed easily, again almost a range deeper than would be expected for a woman of her height and age.

"I phoned ahead and made dinner reservations on the way over here," I said. "Over on the Hong Kong side. I hope you like Indian food. There's a great restaurant in Pacific Place called Bombay Palace. But if you'd rather have something Chinese or Western, just let me know and we can easily change it."

"Well, we could start with Indian and then perhaps graduate to Vietnamese or French, and then end up with Chinese. Or should it be 'descend' rather than 'graduate'?"

"You don't mean all in one night, do you?"

"No, silly, I mean on subsequent occasions when we go out for dinner."

I looked at her out of the corner of my eye. This was interesting. She seemed in a mischievous, almost frisky mood. I thought it boded well for a fun evening, and I hoped her serious side wouldn't spoil things.

We took a cab to the Star Ferry, which I always preferred for getting across Victoria Harbour, rather than the MTR, Hong Kong's fast, efficient, clean, but generally uninteresting underground rail system. Of course, we would have gotten to Pacific Place, the ritzy multistory, multifunction waterfront mall complex (office towers, three five-star hotels and luxury apartments, and upscale shops and boutiques), faster and more directly by MTR, but it wouldn't have been nearly as romantic as the Star Ferry.

The distinctive green-and-white double-decker passenger-only boats have been plying the Hong Kong harbor for more than a century and are as much a symbol of Hong Kong as the more recent controversial Bank of China Building designed by the world-famous architect I. M. Pei. Called the Star Ferry because each ferry's name includes a "star" (Morning Star, Evening Star, and, for the fleet's first diesel engine-powered boat, Electric Star), they remain one of the most economical ways of getting across the harbor.

Fare for the air-conditioned upper deck was the equivalent of just twenty-eight cents U.S., but I opted for the even cheaper fifteen-cent lower deck, not for penny-pinching reasons but because I wanted Trish to experience the crossing in all its dimensions: the refreshing breeze that alleviates Hong Kong's often oppressive humidity, the blaring horns of the other vessels—fishing boats, ocean liners, transport ships—on the harbor, the smell of the sea water (and sometimes some not-so-pleasant smells too), and the ocean spray if we managed to get a seat close enough to the bow.

I loved it when the ferry, after rumbling and shaking as if in protest at its constant chugging back and forth across the harbor, disengaged from the clattering wooden pier where it had just disgorged passengers and slowly gathered momentum anew in the six-minute crossing. For me, those six minutes almost always were an interlude of contemplation, a rare moment of quiet and calm amid the constant hubbub and ceaseless energy of Hong Kong.

As we sat together on the wooden benches, Trish became thoughtful and quiet as Hong Kong's great urban nighttime skyline came into full view, a riot of neon lights and a nearly endless line of skyscrapers with the occasional buzz of a helicopter overhead. It seemed to sum up the city's great achievements as a center of international commerce and finance, a model of order and stability on the rim of the now-waking giant of China.

When we disembarked on the Hong Kong side and found ourselves swept along by the crowds in Central, though, Trish's perkiness returned. "You know, Rick," she chattered, "we learned today in the training seminar that people decide whether they love or hate Hong Kong in the first twenty-four hours. Our trainers used that illustration to remind us that every single moment counts when dealing with a new guest."

"And is the same true in Manila?" I asked.

"Of course," Trish said without hesitation. "The principle of instant, or nearly instant, judgment applies to everything. And to everyone. Don't you find that you make up your mind almost instantly, and probably unconsciously, too, about whether a person's going to be interesting to talk to or not?"

"Well, when we met at the Hyatt reception two months ago, I certainly pegged you as someone exceptionally intelligent and a lot of fun, and I haven't been disappointed."

"Oh Rick, you sure know how to make a girl feel good about herself," she sighed. But any further ego stroking was interrupted because we'd gotten to the head of the taxi line and started to get into the next cab that pulled up. I quickly told the driver our destination, speaking to him in Cantonese even though in this part of Hong Kong, with its high concentration of gweilos, the driver probably would have understood English. But I wanted, I admit, to show off for Trish.

The dinner wasn't sensational. I had eaten better at the Bombay Palace, but it didn't seem to matter. Trish was clearly enjoying Hong Kong, and she seemed to be pleased to be with me. Perhaps because she seemed to have an aura of endless energy, I found her a wonderfully stimulating companion. She could keep up with me no matter what we talked about—China, the challenges of the reporting life, how people respond to different moods in one another—not necessarily because she knew a great deal about each of these topics (China and reporting, for instance, were quite unknown to her) but because she had a quick and inquisitive mind. And she invariably came up with some insight that I hadn't spotted. I'd already seen her intelligence displayed in a number of ways, but to my surprise, she was also very well read across a broad range of literature.

Trish had told me at the reception in Manila that her mother had been an avid reader, but she hadn't said anything then about herself. It turned out that in this she was indebted to both her parents. She explained that her competitive-minded father had sometimes required his daughters to read a literary classic in their informal family salons and, extemporaneously, to defend their initial analysis of a book in front of the other sisters. It was his way of countering the quintessentially Asian disappointment of having no sons by training his daughters in this rigorous manner. It had sharpened the ability of each girl to think on her feet in any discussion, but it had been a decidedly eccentric upbringing. I wondered what other surprises there might be for me as I got to know Trish.

Little did I know that I would soon find out.

We finished dinner and took a cab back to Central. The Captain's Bar in the Mandarin Hotel, another of Hong Kong's finest, had long been a favorite of mine, a surprisingly compact area off the main lobby with a small dance floor. Two Filipino performers were singing the usual repertoire of slow, syrupy ballads, accompanied by a three-piece band. Dancing with Trish here seemed the most natural and enchanting thing in the world, and I led her on to the dance floor as quickly as I thought I could, after our drinks arrived, without appearing overly eager.

As the seductive harmonies of the singing kept pace with the guitar, keyboard, and drums, I thought I was approaching heaven itself. The lights were low, the dance floor not too crowded, the music softly soothing. With my hands circling her slim waist, I pulled Trish's sensuous body close to mine and was elated that the move met no resistance from her. Not only that, she tucked her head so smoothly under my chin that, suddenly, all was right with the world, and I knew that nothing and no one could come between us. I felt something in my soul that had slammed shut the day I slammed the door of my apartment with Marcia now opening to Trish's exciting mind, her engaging spirit, and, of course, her drop-dead good looks.

I wanted more than anything in the world to kiss her, and then—the perfect end to the perfect evening—to take her home, and to bed. A warning thought flitted momentarily through my mind: Whoa, slow down, buddy, there's plenty of time for that after a few more dinners. But, to quote one of my father's favorite sayings, "The train had already left the station." I was becoming intoxicated by her, and rational warnings had no effect. Before the next song started, I put my cheek against hers and whispered in her ear, "Trish, this has been fantastic. Let's go to my place for a drink and some time alone."

Her response was almost abrupt. "Are you serious, Rick? You want us to go to your apartment right now? Let me see"—she said the words slowly—"you want me to help you choose the color for your new drapes, right?"

She was smiling, but it was the kind of smile that started and ended at the mouth. There was palpable tension in her words. I wasn't sure whether

I should reply in a similar bantering tone or protest that she had misunderstood. To buy time while I tried to figure it out, I took her by the hand and led her back to our small table at the back of the bar.

She didn't pull her hand from mine when we sat down, but it was clear her tense mood hadn't changed. She looked at me piercingly. "Look, Rick," she finally said, "things were going really well tonight. I thought you were one of the few men who appreciated me for my mind as much as my looks—well, Ludwig did, too, at least I can say that for him—but now you've gone and ruined it all. What in the world made you think I'd sleep with you on our first night together in Hong Kong?"

I wanted to retort, "Well, maybe because you tucked your head under my chin," but Trish was on a roll.

"Look, we're still just getting to know each other. And besides, Clarissa said some interesting things about pre-marital sex. Did you know that couples who live together before marriage have a higher chance of divorce afterward? So much for trial marriages."

I didn't know what to do with this. Who'd said anything about marriage, much less divorce, a topic I was even less keen to bring up? Did she want to talk about our relationship, trial marriages, or what? And why was Clarissa in the picture again? How I was coming to resent her, despite the favor she had done me yesterday. I wished missionaries would just stick to their boring Bible studies and prayer meetings. Why did they have to get involved in other people's love lives?

But Trish was just warming up. Now, she got really feisty. "I told you this afternoon, Rick, that I wanted to stay in the hotel tonight," she said tartly while I tried to recall whether what she'd said had really been that explicit. I seemed to recall that the question was open to discussion. Well, I guess that wasn't the case anymore because Trish was continuing. "And in case I need to spell it out for you, I am absolutely not going home with you now." She withdrew her hand from mine.

I was shocked. I hadn't imagined that a simple invitation to my apartment for a drink would lead to this blow-up. Of course, to be honest, I wouldn't have minded at all if a steamy scene followed our nightcap. But it wasn't as if I'd been planning some elaborate seduction scene. At least, I didn't think I was.

There was a long moment of silence. I still wasn't sure what to say, and now Trish seemed to sense that I was at a loss for words. She softened a bit, "You know, Rick, that was a mistake on your part, but it doesn't mean the end of our friendship. If you don't mind, I'll go back to my hotel now and take a time-out. I didn't mean to slap you in the face, but maybe there are some things we need to talk about. But not now."

With that, she got up from the table and started heading for the glass doors of the Mandarin lobby. I couldn't bear the thought of her taking the Star Ferry back across the harbor unaccompanied. It wasn't that there was any danger; Hong Kong was one of the safest cities in the world at night. It was just that if she were going to take the Star Ferry again, I wanted to be there too.

I thought quickly, trying to take the initiative for the first time since my carelessly worded invitation. "Look, Trish, I understand that you'd prefer the evening to end right here, but can I suggest something different from the Star Ferry? Take a taxi back. I'm certainly willing to pay for that," I said and started to reach for my wallet.

The look of anger that flitted across her face told me I was in even deeper trouble now. And I immediately realized—though not quickly enough to avert the damage—that I'd insulted her. Here she was, a confident, self-assured independent and modern woman with a high-powered job that paid very well, and I was trying to give her money as though she were a call girl.

But Trish was all class. All she did now, in contrast to her earlier outburst, was to say very quietly, "No thanks, Rick. I don't need your money." Without another word, she turned and proudly walked out the door, head high.

I, on the other hand, felt about an inch tall as roiling emotions swept over me: regret for the clumsiness of what I'd just said and done, humiliation because it was surely obvious to the other guests in the small dance area that Trish had just walked out on me, and an inarticulate anger with Clarissa, whose meddling, I was firmly convinced, was the reason for Trish's attitude. I went back to pay the bill and tried as I did so to appear as though nothing unusual had happened between the couple who, just five minutes earlier, had seemed so perfectly happy on the dance floor.

I'd gotten halfway out of the lobby, my thoughts spiraling the more I thought about what a disaster the evening had turned into—though I consoled myself with the thought that Trish had said the breach wasn't irreparable—when my cell phone rang. "Rick," said the voice, "sorry to interrupt you at dinner or wherever, but have you got just two minutes to talk?"

It was Steve Meitnic. I was relieved to be distracted by something more down-to-earth than my damaged romance.

"Sure, Steve, go ahead," I said. No point in telling him about the latest drama in my personal life.

"I'm still in the bureau and just got an e-mail from Reddaway. New York's decided to do a crash cover on how Americans overseas are coping with the anti-American backlash over the Bengali's death in South Carolina. Reddaway wants you to hotfoot it back to Guangzhou to get some reaction there. He's apparently caught on to the fact that there's a rising anti-Americanism, actually, anti-foreignism in South China. They want a file by Thursday."

Great, I thought with an inward groan, and today's Tuesday. "First of all, what is this Bengali thing? Second, Lucinda was telling me yesterday that Reddaway was shouting at Lasch for sending me off to Guangzhou on a wild goose chase. What's gotten into him now?"

Meitnic laughed. I was relieved at his response. At least someone in the universe still had a sense of humor.

"While you were in Guangzhou, an Indian student was knifed to death by a bunch of rednecks in a bar in some town in South Carolina. Apparently, they thought he was Arab or something, and witnesses said they were shouting stuff like "Ay-rabs out, Ay-rabs out" as they piled into the poor fellow. Of course, they were drunk. But his murder comes on the heels of the killing of another foreign student in New York City, some Columbia grad student from Guatemala shot dead outside a university dorm. The New York murder was completely unconnected, apparently didn't have any ethnic motive, and may have been a case of personal rivalry over a girl.

"But the two murders have become a big news item, not just in the U.S. but internationally," he continued. "They seem to have pushed over the top the resentment some people are feeling who think that the U.S. is making it exceptionally difficult to get a student visa, and maybe America just doesn't like the rest of the world anymore and wants to throw out all foreigners."

"OK, Steve, thanks for alerting me. I'm not far from the bureau now, so I'll be right there. Stick around for ten minutes or so, will you?"

"Sure thing."

Oh no, I thought again. Whether I liked it or not, I seemed cursed to spend more time in Guangzhou.

As I made my way to the *Epoch* office, I had the presence of mind to call the Park Century Hotel. Trish wouldn't have made it back yet, but at least I could try to repair the damage by apologizing in a message. I was halfway up Ice House Street beside the Mandarin Hotel when I got through to

Trish's voice mail. "Trish, I'm terribly, terribly sorry," I said. "I really behaved like a goat tonight. Please don't write me off totally. At the very least, let me talk to you by phone." I left my mobile number and hung up. No need to sign off with a name; she would certainly know who it was.

Steve was going over printed e-mails when I got to the bureau, a steaming cup of coffee on the desk. To my surprise, his wife Mary, the redheaded shopaholic, was also there, curled up on the sofa just inside the entrance, looking quite content reading a novel. Well, at this hour, even the Hong Kong shops were closed.

She greeted me with a "hi" as I walked in the door and went back to her reading. A plastic plate with half-eaten noodles lay on the coffee table, evidence of a working dinner *a deux*. It always surprised me how close Meitnic and his wife seemed to be. They did just about everything together.

"Here's Reddaway's e-mail," Meitnic said, tossing a double-folded printout at me. "I've almost finished the sports section roundup. There's a bottle of white wine on Lucinda's desk that we bought at Park'n'Shop on the way over from the Intercon. Help yourself. We even bought plastic glasses so you don't have to resort to Styrofoam or a coffee mug."

"No, but thanks anyway."

"Hey," Meitnic looked at me, fully in the face, "you don't look too cheery. Everything OK?"

"Spat with the girlfriend," I said as laconically as I could. I didn't want to discuss Trish with anyone right now.

"It happens," said Meitnic dryly. "Good reason for marriage. If you have a spat with your wife, she'll choose a lousy wine for dinner instead of dumping you." He chuckled.

I did, too, but Mary shouted through the office door before I could reply, "Hey, I heard that. I'll have you know that this is decent French white plonk. It was the noodles you ordered that were lousy." They both laughed and I began to relax. There was something reassuring about a couple who could banter so easily and without embarrassment with each other.

Reddaway was as terse as ever in his all-bureaus query: "Have noticed anti-American outbursts in several cities, from Calcutta to Buenos Aires. Need to know if this latest wave is mainly a reaction to Rajput's murder in Spartanburg, South Carolina, or is part of a bigger turning against America. Specially interested in what's going on in China because memory of Belgrade embassy bombing there is still fresh and we hear reports of a new nationalism brewing. From Latam bureaus need fresh take on student protest. London and Paris usual suspects. Berlin and Moscow should provide fresh reporting.

"Think this thing is a substantive and lasting phenomenon and won't be forgotten in three weeks. Need best reporting as well as analysis from experts in your areas. We are crashing cover so need main, full-bodied takes by Thursday a.m. in New York. Good luck."

"Good luck"? What did that mean? "I'll have you strung up if your bureau doesn't deliver"? Or was it more of a "stay safe if things get tough on Americans in your neighborhood"? I thought it was more likely the former than the latter. Lasch always looked after his correspondents. Reddaway, on the other hand, tended to think of them as annoyances who could occasionally be useful but probably needed to be given a few lashes to "encourage" them to deliver. I groaned aloud.

Meitnic heard me and laughed out loud. "Come on, Rick, it's time to stand up and salute again. That's what we're out here for."

"Yeah, but Reddaway thinks we can turn sources on like a spigot. He doesn't seem to have a clue about the logistics involved in reporting this kind of thing. All I can say is, thank goodness Teresa knows what she's doing in Beijing and Mike is pretty well up to speed now in Shanghai. At least that part of China's covered. By the way, with you here, how are you going to cover India?"

"I've got Singh in Calcutta—he's a terrific reporter—and as it happens I've got a notebook full of stuff myself. Three weeks ago, they had that non-run piece on overseas investment. I got an earful of anti-Americanism then."

I grunted. Steve was a very well-organized reporter who seemed to have an instinct for the direction New York would be heading and was often half a jump ahead of these crash covers. I envied him. I was better at chasing breaking stories, the ones where you jumped into the middle of something and had to cover the story real fast.

"Well, I guess it's off to Guangzhou again. But this time I'm not going to head out until I've gotten to more people in Hong Kong. I don't want to arrive there without some solid leads. I think I know who I've got to see, but I can't get to them until tomorrow. By the way, how're they treating you at the Intercon?"

"Terrific. They keep a record of every guest from the previous visit and take note of quirks and special requests. They already called our room to schedule Mary's Swedish massage. Gave us a pretty good complimentary bottle of Merlot, too, when we arrived. Do you want me to do any foraging in Hong Kong while you head north?"

I thought fast. If Meitnic delivered spectacular reporting from Hong Kong while I was away, it might not make me look good. On the other hand, if the *New York Times* had a Hong Kong dateline on anti-Americanism and my bureau was silent, that would look even worse. I took a chance.

"Steve, there's a great fellow at Hong Kong University, a sociologist called Wang Yinan, who's written a few books on regional attitudes toward Western industrialized countries. He might have some insights. There's also a guy at the American Chamber of Commerce who's been here for decades and is in pretty tight with the Special Administrative Region leadership. His name is Jenkins. He's good at dissecting semi-official attitudes and putting them in context. Lucinda can give you all the contact info in the morning. Meanwhile, I'm pretty pooped. I think I'll head home now and get an early start on things tomorrow. If you need anything—not that the Intercon isn't pampering you enough already—just let Lucinda know. She could probably even arrange a monkey-brains dinner."

"Oh yuk, Rick," Mary shouted from the reception area. "Isn't that where they put a monkey in the middle of a table, slice the top of its skull off, and give all the dinner guests a long spoon to lift out the jellified brains? How disgusting!"

"You got it, Mary. Just joking, of course."

They laughed in unison and said good night in unison. I wondered if I would ever reach that point of such harmony with any woman. With Trish? That certainly didn't look too likely right now.

My two-bedroom apartment in Deepwater Bay had been meticulously cleaned and tidied by Carmencita, a Filipina helper I shared with my neighbors across the hall. Being single, I hardly needed live-in help, and the Ericksons were only too happy to let Carmencita do my place for part of each day. Of course, since I paid part of her wages, it helped them too. Tony was a Brit in a major international accounting firm in Hong Kong, but he seemed to be rather low on the totem pole and constantly in danger of having his job localized.

There was a derogatory label for his type, FILTH, short for "Failed in London, try Hong Kong," that locals used to describe gweilos who probably wouldn't have had much professional success elsewhere but who got by in Hong Kong mostly by virtue of being white and native speakers of English.

I suspected Tony managed to keep his job by telling the firm he would stay in place for relatively modest pay. After all, he did have previous international experience and had proven useful in the office. But he also had four children and a wife whose visa didn't permit her to work in Hong Kong, so his salary was stretched. It helped that I helped out with Carmencita.

Turning on the TV as soon as I walked into the living room, I saw images of some nasty rioting in several different cities of the world. One piece had footage of an American getting beat up by a mob somewhere or other. Seeing that made me realize just why I was reluctant about heading to Guangzhou again right then, but I knew I didn't have much of a choice.

I toyed for a moment with the idea of calling Trish again but decided against it. The message on her voice mail would do for the time being. After all, I had my self-respect, too, and I'd already apologized.

In the morning, I started early with a phone call to Harry Wok. He was something of a fitness buff who worked out around seven o'clock in a club in Kowloon, and I knew I could get him then. Just as important, I would have his undivided attention, which wasn't guaranteed if I waited to phone him after his usual ten o'clock arrival at his office as publisher of *Asian Reflections*, a newspaper he had started from scratch only five years earlier. Harry was a delightful anomaly: a Hong Kong businessman who had worked for several years in the U.S. as a buyer for a Hong Kong plastics corporation. He had connived his way into an MBA program at the prestigious Wharton School and then built his way up in publishing in Hong Kong.

He was a total iconoclast. He could swear in English like an army drill sergeant, was phenomenally well-read in both the cutting edge of scientific discovery and sociology, and was an absolutely fanatical fan of the Washington Redskins. At the same time, he was skilled in Chinese calligraphy and had had several exhibits of his artistry in Hong Kong. He hated communism as a system but was smart enough to maintain close ties with people in Hong Kong who would alert him to anything he needed to know about events in China for his paper.

Asian Reflections wasn't exactly highbrow; its staple diet was a daily digest—usually accompanied by some vivid color photos—of the romances of Hong Kong movie stars and starlets and of the comings and goings of big wheels in the world of Hong Kong commerce. For that reason, it was both feared and respected in the city, an odd combination of luridly illustrated scandals and an insightful guide to big business in Hong Kong. Where Harry got his facts, or even who his reporters were, was something of a mystery, but it made *Asian Reflections* both a source of titillating anecdotes and required reading for people whose livelihood depended on up-to-date business reporting in Hong Kong.

I liked Harry as much for his Rabelaisian lifestyle as his uncanny knowledge of what was going on in China. I had long since realized that his loud buffoonery coupled with his calligraphic skills was a deliberate subterfuge. Some people underestimated him because they couldn't believe such a noisy, Americanized Chinese knew very much about China. Others thought he was less critical of the Chinese government than he actually was because his skill at calligraphy implied a meekness of disposition or a submissive attitude toward Chinese culture and hence, by extension, authority in China.

Big mistake on both counts. Harry could indeed be loud and buffoonish, but I found his uninhibited observations of what was happening in China refreshingly original and insightful. I think he liked me because, being a bachelor, I was available at odd hours for a spontaneous supper and because I kept my cards pretty close to my chest. Basically, too, he liked *Epoch*. It was pretty liberal on American domestic issues but surprisingly conservative and robust on international affairs.

"Harry, don't want to interrupt your workout, but something has come up and I need your insights. Can we have breakfast when you're done with your sit-ups?"

Harry laughed uproariously. "Hey, Rick, you should get into weights too. Makes the girls go ga-ga." He would deploy American and British colloquialisms at the oddest moments and in the most peculiar combinations, and he seemed to amuse himself by doing so. Never-married and long considered one of Hong Kong's most eligible bachelors, Harry was the frequent target of gossip in other Hong Kong papers. He'd enjoyed the company of the pick of the very starlets his own paper liked to write about (of course, his own dalliances were never featured in *Asian Reflections*). But he had recently shown signs of settling down by getting engaged to a young mainland artist named Xialin he had met through his calligraphy. "Come on over. We can have breakfast in the club. I should be showered and dressed by about 8:30. Xialin will join us."

I'd called the taxi company late the night before to warn them that I might need a car early, and by eight o'clock the Mercedes was in the apartment garage, shining brilliantly and purring in readiness. The dispatcher often assigned a driver called Ah-Kong to me, and I had grown to like him because he had an uncanny sense of when I wanted conversational chitchat and when I just wanted quiet. The trip this morning, through one of Hong Kong's three Cross-Harbour Tunnels and to the Kowloon Recreation Club, took less than twenty-five minutes, and it was a quiet twenty-five minutes.

Xialin, in a pair of linen capris and a blouse of matching purple, was reading a French art magazine in the lobby of the club when I arrived. She was pretty in a sort of French *gamine* way, slight pixyish but with a startling repertoire of different facial expressions, almost all of them intriguing. It was easy to see why Harry had forsaken the starlets for this French-educated, artistically inclined beauty.

"Sorry I wasn't ready when you arrived," Harry said as he charged out of the changing room. "Hey, Xialin, have you said hello to Rick?" She was used to the peremptory social graces of her fiancé, and in fact rather amused by them.

"Oh yes," she said, "Rick and I have been discussing French post-modernism for the past half hour." Her sarcasm delighted Harry, who was used to having underlings respond with servile obedience to his every summons. Her sass, by contrast, stimulated him. He roared with laughter.

We strolled into the dining room where a breakfast buffet was waiting. I was especially pleased by a large bowl of peeled, fresh lychees and piled them on my plate. I took it as a good omen for the day.

"Harry," I said after we had exchanged pleasantries about his and my own recent trips to New York (they had coincided in time, but we had not met there), "our editors are really on to the recent anti-Americanism that has erupted over the murder of two foreign students in the U.S. I'm going to Guangzhou later today, but I wanted to pick your brain a little first and see if you could give me some contacts there."

Harry didn't reply immediately, seeming to concentrate on his bacon and eggs. Then he wiped his mouth with a napkin and looked at me full in the face.

"Rick, this is really serious, and I mean serious. South China has been buzzing with rumors of a nationalist clique in Guangdong's military and political leadership for months. You probably know that. But I think this global change of mood toward America could trigger something really big at the national level. If these guys in the south are able to carry with them a large part of the central committee, it's time-out for China's current leadership. You know, in spite of big noises the leadership makes toward Taiwan from time to time, they don't want to seriously damage the relationship with America by doing anything really provocative. They're actually pretty moderate. But that could change in a hurry if these Guangdong people make a successful move."

He stopped and looked at his coffee cup as if deep in thought. "When do you have to write this up?"

"Well, actually they're doing a cover story this week, so I've got to file by tomorrow night."

"I thought so. Look,"—he looked me full on again—"there's a man in Guangzhou who will know everything that's happening in the city, a businessman, if that's not stretching the truth, called Tung Chi-keung. But he's a bit dangerous, you know. He's up to his chin with the Triads, and he's pretty ruthless. If he thought you were an American spy or just someone doing the CIA's business, he wouldn't think twice about slitting your throat and dropping you into the Pearl River. You want to take that risk?"

"I guess so," I said, without much conviction. "But how do you know someone like this if you don't mind my asking?"

"Oh, simple. He used to be married to my sister. She still lives in Guangzhou, you know, as does my mother."

"So in effect, he's your brother-in-law?"

"Used to be. She split with him three years ago when she discovered what he was into. I would meet him on trips up to Guangzhou to visit my mother and sister until the authorities there put me on a blacklist. Occasionally, this guy shows up in Hong Kong, and he usually looks me up. He's probably the most dangerous Chinese I've ever met. But he knows a lot."

Xialin interjected, reverting to sarcasm again, "Thank you, Harry. You have just told this nice American reporter that his best contact in Guangzhou is the most dangerous Chinese you have ever met and may slit his throat. Rick, I hope you are fully insured."

I was amazed at her dark humor, but I realized that it was part of the total package of her unique style that had completely won Harry over: outwardly so Chinese but inwardly the antithesis of modest grace normally associated with Chinese femininity. He loved her because she was thoroughly independent.

"Don't worry," I replied, keeping in the spirit of the conversation. "It will all go to my mother in Grand Rapids."

Harry laughed, then looked at me intently, his face showing real concern. "Rick, are you sure you want to do this?"

"Well, Harry, I wouldn't have called you up unless I thought you could deliver the King of Diamonds."

"Better make sure he's not the Joker," Xialin chimed in. Harry laughed again, and I saw once more why Xialin had totally beguiled him. She was one of the few human beings he couldn't order around. He loved her for it, and she loved him for never being put off by her unabashed sauciness.

Harry slid my notebook, which I had out of habit placed on the table when we sat down, next to his plate and carefully wrote down a phone number and handed it to me. "It's a mobile number," he said. "Tung Chi-keung never likes to stay in one place very long."

"Of course not," commented Xialin. "He would make too fat a target." This time Harry didn't laugh but looked at me steadily. I wasn't sure which was more unnerving, Xialin's black humor or his steady gaze. But it was time to move and Harry got up to leave. Xialin, however, wanted a last word. "You know, Rick," she said thoughtfully, "I've only met you a few times, but I like you. I hope you get a fabulous story. We'll celebrate when you get back." Then she got up and kissed me on both cheeks, French-style, as Harry beamed in the background. I didn't know what I had said or done to earn this show of affection, but I was certainly grateful for it. I felt like I needed all the encouragement I could get.

Armed with the Tung Chi-keung contact, I could have headed for Hung Hom and hopped on the train to Guangzhou then and there, but I had one more thing to do in Hong Kong. I had to find out from Clarissa what on earth she had said to Trish that had upset the whole plan of her staying at my place during her visit. It bothered me, and I was still angry with Clarissa for her interference in my love life. But I knew that whatever thin membrane of connection I might still have with Trish would probably pass close to Clarissa.

I took a cab straight from the Kowloon club to Mongkok and Clarissa's walk-up. I hadn't phoned in advance, and I knew there was a chance Clarissa might be out. In fact, in my jacket pocket was a note I had written to her saying that I had probably offended Trish and hoping that she, Clarissa, would act as a peacemaker for me. It was a groveling sort of message, and it went against all my normal macho instincts. But I decided I would rather grovel to Clarissa than to Trish.

There was no more than a delay of a few seconds after I pressed the alarm-clock doorbell before the door swung open and there was Clarissa, beaming at me again as if I were just the person she was waiting to see. Her ebullient greeting dissolved my hostility somewhat. I half expected to see

Trish in the tiny living room as Clarissa, clucking away, showed me in. But she wasn't there, and I was relieved. I knew that I didn't have much time and had to talk fast.

"Clarissa," I began, "I'm sorry to bother you twice in just two days. I hope you don't think I'm a real pest."

"Pshaw," Clarissa interrupted my carefully rehearsed spiel. "You and I have started to become really good friends, and I never feel pestered with my friends." I was glad she thought that way, because I certainly didn't. But I could see that she wasn't just being polite. Clarissa was polite to everyone, but with people she liked her response went far beyond mere courtesy. She must have sensed my tension and became serious. "What's on your mind, honey?" she asked.

"Has Trish been in touch with you since yesterday morning, I mean last night or today?"

"No, honey. Has something happened? What's wrong?"

"Well, no, nothing's really wrong, but, well, she is kind of ticked off with me, and I wanted to patch up any misunderstanding there may have been."

"What are you saying, Rick? Did she tell you she wasn't going to sleep with you?"

I felt I had been not just slapped in the face but punched in the stomach. For all of her Miss Missionary politeness, Clarissa had now cut to the chase with savage speed. She had instantly put her finger on the problem and seemed to know that Trish had put her foot down, hard. I reddened and coughed. What was there to say? My concept of missionaries had been that they usually beat around the bush, never saying directly what was on their mind. That stereotype had been completely shattered by one unerringly well-aimed question from Clarissa.

"Clarissa," I said, attempting to defuse things a little, "you know, I didn't grow up in a churchy family, and I sure don't know that much about what you missionaries believe. But look, this is the twenty-first century, and this is the way things are now. You meet someone you like, maybe you fall in love, but getting to know someone usually means having sex with her. I mean, how else are you going to find out if you're compatible? Trish wasn't being forced to do anything she didn't want to do. In fact, all I did was suggest going back to my apartment. Of course, I wouldn't have minded at all if we wound up in the bedroom, but I wasn't going to force it. But if she'd been willing, what would have been the big deal about making love?"

"Actually, Rick, I happen to think that sex is a pretty 'big deal,' and it explains why, for most of the past two millennia, Christians have taught that it's a no-no outside of marriage. You probably think sex is OK, any day, so long as it's between two people who are willing. Well, I'm sorry, I don't think that's true at all, and nor, at this time, does Trish. Call me old-fashioned, prudish, puritanical, interfering, whatever name you want, but give me credit for standing my ground on something I think is very, very important."

I sighed. I really didn't want to head into China on the tail end of a heavy religious discussion with Clarissa. I suddenly felt very tired. I wished now that I had never set eyes on Clarissa, much less asked a favor of her at short notice. But I knew that if I didn't at least get my foot in the door with her, I would be at a dead end with Trish. Somehow or other, Clarissa had gotten inside Trish's head.

"Clarissa, just tell me one thing, please, before I have to get going. Just what exactly did you say to Trish that turned her from being a very sweet, very intelligent, very attractive girl who agreed before coming to Hong Kong to stay at my place to being someone who reacted to my invitation to go back to my place and have drinks as if I were trying to recruit her as a sex slave?" I knew I was exaggerating, but I was fighting my frustration.

Clarissa flinched. Apparently, Trish had not told her that the original plan was for me to pick her up at the airport, take her home, and only later would she show up at the Park Century for the training sessions.

"Rick, I'm going to be very straight with you. When I met Trish at the airport and began to show her around Hong Kong—not that I'm any expert—she was very curious about what I was doing here. So I told her. I just told her how I grew up in a very chaotic home and became a Christian nearly fifty years ago. I told her how I felt God was telling me to come to Hong Kong. Very quickly, and without any prompting by me, she asked me what I thought about relationships between men and women who weren't married. Now, you don't have to be a rocket scientist to figure out where she was going with that. She never mentioned you at all, and neither did I.

"But I told her straight out that, as a Christian, I think God's best is for sex to be delayed until marriage because it always works best when the commitment to the person has already been made, and statistics show that if you live with someone before you get married, you have a higher chance of divorce than if you don't."

I could see now that that statistical claim by Clarissa had made a big impact on Trish.

"She—like most people, I've discovered—didn't know that," Clarissa continued. "If something I said reinforced what she had already heard previously—you know the Catholic church still teaches strongly against sex outside marriage—"

The doorbell rang sharply with three distinct rings, startling both of us. "Excuse me, Rick," she said, interrupting herself. "Let me see who that is."

She went out into the hallway, and I heard her saying, "Oh, hello Herman, forgive me, I've got another visitor here right now and I completely forgot that you were coming by. Please come in."

There was the briefest pause before a tall, skinny man with receding gray hair and a plastic shopping bag clutched in his right hand shuffled, shy and slightly stooped, into the room.

"Rick," Clarissa said, "this is Herman Fielding, also a missionary in Hong Kong. Herman, this is Rick Ireton, a reporter from *Epoch* magazine." The newcomer squinted at me when he heard the word *reporter* and turned immediately to Clarissa. "Look, Clarissa," he said, "I'll come back another time. You go ahead with whatever you were doing. I can do some things in the neighborhood." With that, he turned around and would have been out the door, but Clarissa, with surprising forcefulness, grasped his left hand with her right and pulled him back into the living room.

"Herman," she said jubilantly, "I think your arrival is providential. Rick here travels to China often to report on developments there. You travel to China a lot too. I'm sure he'd be very interested in hearing what you do."

"No doubt he would, Clarissa," Herman said, "but I make it a habit never to talk to reporters. They don't understand anything we do, and they always misquote us."

I couldn't let that pass. "You know, I've never met you, but you've just insulted an entire profession. What is it you have against reporters?"

"Herman, you can trust Rick," Clarissa interrupted. "I promise you that. He would never do anything that would betray me or one of my friends. Would you, Rick?"

"Of course not," I said mechanically. This was baffling to me. Why would Clarissa, having just told me that she had told my girlfriend indirectly why she shouldn't sleep with me, now put herself out on a limb for me?

Without waiting for Herman to collect his thoughts, Clarissa charged ahead. "Herman smuggles Bibles," she said bluntly. "Well, not just Bibles but all different kinds of Christian literature. You see, the Christians of China are not free to read whatever they want and, although Bibles are not illegal, they're often hard to get in the numbers the underground church needs. Herman knows a lot of people in the house church movement in Guangzhou and often goes there with suitcases of Bibles and other Christian literature."

Out of the corner of my eye, I saw Herman become progressively more alarmed, then even somewhat angry, at Clarissa's disclosure of his work. But I suddenly wondered if there was more to it than just Clarissa foolishly prattling on. What if she thought that Herman had information that, when I realized what it was, I would want access to. That, of course, would indirectly keep me under her wing. I felt distinctly uncomfortable.

"Herman, Rick's not a Christian yet"—what a brazen attempt to manipulate me emotionally—"but he does know a lot about China, and I'm sure he could learn a lot about the country from your work."

I decided if Herman had anything to tell me, he'd probably be more willing to trust me himself than if he relied only on Clarissa's say-so. "Look," I told him, "you don't know anything about me and you probably think I'm just like every other irresponsible reporter you've met. You don't have to tell me a thing if you don't want to, but you need to know that you're not the first Christian missionary to China that I've met and that I've actually written about Christianity in China before."

"Oh, when was that?" Herman seemed genuinely interested now.

"*Epoch* last summer did a report on American missionaries in Asia. I reported on the China piece of the story."

"That was you? I thought that was well done, surprisingly fair, in fact." I ignored the backhanded compliment. If Herman knew anything I needed to hear about Guangzhou, I wanted him to tell me right away, not after beating around the bush for half an hour. "Why are you going into China now?" he asked.

I sighed again. Now it was my turn to worry about how far I could trust Herman. If Lasch were listening in on the conversation, what would he say?

"I'm doing a story on anti-Americanism and China's rising new nationalism," I said, seizing on Reddaway's project. "But there's a connection with an American whose whereabouts I'm looking for in Guangzhou."

"Then I know who could really help you out," Herman said, suddenly eager. "He's a church leader in Guangzhou who operates safe houses for literature supplies and"—he paused for dramatic effect—"for church leaders from other parts of the country who are on the run from the authorities."

"And why would he be able to help me?" I asked.

"Because if your American friend is hiding out in the city for any reason, my contact would probably know where he is."

"And why would he want to help me?" I countered.

Now it was Herman's turn to sigh. "Normally, he wouldn't," he said. "He's extremely careful about who he helps. The only reason he might help you is if I vouched for you."

Now the shoe was on Herman's foot. Things were getting decidedly awkward. This was the last place I expected to find any Guangzhou contacts, but now Clarissa's missionary cohort just might have the key to McHale's whereabouts. But first I had to get Herman to trust me.

"Clarissa, this is complicated," Herman said. "We've got a long chain of indirect trust going on here and it's pretty fragile. I could decide that I'll trust Rick here because I trust you, and the only reason that Brother Li will trust him is because he trusts me. But"—and now he looked at Clarissa and me sternly—"nothing personal, mind you, but why do you trust Rick?"

Clarissa looked at me for a few seconds with an intensity I had never seen in her before. It was her turn to sigh. "I trust Rick," she said, "because he entrusted to my care someone very precious to him, his girlfriend, in fact. Rick may not be a Christian, Herman, but he's a good man and he's shown me great kindness. I know he won't let you or Brother Li down."

Well, that hardly would have done it for me, but these missionaries seemed to operate in a different way from ordinary people. Without further ado, Herman took out a notebook, searched through it carefully, then wrote down an address and a phone number on a piece of paper and handed it to me. "When you call this number, let it ring twice, then hang up, and then call again. Brother Li won't pick up unless you do that. Security, of course. Tell him that you are a friend of Brother David, *dawei dixiong* in Mandarin. That's the name he knows me by. Don't say the address on the phone, but let him know you know where he lives. He'll tell you when he can see you."

"Thanks a lot, Herman. Don't worry, I won't get your friend into any trouble." I knew I was being rash to say that, but what could I say? "Clarissa, you've bailed me out again—thanks. And as for Trish . . . " I didn't know what to say.

"Don't worry, Rick, I'll know what to tell her."

"Thanks, Clarissa. And thank you, Herman."

When I walked out of the apartment building, a cab was right outside letting off a passenger. I waved to get the driver's attention, got in, and headed immediately for Hung Hom.

Chapter Seven

On arrival at the Golden Panda, I made straight for the lobby pay phones. I could have used my mobile, of course, but the disadvantage was that the sometimes poor signal quality in public areas meant that conversations often had to be shouted—to the annoyance of people around you—or that, even if talking at a conversational level were possible, there was still the risk of all and sundry hearing everything. But actually, more than the fear of being overheard was the fact that cell phone conversations are ridiculously easy for anyone with surveillance equipment to pick up. Not only that, but when turned on, cell phones effectively become tracking devices, because they constantly transmit signals to and from the coverage network, signals that are easily intercepted to determine a person's exact location.

Not that I thought the Chinese security was monitoring my movements that closely—yet. But it was always a good idea to be careful and not take any unnecessary risks. After all, I was going to be taking a big risk if I had anything to do with the scary Tung Chi-keung. So going to the pay phones was the best move, not just because of security considerations but also because yet another group of Americans, couples who had come to China to adopt babies, was clogging up the reception desk area in the vast lobby. It would be a long wait.

These Americans were part of a growing contingent—despairing infertile couples, powerful East Coast career women who'd heard the alarm of their biological clocks, traditional middle-class heartland families who wanted to give a disadvantaged child the same opportunities their own natural-born children enjoyed—who were eager to bring home and love China's seemingly endless supply of unwanted baby girls. A few days from now, a joyful scene of introduction and bonding would be repeated dozens of times in the hotel as dazed infants and overjoyed new parents met for the first time to become newly minted families. And the U.S. consulate next door would be inundated with another avalanche of documents to prepare so these new little Americans could go home to start their new lives.

I'd been relieved during my previous stay at the Golden Panda that it hadn't coincided with the arrival of one of these groups of adoptive parents. They could literally take over the hotel, and the Golden Panda was said to have a fleet of baby cribs—significantly more than any ordinary hotel would have—ready for these occasions. The reason for the flood was because only the U.S. consulate in Guangzhou handled the processing of papers for the adoptees, so every Chinese baby adopted by an American had to go through Guangzhou before she left China for the United States. And of course, the Golden Panda's location right next door to the consulate meant that everybody stayed there.

I'd been there in the past when the hotel was full of these new families, and the wailing babies and the sound of jet lagged, harried, inexperienced parents trying to keep their new "bundles of joy" happy kept me up half the night. And where other hotels might be plagued by the smell of stale cigarette smoke in the halls, the Golden Panda's had a faint odor of what I could only assume was a combination of baby spit-up, urine, and talcum powder. But despite my annoyance, I had to grudgingly admit that whenever I saw these new families in the public areas, the lobby or the elevators or the restaurants—dad with the infant slung in one of those expensive baby carriers across his chest, mom expertly, fussily, and indulgingly wiping up drool, baby looking about in wide-eyed wonder at these two strangers who were treating her like a princess when all she'd known in her short life was abandonment and rejection—well, even my jaded reporter's cynicism took a rest and I couldn't help a smile myself.

But I had little time today to contemplate such heartwarming scenes and needed to contact Tung Chi-keung before anyone else. He certainly seemed to be the best of any of my possible sources who might know about Great Master Wu and the nationalism apparently gathering strength in Guangzhou. I toyed with addressing him in Mandarin, but precisely because I was quite fluent in it, I decided against it.

I also considered, and rejected, my serviceable Cantonese. Nothing would be more likely to trigger in Tung the suspicion that I was from the U.S. government than a good performance in any Chinese dialect. You could assume that Feds from Tobacco and Firearms, or DEA, not to mention the FBI or CIA, would hit the ground here rattling off pretty fluently in the local tongue; that was precisely the impression I didn't want to give when I addressed a dangerous Chinese mobster. Besides, because he spent at least part of his time in Hong Kong and had "business" there, I assumed Tung would have at least a rudimentary command of English.

Well, rudimentary it was, as I quickly discovered when I called. As soon as he answered the phone, I told him my name in English, that I was a friend of Harry Wok, and that I lived in Hong Kong.

"What you do in Hong Kong?" Tung wasted no time in asking.

"I work for the American weekly newsmagazine *Epoch*," I replied.

"What you write for them?" Tung continued. I guessed that this was his standard interrogation of any stranger who contacted him out of the blue.

"Oh, news from Southeast Asia, regional business developments, even sports." It was all true; it just wasn't the whole truth.

"What you write now?" Tung continued. It was not only an interrogation; it seemed like some kind of catechism that he probably went through with everyone when they first contacted him. I wondered what he looked like.

"I'm reporting for a piece the magazine is doing on American business executives living overseas. You know, there have been reports of anti-American rioting in many parts of the world."

"Yes, I know. Some foreign students in America get killed last week. Many people think Americans don't like other people in the world," Tung said, summarizing international perceptions tersely and rather well, I thought.

"Why you want see me?" Tung went on, relentlessly. But I was prepared and offered what I hoped would be a smooth-sounding reply. I'd already edited it down in my mind to something simple on the assumption his English would be limited. Now I had to edit it even more because his acquaintance with the language of Shakespeare seemed to be but a glancing one.

"Harry said you know more about business conditions in South China and Hong Kong than anyone. Harry said you are an expert on business here." I was working hard to resist the temptation to mimic Tung unconsciously in my own speech ("Harry say you big expert on business in South China"). "He said you had many years of experience and know the government situation and the local situation very well. I know I can talk to some Americans, but I really want the views of a Chinese businessman who has been in business many years."

There was a pause after I finished my spiel. Of course, flattery is one of the oldest techniques in the hack's book to get in good with a source. I took a chance that Tung hadn't come across it much from Western reporters for the simple reason that he probably hadn't met very many. But I was under no illusions. I knew that if Tung agreed to see me I would want my wits about me.

"How many days you stay in Guangzhou?" The interrogation was continuing.

"Oh, maybe four days."

"Good. You come, dinner tomorrow night?" Tung pressed on. "I meet people maybe you find interesting. Harry good man. He crazy and his sister crazy, but he good man. You know Ming Garden Restaurant?" I didn't, which Tung must have assumed because he continued without waiting for an answer. "Ming Garden Restaurant very big restaurant on Er Sha Island. Everybody know it. You know its Chinese name: ming chao yuan. Every taxi driver in Guangzhou know it. Very famous. Big restaurant. You come, 6:30 tomorrow. I have special private room on third floor. You say my name, Dong Zhiqiang in Mandarin. Everybody know me in Ming Garden. No problems. Oh yes"—an afterthought, apparently—"You come alone?"

"Yes, there's no one with me."

"Good. Many reporters not a good thing." For the first time, I heard Tung laugh. He'd made "many reporters not a good thing" sound like a Confucian proverb, and he probably realized this just after saying it. I was relieved. At least he appeared to have a sense of humor.

But I was still worried. To walk alone into the social lair of the "most dangerous Chinese" that Harry knew might not be the smartest move. My only sliver of hope was that his apparent liking for Harry would translate into some sort of benevolence toward me.

But Tung was not finished. "You very lucky," he said. "Next week I travel many places. You lucky because I see Harry only one month ago in Hong Kong. I like Harry. But he have many problems with Hong Kong government. Tax problems. That why he still like talk to me." He laughed. I had not been aware that Harry had any tax problems, but it seemed Tung knew more about my friend than I did. I was relieved that he had agreed to see me.

"OK. See you tomorrow. Goo-bye." In a happy blending of Chinese pidgin and English colloquialism, Tung had at last conveyed the impression he spoke English.

I hung up the pay phone and was relieved to see that the long line of

Americans checking in had dwindled to three couples, all in their forties with earnest-looking faces. Perhaps this was their last chance for a family, I thought. I got in line, registered, and went up to my room, this time on the twelfth floor. It had the unmistakable scent of inexpensive industrial air freshener, and I suspected that the previous occupant of this "non-smoking" room I had requested had lit up. I looked out the window at the normal chaotic water traffic in the muddy-brown Pearl River below. The sounds of the scene—blaring boat horns, shouts of the boatmen, loud chugging of slow-grinding tugboat motors—were muted by the twelve stories separating me from the river and the tight seal of the hotel window.

It was mid-afternoon, and I could still get some reporting done and start getting appointments lined up if I hopped right to it. Going through my list of contacts, I decided to leave off for the moment two American teachers I had met on a couple of previous trips; I could see them tomorrow. I turned my attention to three businessmen I often met with on my reporting trips to Guangzhou. One, an oil company executive, was on home leave in Dallas, according to his secretary, but the two others, who knew each other well, agreed to meet me for dinner that night. Anticipating that they might want a Western meal for a change from the local diet, I invited them to the flashy French restaurant on the top floor of the Golden Panda. *Epoch*, of course, would pick up the tab.

I e-mailed Burt again. Prudence suggested that I at least let him know I was back in Guangzhou. On the spur of the moment, I decided to call Clarissa. Her intuition about Herman's specialized knowledge of the Christian underground church scene in the city had turned out to be a useful break and might come in handy. I still wasn't happy about the role she had played with Trish, but I certainly didn't want to cut off all contact. She seemed, strangely, to be expecting me to call, and we chatted about the train trip between Guangzhou and Hong Kong, which she had yet to do, and about other cities in China she should visit. But she also had news for me. "Oh, and I heard from Trish," she said. "She says she still likes you and wants you to call when you can."

That, at least, was one less thing to worry about while I was on this risky assignment. "Oh, and a message of sorts from Herman," she added, "though he didn't know you would call. He says he's heard from friends there that it's getting very tense where you are. Be careful, he says."

"Thanks, Clarissa. And thanks for the introduction. He wouldn't have talked to me otherwise. Must go now. Talk to you later."

I got off the phone and wondered for a moment if Tung's pidgin had infected the way I was now speaking. I chuckled a bit, which was not a bad sign though I wasn't at all encouraged by the "very tense" message. I already felt enough "tension" just being in the city again.

I called Trish at her hotel even though I was certain she would be in the middle of an afternoon training session. But I wasn't sure how the rest of the day would play out or whether I would be able to call later, and now that I had Clarissa's assurance that Trish still wanted to hear from me, I didn't want to delay for a minute. As I suspected, she wasn't in her room, and when I had the hotel operator chase her down, the hotel staff confirmed that she was training and could not be interrupted. In fact, they told me it was "impossible" to call her out of the meeting room.

Telling a reporter that getting access to somebody is "impossible" is a bit like waving a red flag in front of a bull. Now, I was more determined than ever to get hold of her, so I tried her Philippines mobile number, not sure whether she even had it with her or whether it would work in Hong Kong. To my surprise, it did connect, then rang for a long time before transferring to her voice mail, at which point I hung up.

If I was going to leave a voice mail for her, it made more sense to do so on the phone in her Hong Kong hotel room. But when I dialed the hotel again and got to the voice mail system, I found myself momentarily at a loss. What could I say when our last parting words had been so awkward? I didn't want to sound puppy-like in missing her, but I didn't have any great witticism at hand. Finally, I simply said, rather lamely, "Trish, it's Richard. I just wanted to see how the sessions at the hotel were going. I'll try to call back later." I also left her the Golden Panda number and my room number.

With still some time to kill, I wandered downstairs to the hotel bookstore on the level below the lobby where I was delighted to find two books on Qi written and published in China. I bought them and took them back upstairs to read until dinnertime. I was hoping Trish might call and didn't want to be out of the room for too long if I didn't have to be. Just before dinner, I tried her again, but this time no one at the hotel could find her. I could only guess that she and her colleagues had gone out for a drink at the end of the day's training and she hadn't been back to her room to get my message.

The two businessmen showed up promptly at 7:00 p.m. in the hotel lobby where I'd arranged to meet them. For a change, I wanted to be seen doing something "normal," in case anyone had me under surveillance.

Josh Wilkins was a giant of a man at six feet five and probably close to three hundred pounds. He stood out like the proverbial sore thumb in South China, where the locals are petite even by Chinese standards. A native of Louisiana, he was in China to oversee the manufacture of fishing tackle products at a local factory. As he slowly waddled across the lobby, light pants and a plaid jacket so loud it might have gotten a used car salesman fired, groups of Chinese stopped their talking to gawk. Wilkins had once wryly joked to me that the authorities knew he couldn't be a spy because he attracted too much attention wherever he went.

Tom Sperapani, the other businessman, was from Chicago and an executive for an American cell phone company. Trim, balding, probably about five foot nine, and neatly dressed in a blue mohair summer suit, Sperapani was Laurel to Wilkins' Hardy. It was a bizarre sight, and not just for Chinese.

After some quick greetings, we immediately went up to the Versailles Restaurant on the top floor of the hotel, which had a panoramic view of Guangzhou. "Josh," I joked after we were seated and had ordered both food and drink, "you're more inconspicuous than ever. How do you do it?"

Sperapani cracked up but, Chicagoan to the core, turned serious and followed up with a question of his own as he glanced at the notebook I'd put on the table next to my place setting in anticipation of gleaning much useful information from these two. "Well, we having a revolution or something, Rick? What brings you here?"

"I was hopeful you could fill me in on what's going on here," I replied. "I don't need to tell you what's been happening all over the world in the past few days. But I need to know about this city. What's the mood toward Americans in Guangzhou these days? How has the killing of the foreign students in the States affected things? Has it stirred anything up?"

"I'll say." Wilkins needed no prompting. "It's gettin' nastier than the bayous in a hurricane just goin' to the corner store. I don't speak the language, you know that, but I get calls behind my back and they sure ain't wishin' me no merry Christmas."

"When did this start?"

"Well, the real catcalls got goin' only after the news got around of that Bengali gettin' killed. But we seen leaflets posted up that don't make us feel welcome. Tom here reads the language a little. He can tell you what they said."

Sperapani took over. "Josh is talking about some printed pages some foreigners found stuck to their car windshields a few weeks ago. It was the 'foreigners get out' stuff, not specifically against Americans. But recently we've seen notices posted on utility poles signed by a group called Defenders of the Motherland. My wife even got a call yesterday from some strange man, speaking broken English, saying that foreigners should get out of China right away."

"Yeah, we've never had stuff like that before," Wilkins joined in. "I've always found the Chinese the most gracious people you'd want to meet anywhere. Why, our kids play with their kids in the parks. But I tell you, what's been happenin' in the past few days has really upset my wife. She don't want to spend another week here."

"Do you plan to leave?" I asked.

"That's gonna be hard," Wilkins replied. "The factory that does our fishing tackle is the only thing I've got."

"But if things get really scary?" I persisted.

"Yep. I ain't stayin' here to see my family terrified like a treed 'coon. The family business ain't worth that."

"And you?" I asked, turning to Sperapani.

"It depends," he said. "If the Chinese we do business with tell us it'd be best for us to go, we will. But corporate has told us to stay put and keep our heads down on the assumption that this will all blow over."

"Do you think it will?" I asked, looking first at Sperapani and then at Wilkins.

Sperapani was cradling a glass of Merlot and didn't answer immediately, but Wilkins jumped right in. "Tell ya what," he drawled, more Louisiana than ever, an indication of his agitation, "I just got this feelin' that this is the beginnin' of somethin' real big. It don't seem to be happenin' yet in no other parts of China. I got a buddy in the toy manufacturin' business outside of Shanghai 'n' he says it's all normal there. But you don't know with them Chinese. I mean, look what happened after them Boxers got busy back in the 1900s. Loads of foreigners got killed, and the rest of 'em holed up in the diplomatic area in Beijing, and it took two months to rescue them. Why, they had half the European armies marchin' into the country to do the job. I read they messed up Beijing real good while they did it too. Didn't do the Chinese much good, I'll tell ya that. They had to pay through the nose for all the missionaries that got killed and stuff. What do you say, Tom?"

"You know, I don't always agree with Josh, either on American politics or on what's going on here. But I have to say, I don't think there has been this degree of anti-foreign feeling in the air since the Cultural Revolution. Of course, I wasn't here in the 1960s so it's not like I know, but I've read about it. Even then, as we now know, some of the violence was the result of squabbling between different radical factions, and it didn't spread much beyond Beijing. This is different. I think it's too early to say that it's a movement yet, even just in South China, but it's getting pretty close, and I agree with Josh that it's certainly beginning to get scary. I haven't experienced this sort of thing in any foreign country, even in the Arab world where I was for four years.

"Another thing," he continued. "And I don't know if it's connected, but the Daoist temples around here seem to be doing a lot more business than usual these days. I never thought of the Chinese as being very religious, but I think I've seen more josh sticks and pieces of burnt paper in the street in the past few weeks than I ever have."

"What's the burnt paper for anyway?" Wilkins asked, and Sperapani replied before I could. "Sometimes it's just a custom to honor the dead, like the Ching Ming in the spring when they tend the family graves. But burning paper can have more specific meanings, too, kind of like burning the symbolic representation of something you don't like."

"You mean like stickin' pins in wax dolls?"

"Well, only sort of. It's not voodoo, you know."

"Well, if someone wrote my name on a piece of paper and then burnt it, I'd feel it was like voodoo," said Wilkins. Sperapani laughed and added, "I've got to say something else though . . . and the problem is, I can't exactly put my finger on what's bothering me. But what it feels like is that the Chinese are at a turning point. I feel this kind of mood, this strange, somewhat hostile atmosphere, and it has to either develop even further and take the country in a completely new direction or it will be thoroughly submerged by some kind of pro-foreign reaction that follows. Either way, we could see big political changes."

I generally tried to keep my reporting dinners from ending on a serious note, and this one was getting grim indeed. I changed the subject from anti-foreignism to teasing Tom about the lackluster performance of the Red Sox this season. Josh joined in with some enthusiastic support of the New Orleans Zephyrs, and we ended the dinner on a lighter note. But as we parted ways in the lobby, I worried about their families. If the anti-foreign feelings could not be contained, things could get really ugly.

The next day, I took a cab out to the metallurgical institute to meet the two Americans who were English teachers there. The campus was on the outskirts of Guangzhou, and before long the cab was picking its way through the city's clogged minor arteries. Great wheelbarrows of watermelons, flatbed tricycles loaded down with lychees, uniformed girls selling cigarettes from vehicle to vehicle—all brought to mind the China of days gone by, with old commercial traditions superficially modernized by motor transport.

When I finally arrived at the restaurant the teachers had selected, it was squeezed, as so often happens in China's fast-growing cities, between a tire repair shop and a huge construction site. Getting out of the cab, I was assaulted by a deafening cacophony created by jackhammers and lurching cranes, and I wondered if I'd be able to hear a thing these teachers might have to say over lunch. I was relieved that they had anticipated the need for quiet and had reserved a room at the back of the Hong Bin Lou Restaurant on the third floor, where a row of private dining rooms indicated that the establishment was popular with the rising class of Chinese entrepreneurs.

The two teachers arrived just a few minutes after the hostess had shown me into the room. Jake Evans and Jennifer Hofstadt were both quite tall, even for Americans. Each wore jeans and a short-sleeved polo shirt, so similar in appearance they could easily have coordinated their attire. Jennifer had a large, upturned nose in a round face, reminding me of the sweet-faced yellow-and-green budgie my sister had had as a pet for many years. Jake was clean-shaven but still pimply. I didn't think either had been out of college for more than two years or was more than twenty-four or twenty-five years old.

And they were so polite and clean-cut I suspected they might really be missionaries, a phenomenon Clarissa had clued me in on in one of our first conversations when I'd questioned her about being a missionary. It seemed that coming to China to teach English was a favorite ploy—and to hear Clarissa tell, a very successful one—used by American churches. Of course, I had never asked these two directly if they were, but they certainly acted the part. For one thing, they'd told me in past conversations about how they made a point of getting to know their students, and I'd been surprised at how much they knew about the ordinary lives of Chinese from what can only be called the lower middle class.

They weren't a married couple, but life had thrust them together in this unusual workplace far from home; and it was obvious they had become close. Watching from the restaurant window just now, I'd seen Jake show touching concern for Jennifer's safety as they got out of the taxi in heavy traffic. No doubt recent events in the world and in Guangzhou had only intensified that protectiveness.

Soon after our dishes arrived—a shrimp and cashew stir-fry and pan-fried dumplings—they opened up about the situation in their institute.

"You know," Jake said, "things have gotten a bit wild here. We haven't experienced any anti-foreignism directly, and the school tries hard to protect us from any problems. Oh, sure, we've both gotten sour looks and some muttered derogatory comments as we've passed vendors in the street and stuff like that, but nothing that's really a big deal. But what's really surprising is that some of our students have been targeted. Some have even been threatened for studying with foreign teachers. Clumsily written Chinese notes left on desks in the classrooms warning them not to get too close to the foreigners and so forth, and in the past few days, they're using 'Americans' a lot more. Before it was mostly just 'foreigners.' One of Jennifer's students actually got beaten up off-campus. Do you think that was connected?" He turned to Jennifer to ask.

"I don't know, but it's possible. Anyway, some of the other students got really nervous after that incident."

"Do you feel in any personal danger?" I asked, even though I knew it sounded like the kind of "how-does-it-feel-to-be-the-mother-of-a-road-side-bombing-victim?" question that most journalists hate asking but can't always avoid.

Jake looked at Jennifer before replying, and she returned the look. They had obviously discussed this with each other. Jennifer spoke: "You know, we've never had any trouble with the Chinese in all the time we've been here. They've always been nice as can be to us. But, you know, it's so hard to know. We don't know, for instance, what they're saying in their homes about these student murders in the U.S. And also, we have this feeling that there's some kind of new mood, something that's gathering strength that isn't"—she paused, seeming to be aware that she was being increasingly vague—"well, normal. It's as if a new spirit has descended on Guangzhou and affected people's attitudes in a weird way." She half shrugged as she ended lamely.

I definitely wanted to hear more about this. "You mean, the atmosphere of the city has changed in someway that you can actually detect?"

"Well, yes," Jake said slowly.

"Would you say the Qi of the town has undergone a change?"

Jennifer looked startled and glanced at me sharply, asking, "How do you know about Qi? Have you studied Chinese medicine or martial arts?"

"No, but I've encountered people in Hong Kong who believe in Qigong," I said. "Frankly, I think it's a lot of hocus-pocus."

"We don't," Jake said, suddenly very serious. Then he looked at Jennifer as though uncertain if he should say more. He asked her, "Do you think I should tell him what happened last November?"

"Why not?" she answered. I was immensely grateful to her. There's nothing more irksome to a reporter than knowing that someone knows something that he's not going to tell you. "It's part of what's going on," she said.

"Look," Jake explained, "you might as well know something about us. We're here to teach English, and we love the Chinese people. But when we have an opportunity—it's all above board and legal, according to our contracts"—he hastily added, "we feel free to share our own spiritual testimony." He stopped, then added, to make sure that I understood, "We're Christians," and continued, "We tell our students the Christmas story, and we are allowed to refer to Bible passages in the classroom to explain it. We can do the same at Easter. Of course, with a few of our students and not during class time, we have prayer meetings.

"Well, last November some young members of a Qigong group in town visited our school. They were associated with someone called Great Master Wu."

If he didn't have my attention before, he certainly had it now.

Jake continued, "We'd heard the name from time to time but never met anyone who claimed to actually know him. The Qigong group put on a demonstration of their meditation and martial art skills—you know, breaking bricks with karate chops, having people poke swords at their stomachs without any blood. I tell you, when our prayer group met that night we all felt as though we were facing tremendous opposition when we prayed."

"Opposition?" I asked. "You mean your meeting was interrupted?" I didn't get it. Were the Qigong folk now raiding Christian prayer meetings?

"No, not that kind of opposition," Jake said. "I know this may sound goofy to you, but, like, sometimes, when you pray, you feel like you've got a private phone line to God? You feel your prayers are, well 'getting through'? But other times you don't feel anything one way or another. And then there are moments when you have the sense that your prayers are, like, not going anywhere? Because there's a sort of brass covering over the place where you are that's stopping the prayers getting through?" He seemed to know that he risked coming across sounding like a religious freak and had lost some of his confidence; each sentence and sentence fragment now ended questioningly in that annoying way that teenagers often use.

"I'm sorry, but I don't know what you're talking about," I said, then realized how harsh that must sound to these young, well-meaning kids and added quickly, "I'm not questioning what you are saying. I just mean that I've never had that experience myself."

Jennifer was looking more and more anxious as Jake spoke, apparently also worried about what I might think of them. "You know," she interrupted with a sweet look, "I'm sorry, Rick, because we don't know you that well and we haven't asked what your religious background is. It's unfair to dump all this stuff on you."

I was relieved that she saw the difficulty of accepting Jake's story as anything but a very subjective experience. But it struck me that whatever they had experienced had been very real to them, even if subjective, and that they weren't making this up.

I was reminded of one of my first big stories, as a summer intern in a small Arizona newspaper. It was a "where-are-they-now?" kind of story about someone who had made national headlines about ten years earlier with a wild story of being kidnapped by aliens and taken aboard a space-craft where medical experiments were conducted on him. The fascinating part of it was that his coworkers at the logging company had corroborated his story, saying they'd all seen the alien craft and seen it take their friend away, and there were unexplainable burn marks in the clearing where this had happened. And the guy had disappeared for several days and was finally discovered, slouched and groggy, in a phone booth in a town miles away.

I remember when I finished interviewing him I was sure of only one thing: This guy really believes that what he says happened to him actually happened to him.

But of course, I couldn't tell these earnest young teachers that they re-minded me of a guy who thought he'd been kidnapped by aliens. So I said, "Look, you can relax. I've met Christians before, and I don't think you're all a bunch of Bible-thumping hokies."

They smiled wanly but seemed relieved by my attempt at humor. "Well," said Jake, taking up my jovial tone, "I can show you my polyester jacket if you like, I've got a toupee in my closet, and Jennifer can put on her spidery fake eyelashes." Now I laughed, glad that they also could poke fun at ludicrous American televangelists.

"Let me just ask you this," I resumed my questioning. "Have any of your students, maybe those who know something about Great Master Wu, suggested anything political behind this Qigong thing or even the anti-foreignism and anti-Americanism?"

Jake looked at me and shook his head. But Jennifer replied, "Yes, I think there is a connection. I have the impression that Qigong is being used as a spiritual force to rally Chinese nationalism. You know, the only religion that the Chinese can call native, or their own, is Daoism. Buddhism was imported from abroad, Islam was imported from abroad, and Christianity was too. Daoism is the only religion in the world that's totally Chinese." She added, "I studied Chinese religions in college."

"Well, some people would say that Daoism is more a philosophy than a religion," Jake corrected her.

"Yeah, but if it's a philosophy," she retorted, "how come they have temples and rituals and beliefs in spirits and things? They even have people who claim, today, to become possessed by some local spirit of the Daoist temple they're in." Jake looked nervously at me as she said this, probably wondering if I thought they were getting into a very subjective world again. All I said was, "Go on."

"Anyway, it doesn't matter whether you believe what the Daoists say or not," she continued. "Daoism has always been anti-Christian, and often pretty anti-foreign, too, since they think Christianity is entirely foreign. Look, I know I'm getting speculative here, but the Chinese have had this great spiritual vacuum ever since they stopped believing in communism, which I guess happened when Deng Xiaoping and the reformers came to power in the late seventies. I can't prove anything, but I wonder if the Qigong people are stirring people up with this nationalist stuff."

"Well, that is pretty speculative," I said. "I'd want to see a clear connection, a sort of unbroken chain, if you will, before I accepted any of that."

"What are you doing tonight?" Jake asked.

"I've got a dinner meeting with a local Chinese businessman," I replied.

"Too bad. There's supposed to be some public performance of Qigong at Yuexiu Park, and word is that Great Master Wu might show."

"Where in the park?"

Jake looked startled. "I don't know," he said. "Why? Is it important?"

"Because," I said, "Yuexiu Park is the biggest urban park in China, and it has some powerful symbols of China's resistance to Western imperialism in the nineteenth century, including cannon from the Opium War. What time is this Qigong gathering?"

"It starts at 8:00 p.m., and I think goes on until late in the evening."

Jennifer interjected, "My students who have been keeping up on this stuff say that it's the first time the Qigong people have had something resembling a political gathering. I think they're testing the waters. If they don't face any opposition from the Guangzhou authorities, they'll develop it further from there. At least, that's what I think."

Now Jake interrupted. "Listen, Rick, I've got to get to class, but if anything happens, how do we reach you?"

"I'll give you my mobile number." I wrote it down on a page in my notebook and tore it out for him. "But don't call unless something really big comes up. It's entirely possible the authorities have my number, and you don't want to be caught calling me." Whatever I might have thought about their religious beliefs and what they were doing in China, I didn't want these two youngsters to get into trouble because they'd been naïve enough to accept my lunch invitation.

"Right," was all Jake said, and I couldn't tell if what I'd just said had been the first time he'd made the connection that someone who was a secret missionary in China shouldn't be associating with a person whose job the Chinese government widely believed was just thinly disguised spying.

They got up from the table, shook my hand, and quietly headed out to the street. I sat back down and poured myself some more Maojian green tea from the pot on the table and thought over the whole conversation. I didn't know what to make of the spiritual mumbo jumbo Jake and Jennifer had been saying about Qigong. Journalists are supposed to deal with facts: who, what, where, when, how, and why. That was what my instructors at Medill, the journalism school at Northwestern, had drilled into me in those grueling three- and four-hour-long evening newswriting labs and in every lecture. I was feeling out of my element.

That reminded me that I had another religious type that I had to contact. I paid the bill—chuckling that the *Epoch* accountants would probably question this expense account item: Seven dollars for lunch for three people? I walked down the street from the restaurant and found a side street pay phone—again a precaution against the hazard posed by using my cell phone—to call Brother Li. This time, I knew that speaking Mandarin would be an asset and not a liability. Following Herman Fielding's instructions, I dialed first and let the phone ring twice, hung up, then dialed again.

"Brother David in Hong Kong told me about you and said I could see you," I began, without any elaboration.

"Shide, shide, wo zhidao. Ta gen wo shuole (Yes, yes, I know, he told me)," he said. "You know the address. Come tomorrow morning at seven o'clock. I will be here." That was all he said, and he didn't wait for a reply before hanging up.

It was time to head back into the city. Traffic was sure to be bad, and I needed to change and do some writing before the evening meeting. I had to walk to the next corner where the busier intersection increased my chances of finding a cab. But just as I got there, a road construction crew that had been taking a cigarette break sprung into action, and I involuntarily grabbed my ears when one of them started his jackhammer. A couple of passing bicyclists looked at me strangely, but before I could react, my eye caught sight of a poster on a nearby utility pole that stopped me dead in my tracks.

Trying not to be too obvious, I pulled out a small, older model Olympus point-and-shoot camera, so simple it didn't even zoom. The flash was easy to turn off, which I now did because I wanted to photograph the poster without drawing attention to myself. "Cleanse China of foreigners," it said in a bold print headline. "America's recent actions show clearly that it is time to strike back." Beneath was a brief commentary on the student shootings in the United States followed by a call to all citizens to mobilize and protect China from foreign interference.

"Cleanse China of all foreign influence," it said. "Down with all foreign religions, especially Christianity. Long live the Defenders of the Motherland!" Another example of the shadowy group, Defenders of the Motherland, at work.

I quickly took three snaps: horizontal, vertical, and a close-up. As I was putting the camera away, an angry, red-faced young Chinese was suddenly at my side, seemingly from out of nowhere, shaking his finger vigorously in my face. "Bu xing! Bu xing! (No! No!)," he said vehemently but without giving any clue as to his identity. My knee jerk reaction was to ask him what gave him the right to tell me what to do when I wasn't breaking any laws. But I quickly thought better of it. I realized that I risked stirring up something that could quickly get nasty, so I said in English, "Tourist, tourist." Then in deliberately mispronounced Mandarin, "Wo ai Zhongguo (I love China)."

He scowled, then said half aloud, half to himself, "Stupid foreigners, stupid Americans," before disappearing into the small crowd that had gathered.

The taxi ride back to the Golden Panda was eventful. As the driver tried to navigate his car through throngs of motorcyclists and bicyclists, I was suddenly very conscious of being a highly visible foreigner in a very Chinese part of town. I caught sight of myself in the driver's rearview mirror with a deeper frown than usual on my face and my hair flopping across my forehead in a disheveled mop. Several times as bicyclists pedaled slowly by at intersections, there was a rap on the car window.

Even the driver seemed to notice and got annoyed. Well, at least there was one Guangzhou citizen who might not immediately join up with a rampaging mob. "Why are they doing that?" I asked him when we got rapped twice in less than five minutes. But this fellow seemed unusually reticent for his usually voluble profession because all he did was shrug and tap the side of his head as if mental instability alone were enough to account for this behavior.

Back in my hotel room, I e-mailed another file on anti-foreignism to New York, updating the story with an account of my meeting with Jake and Jennifer. I also sent a "personal and confidential" message to Lasch, with a copy to Reddaway. I wanted to alert them that events in China might be moving much faster, and in a much more specific direction, than the inchoate anti-Americanism that was being expressed in many parts of the world. I was protecting myself. If things really got out of hand in Guangzhou, I wanted clear proof in hindsight that I had been on top of the story. If things blew up in South China, they couldn't say I hadn't warned them.

Shutting down my laptop and changing out of my sweaty shirt, I turned my mind to the intriguing invitation from Tung to dinner at the Ming Garden Restaurant. I had never heard of it, and I had only been to Er Sha Island once. It was one of Guangzhou's most affluent new residential developments, an island in the Pearl River distinguished by broad, suburban boulevards, upscale apartments, and villas with gardens, featuring every conceivable kind of facility from health clubs and tennis courts to gardens and swimming pools. In advertising brochures, it boasted proximity to the Canton Trade Fair and Guangzhou's main business district as well as the new high-tech Guangzhou Bridge, which cut through its eastern part in a north-south direction.

Er Sha was, in some respects, a twenty-first-century version of Shamian Island, site of the Golden Panda. It was located east of the Golden Panda and Shamian, downriver on the Pearl and directly opposite Zhongshan

University, where Petrolucci was doing research. The boulevards were broader and the streets less crowded than on Shamian. But the selling point pitched by the dozens of Internet real estate sites to the thousands of expatriates living in the city was that Er Sha was a Mecca of European and American comfort and style amid the teeming chaos of Guangzhou.

But there was another group that also found Er Sha attractive, and it was one that the municipal authorities didn't want to draw any attention to: the Triad bosses and big business kingpins who lived in the indeterminate no-man's-land between legitimate business and organized crime in China. Prominent bosses of Guangzhou's underworld had moved into the apartments and villas of Er Sha's leafy residential neighborhoods. It was rumored that many of the deals sealed over toasts of Scotch and fiery maotai were put together in the opulent restaurants planted on Er Sha by the city's own business leaders.

I'd called Lucinda from the train yesterday and asked her for information on Tung. Bless her heart, she had faxed over a whole sheaf of clippings from Hong Kong's English-language press early in the morning. Going over the material before heading out for lunch with Jake and Jennifer, it was clear that Tung not only was as dangerous as Harry Wok had suggested; he was also one of the kingpins of the South China Mafia with a huge "business" network. No wonder he said that everyone at the Ming Garden Restaurant knew him.

Knowing all this, I was still unprepared for the astonishing reality of the Ming Garden. The driveway was like Vegas East: on either side, giant stone-crested ponds surmounted by cascading fountains and fake Renaissance statues of heroic figures from classical antiquity, lines of columns suggesting a gigantic Roman aqueduct, and stone gazebos every fifty yards. The entrance to the building, which was at least four stories high, glinted and sparkled as the headlights of arriving limousines and Mercedes bounced off the marble columns and façade.

Two doormen, dressed elaborately like those of big London hotels, no doubt sweating profusely in their thick coats, kept the traffic moving while also bowing and scraping to welcome the big shots getting out of their luxury vehicles. Many of these Guangzhou glitterati emerged accompanied by wives, girlfriends, daughters, and other varieties of female escorts. Clearly, the Ming Garden was the place to see and be seen in Guangzhou.

Inside the restaurant's gigantic lobby, teams of uniformed waitresses and hostesses scurried about trying to ensure that, if there were a Chinese version of Thackeray's Becky Sharp, she would be noticed before it became an embarrassment to management that she had not been. The hostess-in-chief, if such a title existed, was an exotic-looking Chinese in her thirties in an eye-bugging, figure-hugging cheongsam of pale green with vibrant pink and red peonies. She saw to it that arriving guests were quickly shown to whichever part of the sprawling, three-story, nine-hundred-seat restaurant they most appropriately belonged. When I walked in, she looked at me questioningly, apparently wondering if I were a tourist on an American Express tour who had been misdirected.

"Dong Zhiqiang Xiansheng (Mr. Tung Chi-keung)," I told her rather loudly. In return, I received another questioning look, as if to say, "You're a gweilo. What business could you possibly have with Mr. Tung?" But she didn't voice her doubts, and in short order I was being escorted by one of the uniformed waitresses to the private dining room on the third floor where Tung had installed himself and his cohorts.

But even if the waitress hadn't led the way, I could have figured out which room the alleged kingpin of crime in Guangzhou was to be found because of the two stocky, suit-wearing bodyguards—their role obvious from their bulging bodies and the way they carried themselves—posted outside the door who carefully examined everyone who came near. As the perky waitress approached them with me trailing close behind, one glanced briefly at me before asking in Mandarin, "Ni shi shei? (Who are you?)" "Wo shi Ai Erdun (I am Ireton)," I responded, with as much languor as I could muster. He tersely demanded, "Huzhao (passport)." I had been prepared for this and took my passport out of a side pocket of my jacket. He examined it carefully, looking for the China entry and exit stamps, then handed it back to me. Still unsmiling, he waved me through the door into the room where Tung was holding court.

They were all standing and had their backs to me when I entered the room, which was surprisingly compact, perhaps thirty feet by thirty. I noticed in one corner a large round table where, I assumed, we would eat. It was already carefully laid with the elaborate chinaware of a Chinese banquet. Behind me, one of the bodyguards who had been outside shouted into the room. Immediately, another security guard in the dining room turned toward me and said, in good English, "Mr. Ireton, from *Epoch* magazine, I presume?" I smiled inwardly at this quaint greeting and wondered where he'd learned to mimic Henry Stanley's famous words to Dr. Livingstone in Africa.

I said yes and reached out to shake his hand. But instead of taking it, he turned to by far the largest man in the room, a roly-poly Chinese of gigantic girth but probably no more than five feet six inches tall. A great double chin rose up from the collar of a glistening blue suit—sharkskin, was my guess—and formed the lower part of a head that seemed, from the front, to be almost perfectly round. But it was the hair that really struck me: totally black, without a trace of gray, and slicked down like someone in a 1940s advertisement for men's clothing. There was already a thin bead of perspiration on his upper lip, surmounting a pencil-thin moustache.

With a surprising show of friendliness and no hint of suspicion, Tung held out his hand and I shook it. It was not a firm grip, and his hand was slightly damp—whether from perspiration or contact with some liquid, I didn't know.

The only woman in the room was a cheongsam-dressed waitress hovering in the background ready, in an instant, to replenish drinks or take new orders. There was no sign of a bartender, and I assumed that the beverages were fetched from outside the room. The twelve other people in the room—my presence, rather ominously, made us thirteen in all—were all men in their thirties and forties except one, who appeared to be in his late sixties and had thick, gray hair.

All were wearing suits and ties, but everyone, except Tung so far, had doffed his jacket and was thus a picture of business informality: crisp white shirts and rather dull ties. I had changed at the hotel into a mustard-colored tropical suit that my Hong Kong tailor had fashioned into an excellent fit about a year ago, so I was suitably dressed. While I was being introduced around, the waitress came by and offered, in Mandarin, to take my jacket. I gave it to her and ordered a plain tonic water. I didn't know which direction the banquet was going to take, and I wanted to keep as clear a head at the outset as possible.

Tung introduced each guest by name but with no description of what they did other than that each was a "businessman." Most of them looked like very hard men, people who make tough decisions—perhaps of life and death—with no regrets. I assumed that they were all lieutenants in Tung's operation. The only exception to this line of introductions was the fourth man in the room, who was smaller, trimmer, and very fit-looking. His hair was shorter than the others', and he carried himself very erect.

"Colonel Su," Tung said in English. "This is man I say on telephone is very interesting you meet." Tung then broke into Mandarin and announced me to the colonel as a reporter for the American *Epoch* magazine in Hong Kong. The colonel, whom I assumed had never met a Western reporter before, appeared to know already who I was and gave me the first firm handshake of the evening.

It was becoming clear that Tung, even if he had already planned this banquet before my call, had given some thought to who the guests were whom I was to meet. I was totally intrigued. Why had Tung, with his reputation as a dangerous crime kingpin with a broad network of suspicious connections, done this? What were his motives in giving a foreign reporter—no, not just a foreign reporter but an American reporter—such unheard-of access to this dark side of Chinese society?

As I chatted with the guests before dinner and finally took my place, after much of the requisite and excessively polite to-ing and fro-ing about who would sit in the place of honor facing the door—it turned out to be me—at the round table, I was eager to hear what Tung might have to say. At this point, he seemed to be the one person who could help me make sense of what was happening in Guangzhou.

Chapter Eight

The banquet was unlike anything I had ever eaten, even at sumptuous events in Hong Kong, renowned worldwide for its gourmet excellence and excesses. No fewer than two waiters and two waitresses appeared as if from nowhere as soon as we sat down and ensured that the dishes moved in a seamless flow on and off the table, that our cups of the high-end hand-picked Phoenix Supreme Oolong tea were kept topped up, and that the glasses of Hennessy XO brandy (for Tung and his lieutenants) and vodka (for Colonel Su: no doubt the vestige of time spent in his very early years with Soviet forces) never came close to being empty.

I stuck with the tonic water that I'd started with; I knew that the toasts with Chinese rice wine and fiery maotai would at some point be coming fast and furious. But I was prepared: remembering a trick learned from old Soviet hands to protect them from vodka onslaughts, I had eaten half a loaf of heavily buttered bread in the Golden Panda before coming, the better to line my stomach.

I was seated to the right of Tung, in the place of honor; next to me I found the mysterious elderly man and next to him Colonel Su. Tung, as befitted an attentive host at a Chinese dinner, plied me with choice pieces from each of the dishes that passed in front of me. I wondered if they had been chosen for their shock value. But then, with a room full of as much testosterone as there was, perhaps the first course shouldn't have been a surprise: three penis soup. The Chinese, particularly the southern Chinese, believe that eating particular animal parts enhances the functioning of that organ in one's own body; hence, fish heads are supposed to improve brain functions. I'd heard that tiger penis was a favorite delicacy because of the power of the tiger, so the choice of animals for this soup baffled me: seal, dog, and bull.

Dog I could understand, it being another common southern Chinese favorite, and bull kind of made sense, too, but seal? The men around the table made a great show of telling me the contents in the elaborate tureen, but I knew better than to show too much interest. To do so is always a mistake at banquets because it is interpreted as a liking for that dish, and someone will quickly spear more morsels of it for the foreign guest. The other guests knew that I was likely to be revolted by this dish, and the requisite cold dishes that followed, and they were right. I found them thoroughly disgusting. Cold hot and sour jellyfish that looked like rubber bands; some vague, quivering black-colored jelly entities whose name I didn't catch; and braised goose paw in abalone sauce.

The men watched me closely as Tung piled the servings onto my plate from the lazy Susan that rotated in front of us. But I knew I could not afford to blow any part of the dinner, to offend anyone in sight, least of all Tung. So I put on my best grin and forced the stuff into my mouth, suddenly filled with gratitude to my dad for having forced me to eat brussels sprouts and spinach as a boy, making sure that every last mouthful of the large helping he had ordered me to put on my plate went down my gullet. I had learned then that obedience plus pretence was the best protection against a violent temper, which my dad could demonstrate without much warning if he thought he was being defied. The sprouts and spinach forced by willpower (mine) down my throat without protest at age seven turned out to be good preparation for the seal testicle, goose webbed-feet, and dog scrotum that I now had to eat.

After this initial trial by ordeal, the meal got considerably more pleasant. I had heard the oft-cited saying about the Cantonese and their food: if it has four legs and isn't a table or chair, if it moves on the ground and isn't a car, if it swims in the water and isn't a boat, and if it flies in the air and isn't an airplane, the Cantonese will eat it. Mercifully, there were no fried scorpions or sautéed silkworm cocoons as in northern Chinese restaurants in the summer, and there were some dishes that even an American whose experience of Chinese food was limited to the local Dragon Express take-out would have enjoyed: chicken with cashew nuts and sweet and sour shrimp.

But the truly muscular dishes at this banquet were exotic in the extreme: fried duck tongues with tangerine peel, Chaozhou-style minced pigeon served in lettuce leaves, braised baby Tianjin cabbage and bamboo pith fungus with supreme broth served in a casserole, sinew of camel's paw, braised whole carp delivered sizzling from the wok on a gigantic plate.

Once I had successfully traversed the ordeal of the three quivering cold appetizers and the really objectionable soup, Tung's guests seemed to relax considerably and began to enjoy the food as much as watching me eating it. Some of them showed surprise—always annoying to me because of its condescension—that a gweilo could manipulate chopsticks unself-consciously and with some skill.

I put up with the combination of teasing and praise that is common when a foreigner is admitted to a really sumptuous Chinese meal because I knew it would break the ice with Tung's lieutenants, if not with Tung himself. His English, as I had suspected, was as rudimentary in person as it had been on the phone, and I was relieved when, after a few stabs at conversing with me for the sake of politeness, Tung pointedly asked the gray-haired man on my right to take over for him. Colonel Su, I noticed, listened attentively to all this, which surprised me, because "Gray Hair" chose to speak English.

He said his name was Chen Yuxian, a name that certainly didn't sound Cantonese and in fact wasn't. Chen was from neighboring Fujian Province and had been in Guangzhou for only five years. He admitted that he hadn't been able to learn Cantonese and had basically given up trying. Enough people in the city spoke Mandarin, he said, for it not to be worth the effort to keep on studying. After a few minutes of polite banter between us—Chen wanted to know what kind of stories I wrote for *Epoch* and I was trying to place Chen's profession—Tung added his own contribution to my knowledge of Chen. Jabbing at a big piece of braised carp before placing it on my plate, he said, "Chen very experienced man. He know all about Guangzhou. He very smart. He have much experience."

At this, the great mounds of flesh emerging from Tung's collar quivered and shook in his mirth. Sweat was now breaking out all over his face. I had no idea what the "experience" was that he was referring to. I noticed that the waitresses came with many more plates of hot wet towels than would have been usual at such a feast, most of the towels winding up in Tung's hands as he sweated from the double exertion of eating enthusiastically from every dish and the occasional attempt of trying to communicate with me. As they entered the room, a bodyguard watched the waitresses carefully. Gang murder had become a frequent feature of expensive restaurants not only in Guangzhou but also in other Chinese cities.

"So what brings you here to Guangzhou?" Chen asked smoothly as we transitioned to a vibrantly colorful dish of mixed vegetables: ruby-red cubes of red pepper, emerald-green snow peas, and gingko nuts like antique pearls.

"Oh, *Epoch* wanted to know about the living and working conditions of Americans living overseas in light of the recent worldwide outburst of anti-American demonstrations," I said as offhandedly as I could.

Chen took his time to respond, leaving me with a vague feeling of disquiet. There was something extraordinarily focused about all of his movements, from eating to drinking to placing his hands on the table between mouthfuls. I had the disturbing feeling that he was not just examining me very closely, but somehow was seeking to project some sort of mental control over my thoughts and actions. At first, I chided myself: How could a complete stranger who happens to be seated next to you at dinner be playing mind games? But after awhile, I felt the beginnings of a headache and that alarmed me. Something strange was happening.

"Many American businessmen don't understand China," he said with deliberateness, as though he wanted to be absolutely sure I remembered every word. "They have interpreted China's rapid growth in strength as a desire to imitate America. Nothing could be further from the truth." He stopped speaking and resumed eating in his strangely focused way. He didn't give me much eye contact, but I was aware with a certain unease that he seemed to be keeping me under constant observation, as though calibrating my every response.

Awkward and uncomfortable, I turned to the man on his right, the colonel with the firm handshake, whose family name—Su—I had been told but not his given name. It turned out, on my inquiry, to be Duxiu, which gave me immediate access to his past. He had been named after Chen Duxiu, a prominent Chinese intellectual and editor and a founding member of the Chinese Communist Party in 1920. "Colonel Su," I said in Mandarin, "I understand that your given name was taken from one of the founders of the Chinese Communist Party."

"You are very well informed, Mr. Ai Erdun. Where did you study the history of the Chinese Communist Party?"

"In graduate school, at the University of California at Berkeley. And if I may follow up, that would mean that you are in your mid-forties?"

"And how would you know that?" Su replied.

"Because the period of the Great Leap Forward, from 1958 to 1962, was characterized by the naming of children after heroic revolutionary ideas or heroic revolutionary figures." I wondered, as I said this, if I was unwittingly causing them to be alarmed by suggesting that I knew China better than most foreigners.

"You have studied Chinese history well," Su commented, "I hope you will apply what you have learned to the good of the Chinese people."

What did he mean by that? But I couldn't follow up because Chen now reentered the conversation, in English once again. He spoke it excellently, as though he had been trained at an interpreter's school, which was a possibility. But the exaggerated deliberateness with which he enunciated difficult English words—Chinese often have trouble with words such as "actually" and "usually"—struck me as highly unnatural. In fact, very little about Chen seemed natural. Although I had earlier been a skeptic about these things, I now somehow just knew in my gut that Chen's behavior had something to do with Qigong. And because Great Master Wu had come up in every recent conversation about Qigong, my thoughts turned to him.

"Mr. Chen," I asked slowly, "are you a practitioner of Qigong?"

He laughed mirthlessly, as though I had committed a great social faux pas and his response was to express amusement rather than to take me to task. "*Practitioner?*" he replied. "That is the word used to describe adherents of Falungong. Are you suggesting I am a member of Falungong?"

"Of course not," I responded, feeling just a little feisty. "But you have some of the mannerisms of Qigong adepts I have met."

"And what do you mean by the word *mannerisms?*" I knew that he understood perfectly the meaning of the English word. He was dueling with me mentally. My head was beginning to pound.

"You are far more focused than most people," I managed to say. "You exhibit a calm that seems a very deliberate selection of mental attitude, and I have noticed that your physical movements are very slow and deliberate."

Chen cracked the slightest smile. At last. I had found his weakness. He was hugely vain. He obviously considered my comments immensely flattering.

"Qigong is one of the neglected secrets of a healthy humankind," he said, and I knew immediately that he would open up.

And so he did. "It is one of China's greatest contributions to the physical and mental health of all human beings. Qigong is the practice of exercising one's inner Qi in such a way that blockages to the free movement of Qi through body and mind are completely removed. When such blockages are removed, we human beings can be open to the uttermost power of the universe."

Chen was on a roll, and I wanted to encourage him. Oddly, I now thought of Clarissa. What would she make of what Chen had just said? How would she handle him? I wondered.

"And what are the origins of Qi?" I asked, striving to mask my growing inner sense of distaste for him. He was, to put it bluntly, a control freak.

"The origins of Qi are as simple and as sacred as the origins of Dao," he replied. "Have you read the *Dao De Jing?*"

Miraculously, as though rising to the front lobe of my mind from an inner recess that I didn't even know existed, came the lines from the first stanza of the great classic of Daoism, the *Dao De Jing* by Lao Zi, a Chinese sage roughly contemporaneous with Confucius (and for that matter, Buddha, in about 500 BC). I had taken a course in classical Chinese at Berkeley, and for a brief period of time was rather attracted to the philosophy of Daoism. Parts of it seemed to me to evoke the paradoxes of Zen Buddhism—"what is the sound of one hand clapping?" the nonsense-sounding question that was believed would lead to satori, that moment of instant enlightenment, when suddenly thrown at a meditating disciple by his master. In the end, I had abandoned it all. I had been put off, I think, by the permanently stoned hippies who seemed to infest Berkeley, many of whom claimed to be Daoists. But I had not, it seemed, forgotten the words of Lao Zi, and I now recited them:

"Dao ke dao fei chang dao. ming ke ming fei chang ming. wu ming tian di zhi shi. you ming wan wu zhi mu." As the words glided off my tongue, I remembered how difficult it had seemed to get my brain around the dense concepts contained in the terse, classical Chinese:

"The Dao that can be told of
Is not the eternal Dao;
The name that can be named
Is not the eternal name.
Nameless, it is the origin of Heaven and earth;
Nameable, it is the mother of all things."

"Hao jile, hao jile (Very good indeed, very good indeed)," Su now chimed in, apparently impressed that any westerner could recite such stuff. Truth was, I couldn't even remember any of the Confucian analects, which I had studied at the same time.

Listening to my Daoist recital seemed to induce a sort of epiphany in Chen, for his appearance of total calm, so disturbing to me hitherto in the conversation, began to dissipate somewhat as he listened enthusiastically.

"If you have grasped that, you have grasped much about China," he said. I wanted to draw him out further, so I resumed the flattery ploy. "Mr. Chen, I am sure you have probably memorized almost the entirety of the *Dao De Jing*," I said, smiling at him. He took my words at face value, as I had anticipated.

"No, not in entirety, but much of it." I felt I had him again.

"You see, Daoism is essentially Chinese. We did not import Daoism from someplace else, like Christianity or Buddhism." He paused, as though uncertain which tack to take now, then resumed. "I can see that you understand that China is a great civilization, which is why Mr. Tung and all of us took a chance in inviting you." I hadn't been aware that there was a test, but I was oddly pleased nonetheless that I had passed it.

"Daoism grew up among the ancient sages of China, a timeless wisdom that we think should be available to all mankind," he continued. "As you know, having studied Chinese history, our ancient emperors didn't always understand Daoism. They considered it a threat to the Confucian principles of ethics by which China was ruled. But much worse, in our view"—I wondered whom he meant by "our"—"was the importation of polluting ideas from outside China over the centuries. Buddhism, at least, learned to live with us, and to become, in its own way, Chinese. But Islam, that barbarian system from Arabia, and even worse, Christianity, which came with the hairy westerners? Those religions have done their best to change China, to block the nation's Qi, so to speak, to stop us from being Chinese, from assuming our Chinese destiny in the world."

I waited, momentarily unsure whether he needed to be prompted by another question. But he didn't. He was really on a roll now.

"Under the reform measures of the last twenty-five years, China has stood up again, as Chairman Mao said in 1949, becoming a major power on the world scene. But in our transition from the economy that Chairman Mao had stipulated after the chaos of the Japanese occupation and the years of civil war to the powerful modern economy devised by Deng Xiaoping, we have had to kowtow again to the rest of the world. Not, of course, as we did in the nineteenth century, submitting to humiliation after humiliation from the foreigners, giving up our territory as 'treaty ports,' paying huge indemnities after we tried and failed through force of arms to resist the military coercion of the imperialists. But now, submitting to international rules and regulations that, in their own way, have been a means of suppressing our national greatness, our global destiny.

"We joined the World Trade Organization, we kowtowed to the Americans at the UN, we forced ourselves to bear the insults of what is foolishly called 'the international community,'" he continued. "Always we had to do what the Americans wanted. If we wanted international trade, we had to join the WTO, which they dominate. The Americans would not sell us the weaponry we needed to protect our national sovereignty, so we turned to the Europeans. They at least were willing to sell us what we needed, but the Americans tried hard to stop them. Of course, the Americans were only doing what the Europeans before them had done, trying to suppress China and prevent her from assuming greatness. But those days are over now. Patriotic forces are even now coming together to ensure that China will never again have to submit to the desires and dictates of foreigners.

"The first thing we have to do is to recover our spiritual greatness, to return to what made Chinese civilization so powerful long before the importation of foreign religions. We must raise up a new generation of Chinese who will release the power of their Qi and unblock the Qi of the great Chinese nation. Have you heard of Great Master Wu?"

Jackpot, I thought. Now to coax him a little further down this road.

"I have heard that he is a great master of Qigong," I said. "But it is not so easy to get to him."

"That is true," Chen said. "He is very busy, and it is also important not to fragment his time. Great Master Wu has become a great treasure of the Chinese nation. His teachings and guidance have helped restore among many, especially the young people, a sense of China's greatness. You must understand, we do not seek to conquer anybody or to control the destiny of other countries, as you Americans have done. Well, not you personally," and he paused as if apologetically, "but your government. We seek merely to recover all of our ancient patrimony and to secure the respect of the whole world. There are many of us who feel China has been patient too long."

Tung, I noticed out of the corner of my eye, had been watching this exchange closely and wanted to jump in himself. "So, Mr. Ireton, Mr. Chen teach you many things, yes?" he said. "You listen what he say. He very intelligent man." He obviously thought this comment was hilarious because the great rolls of fat bulging out of his collar began to shake and perspire again. Then he jabbered a few sentences in Mandarin at Chen, so fast that I couldn't follow it all. But I did catch, "You tell him how we are building China up."

Chen grew pensive for a few seconds, and then resumed his monologue. In a strange way, I think he trusted me. Well, perhaps "trust" was not quite right. He thought he could control me, mentally projecting his own Qi as "external Qi" in my direction. It is true that I had revealed a knowledge of China's past that went far beyond what most foreigners would know, and I had flattered his vanity too. I had also been on my best behavior journalistically too: no notebooks, no tape recorder, no really probing questions. More than anything else, I wanted to keep opening him up.

"Are you familiar with the story of John Reed?" he asked. Again, by a fortunate happenstance, I knew immediately whom he meant: the American journalist who found himself in Russia in November 1917, who sympathized with what Lenin was trying to do, and who wrote a best-seller about the October revolution called *Ten Days That Shook the World*. Now I knew where he was going, and it alarmed me. I knew what his next question would be.

"Would you like to be the John Reed of China's greatest directional change since Liberation? Would you like to be an eyewitness to the beginning of China's new greatness?" Liberation, as every foreign visitor to China since the 1950s quickly learned, meant the Communist victory and assumption of power in 1949. I parried the question.

"What reporter wouldn't want that opportunity?" I replied. "Can I ask when that event is going to take place?"

"It is happening now," Chen said. "Even tonight is the beginning of the greatest event in China's destiny since liberation itself. We have been planning carefully and for a long time. And Guangzhou is where it will start. You will see it all. But you must stay with us. We cannot risk the chance that you will spread the news of what we are doing before we have taken power in the whole country. Tonight is the night when China stands up, stands up for the second time in a century!"

He flushed as he said this, and his voice took on a loud and somewhat hectoring tone. All the others at the table noticed and turned toward Chen. He now reached for his small porcelain cup of dark brown rice wine, which had been until now untouched, and lifted it in his right hand as he looked at Tung. "Long live the glorious destiny of the Chinese people," he declared. "Long live all Chinese patriots!" Tung responded by lifting his cup toward Chen. The two men then downed the rice wine in one draught. The attentive waiters and waitresses instantly refilled both men's cups and ensured that everyone else's around the table was full.

I realized with an inner groan that we were now entering the toasting season of the banquet. Sure enough, maotai, the clear-colored spirit that resembles vodka but is much more troubling for the stomach, was being poured into another cup at each man's place. At least, with the bread and butter in my stomach, I was prepared.

"Mr. Ireton," Tung said, raising his maotai cup toward me and speaking thickly accented Mandarin, "to China's greatness and to foreign countries understanding China." I downed the cup and reciprocated toward Tung.

"Mr. Tung," I replied in Mandarin so the others could join in, "to China's greatness and to peace among the nations." There was much clucking in agreement around the table at this.

Then a mayhem of toasting ensued. Everyone at the table at one point or another wanted to toast me, and many of them toasted Tung and Colonel Su as well. Tung at one point toasted Chen, as I had been sure to do fairly early on in the ceremonial libations. Despite the bread and butter in my stomach, I could feel the effect of the alcohol, at first warming me inside, then making it harder and harder to concentrate.

I remembered a trick I'd seen used by banqueting Chinese officials trying to maintain some degree of sobriety; I put the cup to my lips, tipped my head back, but used my tongue to prevent the maotai either from going down my throat or spilling. I had to be careful as I did this; my host might realize what I was doing if he noticed that the waitresses were refilling my cup less frequently than that of the others.

But I relaxed a little when I saw that several guests were quickly becoming flushed, a giveaway when a Chinese is taking on too much alcohol. The talk became louder, the laughter more boisterous. I wondered how Reed had felt when he was being entertained by the Bolsheviks as they were taking power in Russia.

During a brief pause in the toasting, I asked Chen what he thought Tung's role was in China's recovery of her greatness. "Mr. Tung is a great patriot," he said. "He has made available to our movement all of his many resources in South China."

I wondered what exactly "many resources" meant. I assumed he was referring to Tung's reputed private, Mafia-style armies who protected his sexual trafficking and smuggling in Guangdong and had even muscled their way into Hong Kong, threatening at one point even to kidnap the deputy to the chief executive of the SAR. I was, despite some mental befuddlement, still piecing together in my mind what questions I could ask without alerting Chen to my real agenda. I doubted it would be wise to follow up on "many resources."

But Chen volunteered an explanation himself. "As you know, Mr. Tung has a great variety of business interests," he said. I thought that this was certainly one way of describing the huge network of resources available to one of the great criminal minds of South China. "He is going to assist Colonel Su here." At this revelation, Su looked alarmed and hissed to Chen under his breath, "Don't. Don't. That's secret."

"Don't worry," Chen replied in a loud whisper, his face truly flushed now. "He cannot tell anyone until we have made the move."

Oh boy, I thought. This isn't simply just a story about some foreigner's disappearance in Guangzhou anymore. It's about a political coup d'état in China. Chen, despite the growing loudness of his voice under the influence of maotai—Qigong didn't seem to have much effect in slowing down the power of alcohol, I noticed—seemed to have tracked with me in that thought. "Yes," he said, almost triumphantly. "You thought you were going to be reporting about Americans living in China. But this is far more important. This is one of the great turning points in Chinese history. Oh, and Mr. Ireton, Mr. Tung asked me to show you something to help you agree to stay with us until we have succeeded in our plans. Please follow me."

As Tung nodded his head in acknowledgment of what Chen was now doing, the older man got up quickly from his chair and indicated that I should follow him. My stomach fluttered rapidly. What did he have in mind?

We walked out of the private banquet room, Chen briskly leading the way. Although he had been quite red in the face while drinking, his stride showed no effects of the fiery alcohol he'd imbibed. Now I wondered if perhaps Qigong could slow down inebriation in some parts of the body.

In the corridor outside Tung's third-floor private room, uniformed waitresses were scurrying here and there as though their lives depended on it. Some carried trays brought up from the kitchen, others were bearing large plates with hot, steaming towels, and others were bringing more bottles of alcohol.

We took the elevator all the way down to the basement, and a flash of panic went through me. Had Chen been assigned the task of executing the nosy foreign reporter? I wondered. My misgivings increased when I saw two more bodyguards standing outside a door in the basement. As opulent and excessive as the restaurant had been upstairs, so was the basement gray, dank, and utilitarian. The metal door we were standing in front of now appeared to lead to some kind of storage area. As had been the case in Tung's banqueting room, the bodyguards were sturdy, well-fed Chinese who had obviously spent a lot of time working out. Fear made my skin prickle and grow cold, curiously counteracting the befuddlement that the drinking had brought on. I was suddenly stone-cold sober.

When they saw Chen approaching, the bodyguards opened the door and let us in. It was a completely bare room with cement walls and floor and furnished only with two dented metal chairs placed side by side in the middle of the room. Overhead, an antiquated metal fan was turning. Two glaring neon strip lights threw a harsh bright light over everything. But I was immediately transfixed by the occupants of the chairs. Two Chinese men who looked to be in their twenties sat blindfolded, in soiled pants and "I love Hong Kong" T-shirts, their hands bound behind their backs and shiny black packing tape wound around their heads and covering their eyes. One of them was large and muscular, while the other was skinny and emaciated.

I stood rooted in shock just inside the door, stunned by the sight, my heart pounding like a jackhammer. Leaning against the wall were another two muscular-looking men, presumably guarding the prisoners. Both the prisoners had large tattoos of tigers and dragons on their upper arms, and the skinny one had an earring in his left ear. Dried blood stained the lower half of the face of the larger man. His nose was swollen and misshapen as though someone had beaten him in the face.

"Mr. Ireton," Chen said in a portentous voice, "you have had a unique opportunity and privilege tonight. You have been admitted to one of the momentous secrets of Chinese history, the threshold of a great turning point. Of course, we have taken something of a risk with you. After all, if you went making a lot of noise about this before everything was in order, talking to your editors or, even worse, to the American government, whose agents have been given inexcusable access to Guangzhou from their consulate, you could endanger our entire plan.

"Mr. Tung thought about that risk," he continued, "as well as about the importance of having you present when we make our move. And to ensure you have no misunderstanding about the seriousness of our affair"—his slow speech made the word *affair* seem like a reference to a ceremonial state function—"you are going to be a witness to the swift justice that will govern all our actions as we gain power in China. These men"—and he pointed to the two blindfolded prisoners—"were caught by Mr. Tung's associates"—I was struck that the euphemism *associates* really meant the thugs of an organized crime boss—"trying to listen in on conversations that Mr. Tung was conducting with his business partners. They confessed under pressure that they were collecting information for people who had paid them a lot of money.

"They claim they don't know who their paymasters are, but we think we know. We think foreign forces, perhaps American forces"—and he leered at me as he said this—"have tried to poke their noses into what is not their business. We don't like people who are not our friends trying to sniff around our business, so we have decided to make an example of them both. Maybe whoever their masters are will draw the correct conclusions." Now the leer turned into a sneer.

He paused again. Chen was the master of the manipulative psychological ploy, the unexpected conversational pause. Since it was clear that something dreadful was about to happen, he certainly had my attention. He turned and looked directly at me.

"Mr. Tung has asked me to inform you of something," he said, again portentously. "He wants you to know that he values loyalty and confidentiality more than anything else. He has been so kind as to honor you with what you might call 'a ringside seat' to what is going to happen later this evening. But I must warn you that your presence here comes with a price. Should you turn against us and betray us, or make efforts to report to the wrong people what we are doing, we shall find out where you are, whether you are in Guangzhou or Hong Kong or even America. And we shall deal with you as surely as these men are going to be dealt with." Then, without any hesitation, he shouted at the two thugs leaning against the wall, "Gan diao! (Kill them!)"

The guards stepped forward instantly, each pulling about two feet of stout yellow nylon cord from his pocket. Then, as I watched, rooted in horror, they looped the cords around the prisoners' necks from behind and pulled them as tight as possible, the veins standing out in their temples as they strained. The victims reacted instantly, their faces grimacing and contorting. Though their eyes were covered, the terror still showed on their faces. As the cords were pulled with incredible force tightly around their necks, the two men began to make gurgling and gasping noises. I imagined that, beneath the packing tape, their eyes would have been bulging out as the breath was slowly squeezed from them.

For some reason, perhaps because he was stronger and more fit, the larger of the two men took longer to die, his legs thrashing around in desperation as the strangling continued. The other lost consciousness swiftly and would have slumped forward onto the ground had he not been forced against the back of his chair by the cord held by his executioner. The entire scene seemed to take only a few minutes to play out although it could have been longer. Time seemed immaterial in the face of such violent death. The guards kept the cords tightly wound around their victims' necks for several seconds after they had stopped struggling, presumably to ensure that their victims had actually died rather than merely lost consciousness.

"So much less expensive than a bullet. Quieter, too, and less messy," was Chen's only comment, delivered with eerie calm.

But I only half heard him. Bile was rising rapidly from my stomach, and I threw up, violently and unceremoniously dumping onto the cement floor and the front of my pants and shirt a hefty portion of the sumptuous meal I had just eaten. Chen laughed exuberantly, as though this was one of the funniest sights he had ever seen. My legs felt like rubber, and I could barely stand. I leaned against the wall, head down and still dribbling vomit, as the executioners untied the bodies from the chairs and let them slump to the floor. One of the killers whipped out a cell phone and spoke quickly in Cantonese. I caught only the words *finished* and *box* before he ended the call.

Chen watched me dispassionately as two more men came in carrying a large wooden box, its labeling indicating that it was normally used to transport to the restaurant large quantities of fresh fish. Two metal strips ordinarily used to keep the box tightly closed had been ripped away when it had been opened and emptied of its original contents. At about three feet wide by six feet long, the box was just the right size to hold two human bodies. I realized that this was to be their coffin as well as the container to remove them from the restaurant.

I wondered whether the bodies were going to be unceremoniously dumped out, casketless, into the Pearl River, perhaps weighted down by cement, or simply buried on some anonymous plot in the large box into which they were now being stuffed. Harry Wok had not exaggerated at all in describing Tung as "the most dangerous Chinese" he had ever met. For that matter, he was the most dangerous person of any nationality that I had ever encountered.

I was sweating prodigiously and Chen, uncharacteristically charitable, allowed me to leave the execution chamber and clean up nearby in a small, one-person bathroom that was probably normally used only by restaurant staff. One of the guards who had done the strangling stood at the door behind me, no doubt with instructions to watch me closely.

But he didn't actually come into the bathroom. Traumatized though I was, I estimated I had about a minute to make contact with someone outside before Chen's men came in after me. Perhaps because they realized I had been so shocked by what I had witnessed, they had not noticed that I still had my cell phone in my pocket. My vomit had soiled only my shirt and pants because I'd handed my jacket shortly after being shown into Tung's private dining room to one of the attentive waitresses. Fortunately, my habit was to keep my cell phone, which was quite small anyway, always in my pants pocket just in case I might need it when not wearing my jacket.

I quickly went into the bathroom and retrieved Petrolucci's cell phone number from my recent-calls list and hit Send, praying fervently that he would answer. Miraculously he did, and I quickly flushed the toilet to cover the sound of my conversation. "Giuseppe," I said as loudly as I dared over the noise of the rushing water, "it's Richard Ireton, with *Epoch*. I need your help. It's a matter of life or death. There's a rally for Great Master Wu tonight in Yuexiu Park. Please be there with a car to pick me up. The front gate. Please stage a distraction. Firecrackers or something."

The flushing noise had now stopped, and I pulled the lever again. I hoped they'd be outside chuckling over what a fragile stomach this gweilo had.

"Richard, what's happening? Is your life in immediate danger?"

"No, but it will be if I don't get away from these Triads."

"OK, don't worry. I understand. There will be a distraction."

"Hallelujah," I muttered under my breath. Petrolucci's agile mind had not let me down.

The sound of the second flushing was now dying down, and I knew I would arouse suspicions if I pulled the lever the third time, so I just blurted out a "thanks, bye" and ended the call. I went to the sink, where I concentrated on cleaning up my shirt and pants as best I could, using copious quantities of toilet paper because, as I had found almost invariably in Chinese toilets, there were never any paper towels. There wasn't much I could do about the smell, but at least I didn't look as though I had been worshipping the porcelain goddess at a frat party.

I left the restroom looking a lot better than when I had gone in and feeling a glint of hope in my soul too. Chen observed this instantly, too, and commented, "Good. We can return to the dinner now."

With him in front, me in the middle, and one of the Triad guards taking up the rear, we retraced our steps to the third-floor dining room. There was boisterous laughter and even shouting as we approached, but when they saw that I had come back with Chen they all grew suddenly silent. Tung broke the ice, saying in Mandarin, "I see that Mr. Ai Erdun has been shown how serious we patriots are. Now, Colonel Su, since we can be sure that Mr. Ai Erdun is going to stay very close to us so that he can observe our proceedings, please tell him what role you may be playing in the recovery of Chinese greatness."

Su shifted uncomfortably in his chair, obviously inhibited by years of security training in China's military from saying anything at all revealing to a foreigner. But Tung began to get angry. He didn't like that it appeared as if a guest was defying him at his own banquet. "Tell him, tell him," Tung practically shouted at Su.

Su began his explanation slowly, with a formal historical introduction that was typical of Communist propaganda. "The Guangzhou Military Region," he said, "has a rich tradition of patriotic military action. The villagers of Sanyuanli resisted the British bravely during the Opium War, and our city commemorates that. The great march north to unify China and defeat the warlords in 1927 was planned in Guangzhou. During the Cultural Revolution in the 1970s, Comrade Deng Xiaoping was protected from the Gang of Four by the commander of the Guangzhou Military Region.

"Now it has fallen to Guangzhou to restore the honor of the Chinese nation. Our national leaders in Beijing appear to have forgotten one of the elementary rules of Chinese history: When the whole nation is united and rightly led, no enemy on earth can resist us, not even the Americans!"

He grew animated now, and his voice reflected his passion. "Of course, I am not going to tell you operational details"—and he looked defiantly at Tung as he said this—"but I can tell you something, which you will see with your own eyes very soon: the People's Liberation Army in Guangzhou is lips and teeth with the patriotic citizens commanded by Tung Chi-keung."

Right, I thought cynically. It wouldn't be the first time that Chinese history has been radically changed by a combination of military intrigue, occult mumbo jumbo, and organized crime.

"What is the major unfinished task of the People's Liberation Army?" Su continued. "The liberation of Taiwan! For far too long our leaders have

shivered and trembled in trepidation inside the walls of Zhongnanhai"—
he was referring to the walled compound that had originally been part of
the imperial palace in central Beijing that Communist Party leaders had
claimed for their headquarters and residence—"because they fear what the
foreigners might say or do. I say, 'Down with foreign threats! Down with
China's continuing humiliation! Long live the great unity of the Chinese
people!'" There was a roar of approval from around the table and the raising of maotai cups. I remained impassive in the face of this angry declama-
tion, but from the corner of my eye I watched Tung observing me closely.

"Mr. Tung has asked me to tell you what role we military patriots in
Guangzhou will play in China's coming great change. I will tell you straight:
the officers and men of the Guangzhou Military Region will no longer tol-
erate cowardice and vacillation in the national leadership. We shall initiate
action that will force the nation's leadership to change direction and will
force the whole world to take note! Long live the restoration of China's
greatness! Long live the unity of all China's patriotic soldiers and people!"
More applause and toasts followed this, and Su, flushed and perspiring, sat
down.

Tung watched Su closely, then added dryly to me, in English, "Colonel
Su great patriot. Colonel Su very intelligent man. He not say most impor-
tant thing. Many business groups join me in this big change in China. All
Chinese united for change. You begin to see tonight."

I had seen enough now to grasp what was afoot. Armed members of
Triad groups, many of them under the command of Tung, would join forces
with mutinous People's Liberation Army units in Guangzhou, presumably
under the control of Colonel Su or someone close to him, and challenge
China's national leadership to change policy radically. Put simply, I was
watching the unfolding of a military and criminal-led coup d'état against
the Chinese government. It was the biggest story I had ever covered. I
wished I could call Lasch about it right now. He would salivate. And I
wanted, fervently, to be in touch with Trish to tell her what was happening
to me.

Chapter Nine

The dinner finished soon afterward. There were two more courses, the last being a popular dessert in northern Chinese cooking called silk thread apples, *basi ping'guo:* caramelized cubes of thinly breaded apple which diners pull off the serving dish and plop into a bowl of cold water to seal the caramel glaze. Chinese food traditionally has been sparse on any desserts, and, normally, this was one of my favorites. But after what I had just seen and how my stomach had reacted, I had no interest whatsoever in it.

Suit jackets restored to us, we marched out of the private dining room like a Mafia family at the end of a hard night's negotiation of turf disputes: two bodyguards first, then Tung, then Chen, Su, then me, and then the other guests. Two more bodyguards took up the rear. Waiters and waitresses actually bowed as we left, more Japanese than Chinese, and I half expected to hear the polite greeting of a hundred Tokyo department store clerks to customers as they head out, "Arigato gozaimasu! (Thank you!)"

Their arrival timed with the precision of a White House event, several large black Mercedes limousines pulled up just as we left. I marveled at the ability of a South China crime boss to dispose of these resources and organizational refinements with such precision. Tung sat in the backseat of the lead—and largest—limousine, I was in the second car with Chen and Su. The three of us sat awkwardly side by side on the backseat, the two jump seats already occupied by yet another bodyguard—my minder, I assumed—and a young military orderly in People's Liberation Army uniform who smartly saluted Su when he got into the car. So this is how a military-criminal coup operates, I thought.

We drove off Er Sha Island due north on Guangzhou Avenue and turned left on Huanshi Road East, toward Yuexiu Park. A quick ten minutes later and the park was in sight. We made a left turn again, down Jiefang or Liberation Road North, then drove straight in the south gate. As we did so, I caught a glimpse of a large poster fastened to the park railing: "Great Master Wu Qigong Demonstration. Patriotic Event with Fireworks." Well, no suggestion of a major political upheaval in that. But then I saw a smaller poster tied to the railings next to it. The characters in the main text were too small to read as we drove by, but the large characters at the bottom alarmed me: "Defenders of the Motherland!"

A large crowd of thuggish-looking civilians, perhaps twenty or so, was milling around the gate—Tung had probably mobilized almost all of his Triad retainers for this event—but I was relieved that Petrolucci was nowhere in sight. I had told him to meet me at the little-used front gate, but in the haste of the conversation, I wondered if he might have assumed that I meant the south gate that was most commonly used. I had dreaded the possibility that my guards/escorts might spot him in a parked car not far away from where Tung was going to get out. If Tung saw Petrolucci, he would put two and two together, murder Petrolucci first, and ask me questions later. Then he would probably murder me too.

More remarkable than Petrolucci's absence was that there was not a single Chinese cop in sight. Normally, no mass gathering of any kind takes place in China without a visible small army of uniformed Public Security Bureau officers, so I had to assume that there were plainclothes police all over the place. But who knew how much of what was going to happen was with the connivance of the authorities, how much was being done with a nudge and a wink on their part, and how much was the unanticipated chutzpah of a very ambitious organized crime boss?

It was clear that Tung's men—at least I assumed that was who they were—were carefully scrutinizing the crowd by the gate. It was turning into one of those sweltering South China evenings when even the gnats perspire and Chinese take out a galaxy of folding fans to cool themselves with. Two men perspiring in shirtsleeves were observing the oncoming crowd as we drove through, though they were not asking for IDs. The couple of hundred people lining up were surprisingly orderly, which was uncharacteristic in China, and made up mostly of college-age young people but with a handful of people in their thirties and forties. I wondered who the Triads were looking for. I suspected they wanted to keep out foreigners.

Just then, I saw two westerners having an argument with one of the sweating men watching the entrance. Though they weren't making a big fuss, it was also clear they were not going to be allowed in. The car was moving slowly enough as we passed through the gate that I saw that it was the American teachers, Jake and Jennifer. I was relieved to see—just before my view of the scene was obscured—that they apparently decided not to press the issue further and had turned away, threading their way back though the crowd waiting to get in.

As soon as we had driven through the south gate, I knew where we were headed: the Zhenhai Tower. The tower, also called the Five-Story Pagoda, was built in 1380 by a Ming dynasty official. Situated on a hill on the north side of the ancient walled city, it offered a superb view of Guangzhou and its surrounding terrain. So much so that in various nineteenth-century forays against the Qing dynasty British troops had at times occupied it. Now it was home to the Guangzhou Municipal Museum.

On an earlier visit to the tower, I had been surprised to see a Chinese Bible on display. Clarissa had told me that the British missionary Robert Morrison, one of the first westerners to try to convert the Chinese, had attempted a translation of the Bible when he first arrived in Guangzhou aboard an American ship in 1807, but the one in the display case looked quite recent. Reminders of the humiliations at the hands of the British, however, were obvious enough in the twelve artillery pieces from the 1839–1842 Opium War period—I had never known whether they were Chinese armaments or were captured from the British—that were arrayed in front of the tower.

I stuck close to Chen and Su, who exited the car before me. Ahead of us, Tung was slowly clambering out of the lead Mercedes, putting one fat leg in front of the other with obvious care. Underlings were solicitously ensuring that he didn't fall down or hit any part of the car. In our Mercedes, the bodyguard and the PLA orderly got out first and watched me carefully. Yuexiu Park was the largest urban park in China, at 220 acres about one-fourth the size of Central Park in Manhattan, but it was normally closed to all motorized vehicles. I suspected though that when Tung's people told the park employees to open the gates and let our motorcade in, no one was about to argue.

As we climbed up from the road level to the base of the tower, I was surprised to see that a small, temporary stage had been erected at the foot of the tower. Bleachers had been set up in front of the stage, ready for what

I assumed would be a small and very select audience. Several young men in shirtsleeves waited in knots close by, and just as we approached, about twenty young soldiers in uniform and caps entered the stage area at the double. They came smartly to a halt and sat down on chairs that ringed the stage just in front of the bleachers.

I glanced around as unobtrusively as I could and wondered how on earth I would be able to get away unobserved by Chen, who was still close by, or by Tung and his thick cluster of bodyguards in the VIP seating on the bleachers. But I had forgotten an important point. Tonight was going to be a major event in China's history, an event to take vengeance on the West for all the past humiliations. Neither Tung nor Su, nor anyone else in the assemblage gathering for the evening, would want a foreigner to be visible anywhere.

As I was about to follow Tung and his guards onto the bleachers, Chen put out his left arm and stopped me abruptly. "No, not there," he said. "Come with me," and led me off to an area under a cluster of trees at the edge of the stage area, largely concealed from the bleachers and from the crowd that would gather and be standing nearby. The view of the stage was not particularly good though I would probably be able to see Great Master Wu once he started his act. Of course, to Chen and Tung, their primary concern wasn't how well I could see the show but that I—a foreigner— would not be noticed.

I looked at my watch and saw that it was already 7:45. From my right, the raucous clanging of gongs, drums, and cymbals suddenly started up. It was the unmistakable din of a Chinese lion dance. I had watched many of these in Hong Kong and China, always dazzled by the acrobatic skills of the two male dancers, one acting out the head and the other the hindquarters of the lion. The conventional wisdom has always been that the Chinese don't have much of a sense of rhythm, but every lion dance I had ever seen belied this stereotype. As the drums and gongs clashed away, the "lion" pranced as though stung by bees as it approached the stage.

The dance was something quintessentially Chinese, a requisite part of any kind of big celebration, whether it was Chinese New Year or the open- ing of a new department store. Once they got to the stage, the two dancers didn't actually go up on stage but doffed their lion costumes and walked up the shallow stairs that had been set up by the stage and sat down at the edge of it. The drummers and percussionists stayed a short distance away in a small knot by themselves.

People were rapidly filling up the bleachers and the standing area in front of the stage, and at last I saw uniformed Public Security Bureau officers at the fringes of the crowd. I wondered what Yao Fanmei, the PSB official who had given me his card on the plane, would make of all this.

But I didn't have much time for reflection. A phalanx of thuggish-looking civilians in suits came up, like the soldiers, moving at the double— were they all in such a rush to pull off this coup?—and took up positions in a semicircle behind the soldiers ringing the stage. At exactly 8:00 p.m., the gongs and drums started clanging loudly again. This was the signal for the arrival of Great Master Wu.

He made a simple entry, preceded by two Qigong adepts wearing the loose-fitting colorful silk tunics and pants characteristic of the art, and followed by two others similarly garbed. Wu walked slowly up the steps to the stage as if his energy was coiled tightly within him. Then he stood at the very center of the small area, completely immobile. The four other men began performing various fluid exercises, first placing their hands in front of them level with their solar plexus, and then slowly sweeping them away from their bodies, as if pushing away unwanted presences. They did this for a few minutes, then adopted a knees-bent, semi-bending posture, but without dropping their heads much lower than about chest level if they had been standing.

It looked incredibly simple, even easy, but I had dabbled in tai chi, also called "shadow boxing" in English, during my Daoist phase in graduate school, and I knew that getting the movements correct in tai chi took enormous practice. Even more so in Qigong.

As the adepts were showing off their skills, I studied Wu. His hair was just turning fractionally gray, and it was thinning at the front. But his face, at least from where I could see, was unlined. He was of medium height, perhaps five feet nine, probably in his early fifties, and he looked more physically fit than any person of his age I had ever seen. He wasn't rippling with muscles, but his movements were so well modulated and precise that he seemed to have perfect balance.

From his initially immobile position he had slowly begun to move and interact with people close to the stage. Like Chen, he exuded the impression of being totally in command of himself and those around him. Of course, with a stage and a sizable audience, he was. At first, he appeared to be doing some kind of meditating before beginning his "act," if that is what it should be called. He seemed to move his hands and arms as if everything

was carefully choreographed—which it may have been. Not a single movement was superfluous.

At this point, I glanced around me and was somewhat astonished to
see that the two bodyguards, one People's Liberation Army and the other
presumably Triad, had moved quite a distance away, trying to get a closer
look at Wu. As for Chen, he seemed to be in another world, standing in the
same posture that Wu had adopted and deep in meditation. I realized, for
the first time, that I actually might be able to escape.

Wu now clapped his hands together, that apparently being the signal
for eight of the civilians in suits who had taken up position behind the soldiers to rise to their feet. Wu then stepped forward, closed his eyes tightly
as though powerfully concentrating all his strength. Then he extended his
right hand slowly toward the young men who had positioned themselves
in a row on his right. His fingers gradually extended from a clenched fist to
an entirely flat hand, like a policeman motioning oncoming traffic to stop.
Suddenly, the eight men who had been standing simply collapsed into each
other, falling away from Wu as if pushed by an invisible rod. There was a
gasp of astonishment from the audience, then thunderous applause.

Six of the eight men picked themselves up from the sprawl, quickly
scampered out of the way and made themselves into something of a human
net, arms over one another's shoulders, facing Wu. The other two were
going to be further cannon fodder for Wu's tricks, and they stood in front
of them, facing Wu, in exaggerated martial arts posture. Between the two
groups was a gap of about four feet. Wu swept his arms together as though
he were about to perform a martial arts routine, then once again leveled his
extended palm in their direction in traffic-stopping mode. This time, the
two men seemed literally to leap backward, as though being picked up by
a giant, invisible hand and thrown against the wall. Only there was no wall:
they fell into the "net" of their six colleagues who were bracing themselves
to prevent the two from being hurled off the stage. There was a loud, collective "ooh!" from the crowd.

The audience now warmed up, Wu moved on to what was obviously
a well-rehearsed stage routine. His voice high-pitched and reedy, he called
for audience volunteers to step forward. There was embarrassed tittering in
the crowd; no one, it seemed, wanted to be thrown around the stage by the
unseen forces that Wu apparently was manipulating. In what struck me as
a canned manner, Wu paced the stage with a handheld mike and began to
try to cajole them from this pronounced display of shyness.

"Comrades"—a standard greeting of his performances at military bases, I assumed—"don't be afraid of anything. This force would be available to you, if you were willing to spend a few years becoming a Qigong master. So, to show you that I mean you no harm, I am going to offer you a sharp sword and ask you to try to draw blood from me by stabbing at my bare stomach. Who will participate in this exciting demonstration?"

There was a pause, and then, surprisingly, a young man who looked startlingly like an Asian version of Marcia's detestable Jean-Luc—no older than twenty, with long hair that flopped across his forehead and wearing a Benetton T-shirt above blue jeans—walked forward from the edge of the crowd and approached Wu shyly. An orderly had meanwhile sprung into action and was onstage with a large, theatrical-looking Chinese sword in its scabbard, the kind with a blade so thin that it wobbled as Wu unsheathed it.

It looked to me like something grabbed from an assemblage of stage props for a Chinese opera, but Wu had obviously dealt with this kind of skepticism before. He quickly took hold of the sword, laughed almost maniacally, and drew from one of the pockets of his tunic an apple that he tossed up in the air the way tennis players start a serve. As the apple came down, he sliced it neatly in two. Once again, there was a gasp from the audience; the volunteer stopped dead in his tracks.

Wu handed the sword back to the aide for a moment, then took off his yellow silk tunic, displaying an exceptionally wiry physique without, it seemed, a single ounce of fat. (I couldn't help mentally comparing Wu with his Triad supporter Tung, whose corpulence was quite untypical for a Chinese.)

Stepping back a half dozen paces, Wu turned to the aide and shouted at him to give the sword to the volunteer, who was starting to look uneasy. But Wu, reveling in his nice-guy routine, smiled again at him and shouted in clear Mandarin, "Come on, try to draw blood from me. Come straight at me!" The young man now looked positively terrified and glanced around him as if hoping for some support from the crowd. He got it. Apparently, they knew what to expect from Wu because they began cheering him on. "Go on, attack him!" many of them shouted good-humoredly. I saw that some of those closest to me had knowing smiles as they goaded him.

Reluctantly, the man started moving toward Wu with the sword held firmly in front of him. Wu's face contorted into a fixed grin, as he focused in concentration while the sword advanced slowly but steadily. Then it happened: the sharp point of the blade reached Wu's torso and stopped, as though it had hit a granite wall. Wu, hands on hips, and the ferocious grin still on his face, stood stock still as the sword began to bend into a large arc. I could not believe my eyes. It should have penetrated Wu's skin and be drawing blood by now. But it wasn't.

Wu dropped his hands from his hips and began to beckon the young man to push harder. The volunteer was now straining as he pushed with all his strength, and he was beginning to sweat heavily. The sword continued to bend into an ever-smaller arc as Wu, somehow, seemed to prevent it by sheer force of willpower from piercing his skin.

After nearly a minute of shoving, with Wu resisting strongly, the young man seemed to give up and fell back with the sword in his hands. There was still not a drop of blood from Wu's body, not on the sword, not on the ground. With a triumphant yell, Wu flung his arms wide and the crowd again erupted. In a flash, I recalled reading in graduate school about the Spirit Boxers of the Boxer Rebellion who had performed, in some sort of spirit-enhanced trance, similar exercises in the summer of 1900 before throngs of young and impoverished peasants. Perhaps Michael Young had seen a similar demonstration of skills that had prompted him to say to me, "The Boxers are back." Of course, the Spirit Boxers had failed to inform the young men they recruited that the sword-stopping technique they had mastered didn't apply to British bullets.

The crowd was standing up now, exultant in its applause. Wu, who had masterfully timed every act so far, waited for the clamor to die down and for the audience to resume their seats. Once more, an aide appeared, this time to give him the remote mike again.

"Comrades," Wu began again. "Tonight you have seen a demonstration of ancient Chinese power. I repeat, Chinese power. It is something we learned from our earliest forefathers, something that long ago made the Chinese the mightiest people on earth. Some people thought we had forgotten this power, but it has been available to us all along. Foreigners tried very hard to teach us that this power was not real or that it was a magician's trick or even that it was immoral. But you have all seen for yourselves tonight that this power is real. Not a drop of blood fell from me when that fine young volunteer tried to pierce my body with that sword.

"Today, our great nation has been corrupted by foreign science and foreign ideals, even by foreign religion. Some of our leaders have abandoned the glorious pursuit of making China strong, the goal that Chairman

Mao taught us even during the long revolutionary struggle, and which he demonstrated when the People's Liberation Army liberated the country in 1949."

Applause now broke out again, not universally but from an obviously determined section of the crowd. Gradually, everyone in the audience felt obliged to join in. This was, after all, a "patriotic" event. Wu seemed happy with the crowd's response.

"Some of our leaders," he went on, "seem to have decided that every decision in the world must be approved by the Americans. But can any American do what I have just demonstrated here? Can the Americans communicate at great distances using their external Qi, or are they dependent on mechanical devices? But we Chinese can do everything we want to do when we harness our Qi and decide what course of action is best for the nation.

"I am here to tell you that the demonstration of Qi can be used in the service of the Chinese people, in the service of protecting our national honor. Of course, it would take any of you here many years to become as skillful in the deployment of Qi as you have seen demonstrated here tonight. But you do not need to be Qigong adepts to be part of the greatest movement in modern Chinese history, a movement that is making a decisive move tonight.

"In Guangzhou, there is a great tradition of patriotic fervor on behalf of the Chinese nation. Some people may say that we have difficulty pronouncing the national language"—he meant Mandarin, and there was laughter in the audience at this reference to the mangling of Mandarin by most Cantonese—"but though I am not from Guangzhou, I have noticed that there is no shortage of patriotic sentiment here." There was a murmur of approval from the crowd.

"Tonight is the beginning of a great movement in our country, a movement to recover China's glory. Tonight is the beginning of a change in national policy that will soon liberate Taiwan. Tonight we start to shake off the shackles of foreign attempts to control our great nation.

"I am authorized to tell you that tonight, beginning in Guangzhou, patriotic elements of the People's Liberation Army are going to restore to the entire PLA a sense of national responsibility. Tonight is the beginning of the second great Chinese revolution. As Chairman Mao said in 1949, 'China has stood up!,' so we say now, 'China has stood up again, and will never again bow down to the command of any foreigner.'"

The crowd erupted in applause when Wu finished speaking, rising to its feet and cheering.

At this point, there was a whoosh of rockets soaring into the sky, and at the same time, behind where I was standing, the staccato crackle of a string of firecrackers being set off. I noticed that the two bodyguards who had apparently been assigned as my minders frowned at this development. So did Wu on stage. In the bleachers, too, there seemed to be some confusion. While most of the crowd assumed that the firing of rockets was part of the evening's entertainment, from where I could see him from the side, Tung was surprised by the development and was in whispered consultation with his aides.

A few yards away from me, Chen seemed equally perplexed and ordered the two bodyguards to gather around him for instructions. That move instantly propelled me into action. Betting that this was Petrolucci's diversion, timed to be sufficiently close to the probable start of the real fireworks show to cause confusion, I slipped away in the darkness while Chen was still focused on giving instructions to the bodyguards. I forced myself to walk, not run, but walking very briskly and keeping my head down so that passers-by wouldn't be surprised by a hurrying gweilo.

As it was, though, most of the crowd were distracted by the fireworks and firecrackers, and those who were not looking up at the sky at the pyrotechnics were looking around for the source of the loud staccato tat-tat-tat of the firecrackers. In all the confusion, it seemed no one was paying any attention to me. When I was well clear of the stage area and there were no more bright park lights illuminating the path, I broke into a run, descending the hilly slope leading up to Zhenhai Tower as rapidly as I could.

It was quite a distance from there to the front gate where I had asked Petrolucci to wait for me. I was absolutely flying now, well aware that Tung's men might have stationed lookouts at the various park entrances and exits and even now might have been alerting them to my disappearance. More than once, I was alarmed when I thought I saw dark forms in the bushes, but they made no move for me, so I assumed they were nothing more than young courting couples. The dark corners of Chinese parks often are crowded with dating pairs heavy into petting. With eight students to a dorm room and, of course, no private cars available to them, park benches and bushes are where young lovers do their groping.

Continuing my quick pace, I was grateful that I'd recently resumed running three mornings a week. I was in good shape and wasn't at all winded.

But I had to slow down as I approached the front gate. There were bright lights again, and I wanted to avoid attracting attention as a gweilo in an unseemly hurry. I reached for a handkerchief in my pocket and tried to cover as much of my face with it as possible, trying to give the impression of needing to protect my mouth from dust or moisture.

As I came closer to the gate, I noticed that, miraculously, there seemed to be only a couple of guards there. Presumably, very few people were expected to enter the park from a gate so far away from the Zhenhai Tower. As I slowed down to a brisk walk, wondering how best to approach the gate, there was a sudden explosion of more firecrackers from a location inside the gate but several yards to the east. The two guards left the entrance to investigate. That was just enough time for me to slip out.

I didn't know where Petrolucci would be, but I headed down the nearest side street and looked in vain for a car that might be his. Frustrated, and increasingly worried that at any moment Tung's men would come racing out of the park and spot me, I walked hurriedly to the first intersection and took the cross street leading away from the park. Just as I was walking briskly down the street, I heard a hissed, "Ai Erdun? Ni shi Ai Erdun ma? (Ireton, are you Ireton?)" I froze in panic. I had not noticed the black motorcycle with sidecar parked in the shadows between the street lamps until I heard my name. But now I saw the black-leather-clad motorcyclist beckoning to me insistently. I wasn't sure what to make of this. He could be a Triad member, I thought. But then he said urgently, "Bi Laoshi de pengyou ma? (Friend of Teacher Bi?)"—which I took to be Petrolucci's Chinese surname. "Shi, shi (Yes, yes)," I replied hastily and with relief.

"Shang lai! (Get in!)," he hissed back with surprising firmness, thrusting a motorcycle helmet at me.

I glanced quickly over my shoulder, surprised and relieved to see that there still was no one pursuing me, clapped the helmet over my head, and jumped into the sidecar. The bike lurched forward and roared off.

I was full of questions, but with the helmets, the way the fellow was concentrating hard on getting us away from the park as quickly as possible, and the rushing wind that would have whipped away any words I tried to form, conversation was impossible. I was filled with admiration at Petrolucci's imaginative escape plan. Not only was a motorcycle the fastest way to get through the growing gridlock of Chinese city traffic; the helmet concealed my identity and the fact that I was a foreigner. I wondered how Petrolucci had pulled this off. I'd never seen one of these vintage CJ750 motorcycles in Guangzhou although I knew they were popular with expatriates living in Beijing, where they are quite common.

The CJ750 was modeled after and adapted from the BMW R71 that debuted sixty years ago in Germany and had a very limited production that lasted less than two years. But today, Chinese factories are still manufacturing them, and middle-aged American men trying to recapture their lost youth drive around the streets of Beijing in these black beauties, often with a Chinese babe on display in the sidecar.

I had no opportunity to get any answers, though, as we first roared up Liuhua Road, traveling due east from Yuexiu Park, then pulled swiftly into a small driveway off the street. It led up to a large new apartment building but was well shrouded from the road by bushy trees on either side. I saw Petrolucci immediately, sitting in the passenger seat of a small black Toyota parked there. He waved me over. Pausing to doff my helmet and say a very grateful "thank you" to my unknown escape driver, I leaped out of the sidecar and climbed in the backseat of the Toyota.

"If they did not follow you when Gao was driving, we will be safe here, certainly for a few moments. So how serious is it?" he asked.

"Giuseppe, you're a genius. You probably just saved me life—at least for the time being. For all I know, you may have preserved world peace as well. There's a coup going on right now, and it started right here in Guangzhou. I don't know any of the military details, but the Triads have put together a plot to take over the Guangzhou Military Region. Then they are going to try to spread their rebellion to Beijing. I just heard Great Master Wu in Yuexiu Park. He was doing his magic Qigong routine. You know, sending people sprawling all over the stage. The Triad ringleader had invited me to dinner and for some reason decided to recruit me—without asking me, mind you—as some kind of John Reed of the moving coup scenario. Just one condition: I had to stay with them. Giuseppe, they're trying to change the entire regime in the country." I blurted this all out, in one jumbled mess, aware as I finished that I probably hadn't made much sense.

Petrolucci let out a low, long whistle. "So . . . " he said slowly, "that's what's going on. One of my students alerted me to strange happenings afoot a few hours ago. By the way, I had four of them involved in the unofficial fireworks display just now, and the motorcyclist too. Hey, do you think because I've proven to be such a good organizer that one of your political parties might hire me for the next presidential campaign? Well, maybe not, because I'm European," and his tenor laughter rang out over the hum of the Toyota's engine, dissolving the tension some. My mind, which I now realized had been racing at ever faster speeds since being escorted into the basement of the Ming Garden Restaurant, now finally began to slow down a little, and I could think a bit more logically.

"Giuseppe, I don't think I'm safe anywhere on the streets of Guangzhou right now. I'm sure Tung's men have already got their version of an all-points bulletin out on me to Triad gang members across the city. And if they've got the Guangzhou Public Security Bureau on their side, too, I'm dead meat. I've got one contact there, though, and I have to get to him as soon as possible. But meanwhile I've got the best lead so far on where McHale might be hiding out if indeed he's still alive. There's a fellow here who runs safe houses for Chinese underground Christians—you know, these rural evangelists the government is always trying to suppress. If McHale's alive and hiding out somewhere, this guy'll probably know his whereabouts."

"You mean this fellow is a Christian operating some kind of underground railroad for other Christians in Guangzhou? How interesting. I've never met anyone like that. What's his name?" Petrolucci asked.

"Brother Li or something," I said.

"Can I meet him too?"

"Giuseppe, you've just saved my life. As far as I'm concerned, you can do whatever you want. In fact, let's head there right now. I've got the address. I was planning to make contact tomorrow morning, but it's obvious now that we don't have any time to lose. Can this fellow take me there right now?"

"Sure. But what do you want me to do?"

I thought hard. If there was any hope of getting McHale out, I knew I'd have to get some help from Michael Young. McHale might not even have anything with him that could prove his identity. I thought, too, that if Yao were to get involved in someway, we'd need an OK from the U.S. government to spirit him out of the country and eventually into the United States. Not that I was sure he'd want to come, but it was a chance I had to be prepared for. Somewhere in the back of my mind I knew Burt would be furious if he weren't kept in the know. Reddaway could be—had to be—kept in the dark. But I was sure I'd need Lasch's help in making the arrangements for McHale.

I pulled out of my pocket the piece of paper with Brother Li's address on it and gave it to Giuseppe's driver. "Ni zhidao zheige dizhi ma? (Do you know where this address is?)," I asked. "Zhidao," he replied, and then looked to Petrolucci to confirm that we should go there. Giuseppe nodded.

Brother Li's "safe house" was an old, nineteenth-century European-style dwelling that had probably belonged to a single Chinese family after the Europeans left, been taken over by several families during the Cultural Revolution, and then finally reclaimed by the original Chinese owners. It was not far from Shamian Island, and I was nervous being this close to the Golden Panda Hotel again. But the streets were badly lit and the area was surprisingly quiet. It took only ten minutes to get there, and Petrolucci's driver displayed great skill in weaving his way through Guangzhou's evening traffic.

I looked at the people on the street, going about their lives oblivious to what was happening. Young couples strolling hand-in-hand, three middle-aged men who were probably businessmen or mid-level Communist Party officials coming out of a restaurant, some gawking foreign tourists; all displayed a lack of awareness of the political tidal wave that was about to engulf Guangzhou and possibly all of China. Still, there were signs something was afoot. At one intersection, three military trucks with sullen-faced soldiers in full battle gear waited patiently for the traffic light to change, willing to yield to civilian oversight in at least one area of life.

Petrolucci thought it would be better to approach the house on foot, in case it was under surveillance and we needed to keep moving. We got out of the car, Petrolucci and I, about two blocks away, and Giuseppe sent the driver on a slow loop around the neighborhood, telling him to report any suspicious vehicular activity. But as we approached the safe house, we saw no evidence of surveillance. I wasn't sure it was a good idea to bring Petrolucci along, but he had saved my life and it was hard for me now to play the tough-minded reporter. But I figured at least that Brother Li would be much less suspicious of a foreigner with me than if my companion had been a Chinese.

We rang the doorbell and waited a full minute before anyone answered. The door opened slightly and the young woman behind it, noticing we were foreigners, relaxed a little but asked anyway, "Ni shi shei? (Who are you)?" I had been prepared for this and answered in Mandarin using the code name Herman Fielding had given me in Clarissa's apartment, "Brother David in Hong Kong sent us." The door closed momentarily, and I heard voices behind it having a brief parley. Then it opened again. "Please come in," she said very pleasantly, in English.

"This is Signor Giuseppe Petrolucci, a visiting research scholar from Italy at Zhongshan University. He has made it possible for me to come to you this evening," I said as we entered the old-fashioned vestibule. It had a beautiful mosaic tile floor, chipped and missing many tiles now and yellow with age, and a long old-fashioned brass hanging lamp descended from the second-story ceiling.

A Chinese man in his late thirties then appeared in the long, narrow hallway from a side room. "I am Brother Li," he said simply in Mandarin. "Welcome to our home." He was tall for a southern Chinese, but he had the round face so common to Cantonese. His cheeks were pockmarked, as though he had contracted smallpox as a child.

The greeting seemed a little odd. Perhaps Brother Li did in fact live here, but it certainly wasn't being used as a conventional "home."

"You are the one who called?" he asked, making no move to invite us in or otherwise welcome us, though he did not seem unfriendly.

"Yes, Brother David in Hong Kong told me I could contact you," I said in Mandarin as I wondered about this strange lack of common Chinese courtesy.

"Can you describe Brother David to me?" Brother Li asked, looking a bit embarrassed as he made his request. And it dawned on me: he was just being careful, and until he knew who I was and why I was here, he wasn't going to let me into this house where who knows who was hiding out or what was hidden in it.

When I finished describing Herman Fielding and the conversation in Clarissa's apartment, Brother Li said simply, "I suppose you have come for Mr. McHale. How did you know he was with us?" At this point, the English-speaking young woman, apparently satisfied that everything was OK, left us and disappeared down the dark hallway.

"We didn't," I replied, "but the only contact we had in Guangzhou who might have known where he was, was you. And of course, it was Brother David who told us we should come to you for help."

"He must trust you greatly. Are you a brother?"

This was awkward and embarrassing. He was asking if I was a Christian, a believer, and I wasn't. Nor, so far as I could tell, was Petrolucci. But I had a moment of inspiration.

"Some of my Christian friends have told me to say, 'Not yet,'" I replied. "I am close friends with a missionary in Hong Kong who is well acquainted with Brother David. She, at least, trusted me enough to introduce me to him. And Mr. Petrolucci here just saved my life, so I trust him."

I smiled gratefully at Petrolucci, who gave a slight nod of acknowledgment.

"I am afraid we have very little time to lose," I said. "It is not just a question of getting Mr. McHale out of China. Earlier this evening there was a
rally featuring Great Master Wu in Yuexiu Park. We think that the Triads
and elements of the Guangzhou Military Region together are attempting
a coup in Guangzhou that they will then try to push on to Beijing. If we
don't alert the right people in Beijing right away, it will be too late. The
whole country might be on a war footing in a few days."

"McHale is not here," Brother Li said, "but if this great upheaval that
you have just described takes hold, then you must get him out of China as
fast as possible. I can see that you get to the house where he is staying. It's
nearby. Do you have a car?"

"Yes."

"Good. Sister Li will take you to the house and introduce you. They
would not let you in otherwise. I think you should all come back here with
Mr. McHale."

"But wouldn't that put you in danger?" I asked.

"This house is known to all our brothers and sisters. We can keep a much
better watch on the neighboring streets from here than from the other
house." You would all be in much greater danger if you stayed there."

Petrolucci now interrupted. "Richard," he said, "I will be much more
useful to you back in my own apartment and not getting in your way. Look,
I'll drive you to this other house with Miss Li, pick up McHale, then bring
all three of you back here. If this city is about to go crazy, I want to make
sure that Francesca has someone to protect her. Is that OK?"

"Giuseppe, I'll go along with anything you suggest because you're the
man who just saved my life. Let's go."

Petrolucci's driver was waiting nervously for us when we came out,
looking into the mirror frequently and at passing traffic. He was relieved to
see us but was surprised when Sister Li got into the front passenger seat.
"This is Miss Li," I said, forgetting that Brother Li had referred to her as
"Sister Li." I still wasn't used to these Christian forms of address, and for all
I knew, they were probably totally alien to our young driver.

Sister Li recited an address to him, and he nodded quickly. After glancing once more in the rearview mirror, we pulled away from Brother Li's
safe house. Petrolucci and I looked at each other as if to say, "Well, let's
hope we all get there safely."

"Giuseppe," I said with more cheerfulness than I felt, "I don't know the name of your driver. Can you introduce us please?"

"Oh sorry, Richard, of course." Still speaking English, he said, "This is Weiming, who has a very interesting story. Weiming's parents were among the first students to be admitted to Peking University in 1978. As you know, that was when formal college education was resumed after the Cultural Revolution. Weiming (and he transitioned into serviceable Mandarin), please tell Richard the story of how you got your name." Then, to me in English, Petrolucci said in a half whisper, "I am such an old romantic. I just love this story, and I make Weiming tell it to everyone I introduce him to."

Weiming looked embarrassed and pleased at the same time. "My parents had a very special relationship," he said. "They met their first year at Beida"—he used the Chinese shorthand for Peking University—"which has a very pretty lake surrounded by willows where my father took my mother on long walks every evening after dinner during their four years there. The lake is called Weiming Hu, which means 'no name lake.'" He explained this last part in English. Clearly, he'd told this story to foreigners before. "It was supposed to be just a temporary name until the school could decide on a formal name, but it stuck. The reason I am named after the lake is because my mother died when I was born, so my father gave me the name Weiming to remind me of where he had fallen in love with her."

I couldn't believe such a sappy story could actually be true. If anyone but Weiming had told it to me, I'd have protested that it was too maudlin to be believed. "Oh, that is a romantic story," I said, looking at Petrolucci, "but it is a very sad one too. You and your father must be very close. Aren't you worried that he would not approve of you doing something dangerous like this?" As I finished, I felt Petrolucci jab me in the side, and he shook his head slightly with a deep frown on his face when I looked at him. But Weiming was continuing.

"My father is dead. The Triads killed him," he said simply then fell silent. In the backseat, neither Petrolucci nor I said anything either. After another moment of this pained silence, Weiming took a deep breath and resumed. "My father worked for the Public Security Bureau and was assigned to keep track of the Triads. But a man in his department was an informant and told the Triads where we lived. I was out late that night; it was almost a year ago. I was hanging out at Teacher Bi's apartment after an English lesson with some friends when the men from the Triads came to our apartment, tied my father up, slit his throat, and left him to die after writing the name of their gang with his blood on the floor next to him. They wanted the PSB to know it was them."

Weiming now stopped again. Sister Li had looked uneasy as she heard this story, but when Weiming stopped she put her hand on his shoulder and patted him without saying a word.

The gesture seemed to restore him a bit, and he said, in a somewhat lighter tone, answering my earlier question, "My dad and I were very close. He tried to be everything to me—father, mother, and friend. Many of my friends wished that they had a father like mine because he spent more time with me than their fathers did. One thing we liked to do was to go driving together. We both loved cars, and even though most government employees like my father can't afford a car, we saved and bought one eight years ago. He had learned to drive when he worked in the factories during the Cultural Revolution, and when I got to be as tall as he was, he would let me drive when we were out on empty roads in the countryside. In the PSB, they trained him in defensive driving techniques, and he taught me these too. That's why Teacher Bi asked me to help tonight."

Petrolucci now turned to me and said in English, "Weiming came back to our apartment that night his father was killed. I think he was so shocked he just automatically retraced his steps and wound up at our place. He's supposed to be living with his grandparents now, but when he's not in the dorms, he's more often with us than with them. He's very sharp, and, of course, he's given us insights into aspects of Chinese society that we just wouldn't otherwise have any opportunity to see."

Sister Li in the front seat was now giving directions to Weiming, and it became clear that we were near our destination. But when I saw tall walls and a solid gate guarded by uniformed men, I became alarmed. Had this been some kind of terrible ruse? I didn't want to alarm Petrolucci, but I did want to get to the bottom of this quickly and leaned forward to get Sister Li's attention. As I did so and looked out the front window, I realized where we were. Of all places, we were back on Er Sha Island, and we were pulling up to one of the exclusive gated communities. And as usual in such places, being a foreigner was the ticket to get in; the guards were there to keep local Chinese out. The car didn't even come to a complete stop. All Weiming had to do was gesture to me and Petrolucci in the backseat, and the guard raised the red-and-black striped bar blocking the entrance.

We drove through a maze of winding lanes, bordered on each side by immaculately pruned hedges, and pulled up in front of an elegant, new two-story villa. I couldn't imagine how Chinese Christians had acquired such luxurious property, and, unable to contain my journalist's "need to know," I asked Sister Li.

"Oh, of course it doesn't belong to us," she said, as we walked up to the front door. "Actually, a foreign family owns it but allows us to use it when they are away. They are back in Europe right now."

This time it was a man who responded to the melodic three-note ding-ding-dong of the door chimes. The door opened to a large, spacious hallway with a marble floor, a large curved stairway leading up to the second floor, and, everywhere I looked, a veritable forest of assorted tropical plants in planters. The man who let us in appeared to be in his late seventies, and he took a long time after opening the door to turn around, walk a few paces back into the house to inform the people inside who we were, and then to return to us. He was almost completely white-haired and had the slow movements of someone with chronic back pain. But if he was suffering from some physical handicap, his face didn't show it. He had one of the most charming smiles on any Chinese face I had ever seen.

He didn't speak a word of English, so Sister Li took over the explaining, not that he needed any. He recognized her and was pleased to see her again. Without a word, he went into another room and left us waiting in the doorway. Sister Li smiled at me, saying in English, "I have known that old man for many years. He is one of my favorite people in this city. He is always smiling and is polite to everyone he meets."

"I can see that," I said. "May I know his name?"

"He likes to be known as Brother Matthias, after the disciple in the book of Acts who took the place of Judas. He often says he is only filling a spot for someone else. But as you can guess, he has become quite indispensable to us. He arouses suspicion with nobody."

Just then one of the beautifully carved teakwood doors off the right side of the main entrance opened and a very stout—not quite fat—westerner with gray hair came out, clad in casual shorts, a T-shirt, and a bathrobe. His hair looked slicked back and wet, as if he had just been in the shower. On seeing us, he cracked a grin as wide as the Grand Canyon. "Thank God you've come," he said. "I'm Chuck McHale. You're from the consulate, right?"

"'Fraid not," I replied. "I'm Richard Ireton, a reporter for *Epoch* magazine. This young lady is Sister Li, a friend of Brother Li. Waiting in the car is

Dr. Giuseppe Petrolucci, a research professor at Zhongshan University. The only reason I am here is that Burton Lasch sent me to find you."

"Ah, Burt, thank God for him—what a pal. But doesn't the consulate know I'm on the run?"

"They know you're missing," I said, "but they haven't a clue where you are. And if I were them right now, I wouldn't be out on the streets of Guangzhou looking."

"Why not?"

"Because we're right in the middle of a coup, some sort of alliance of Triad mobsters and units of the People's Liberation Army of the Guangzhou Military Region."

"So it's started," was all he said, but there was an odd expression on his face.

"You knew about this?" I asked.

"Oh yes, I got wind of the planning for it about a week ago and have been doing my best to piece it together since then. Unfortunately, some of the bad boys in this city got wind of me and put out a contract on my life. It's only because I've been in and out of this city for so many years that I heard about that. So I had to go into hiding. As you yourself have discovered, these people"—he gestured at Brother Matthias and then at Sister Li—"operate a pretty effective safe house system in the city."

"How did you find out about it?"

"It's a long story," he replied, "and I don't want to go into that now."

"OK, how did you find out about the coup, then?" I asked, my old reporter's instincts aroused now by this remarkably well-informed foreigner. McHale looked at me with narrowed eyes and replied, even more oddly, "That's not a question you want to ask."

That really got me riled up, and I responded with some vehemence.

"Look, McHale, I've risked my neck getting to you, and these people have risked their necks protecting me. If you're a spook, that's fine with me, only don't play games with me. I'm a journalist, and we don't really appreciate it when people try to use us."

McHale, to my surprise, burst out laughing. "Good old Lasch," he replied. "He sure knows how to pick 'em. Not bad, son, not bad. Stick up for your trade, I say. I obviously won't tell you how I come by my information, but I suspect you got an earful from Burt anyway. I'm a trade consultant, and I've made many contacts in this city over the years. And you can take that as plausible denial."

So he was CIA, after all. I'd met CIA station chiefs before, here and there, and all of them shared this pattern of a sometimes-witty, sometimes-infuriating, mercurial verbal dance, saying something to you but not quite saying it at the same time. Well, no need to pursue that one any further. Now I simply had to let Young know where his colleague—I made that assumption too—was hiding out and have him arrange an extrication plan in the middle of China's most dangerous coup attempt since B-52, the bungled plot by Defense Minister Lin Biao to assassinate Chairman Mao in 1971.

But I had a problem. I assumed that Tung and his friends in local counter-intelligence would have found a way to track my cell phone by now and could locate me within minutes if I used it. My only hope was Petrolucci. It was unlikely that they were also tracking him. At least, I hoped they weren't, though it was possible that if the coup had been as skillfully prepared as it should have been, they'd have the cell phone number of every foreigner in the city, despite the fact that there must be several thousand in town.

"OK, Chuck, touché, and let's call a truce. There's too much to be done to spar over that stuff. Now, first, I've got to get you back to Brother Li's safe house and let the consulate know where you are, and then I've got to make some other arrangements."

"Don't call the consulate," McHale said. "They'll be monitoring phone calls even into the ping pong shed. And don't try any of the staff's cell phones there either because they'll have those monitored too. There's only one way you can get a call through unmonitored. But let's get moving back to the other safe house, and I'll tell you on the way."

Chapter Ten

Sister Li left the house first and looked carefully up and down the street. It was not quite 10:00 p.m. yet, but patrols might be out trolling for foreigners to pick up off the streets. If they came across Petrolucci, McHale, and me, it would be the beginning of a very different adventure. But the coast was clear, and we quickly walked back to the car and got in.

"Giuseppe," I said, "I have succeeded in finding your old friend Chuck McHale."

"Hello, my friend, I hear you've gotten on the bad side of the Triads," Petrolucci said cheerfully. McHale only grunted in acknowledgment. The three of us were in the backseat of the small Toyota, Petrolucci on the passenger side, McHale in the middle, and me behind the driver's seat, a little cramped because McHale was of some girth. Sister Li and Weiming were having their own conversation in the front, and I was astonished to overhear her trying to convert him, going on about how even though his father was dead that he had a Father in heaven who loved him and was watching over him. I thought how these Christians had their priorities all out of whack. Here we were, potentially in danger for our lives in a city entering the grips of a coup, and there she was, telling him how to become a Christian, or, as Clarissa would put it, "sharing her faith." But Weiming didn't seem put off by this.

"Giuseppe," I said, "can we use your mobile phone? Mine is probably marked electronically now, and for sure Chuck's is."

"Of course. All they know about me is that I am an eccentric Italian and I don't chase the Chinese girls because my wife is so pretty." And he laughed infectiously as he said this. Even McHale chuckled.

"OK," McHale now said in a serious vein, "sorry, but I'm going to pull rank and make the first call. Although I said that everyone's cell phone at the consulate is probably monitored 24/7, the goons here haven't cottoned on to American teenagers yet. I know for a fact that Nick Ehrenfold, the consul-general's son, got his first mobile last week. I was at their house when he unwrapped it. It's a pretty good bet that the security authorities haven't gotten around to registering his number just yet. If he's not playing some game on it or photographing his girlfriend, we can use him to get a message to the consulate. Giuseppe, please let me have your phone," he said, somewhat peremptorily, I thought.

Petrolucci didn't object, though, and handed it over to him without comment. We both watched him dial. He listened carefully and then frowned. "Line's busy," he said. "Why are these kids always on the phone?"

"Send him a text message with your number on it," I suggested, trying to be helpful.

"You must be kidding!" McHale shot back. "They've got all of Guangzhou wired for intercepting text messages, and the computers troll through all of that stuff in a microsecond. We might as well call the Waiban at the Public Security Bureau and let them know where we are," he said, using the shortened Chinese term for Foreign Affairs Office, as most China-hands do because it is easier to say than the cumbersome name in English.

"Speaking of the PSB Waiban," I said, rather enjoying this particular segue after McHale had practically jumped down my throat, "excuse me while I make a call."

I plucked the phone out of McHale's hand, pulled out my notebook with Yao's private number, and dialed.

"Who are you calling?" McHale demanded as I waited for an answer.

"Just a friend at the PSB," I replied. I couldn't help toying with him a bit.

"What—?" McHale began to explode, but Petrolucci restrained him with a firm hand on his arm. "Chuck, let Richard do this. I think he knows what he's doing."

I listened as the call kept ringing and then someone finally picked up. "Wei (Hello)," a man's voice answered warily. "Wo shi Ai Erdun," I said, "women qianjitian zai xianggang feiwang guangzhou de feiji shang renshi de. (I am Ireton. We met a few days ago on the Hong Kong–Guangzhou flight). Gangcai fashengle yijian feichang weixian de shi (Something extremely dangerous has just happened). Wo shenma shihou neng jian ni? (When can I see you?)"

"Xianzai jiu keyi (Right now is fine)."

"Where?" I continued in Mandarin.

"Come to my apartment."

I wasn't sure I'd heard him right. How could he suggest having a foreigner come to his apartment on this night of all nights?

He immediately sensed my hesitation and laughed lightly. "Don't worry," he said, "our basketball team is in the national finals tonight. Everyone will be watching TV." I thought grimly that they wouldn't be watching basketball if they knew what was unfolding in Guangzhou at this very moment.

He told me the address, and I wrote it down phonetically in pinyin, the standard Romanization system for Mandarin. I wanted to ask Sister Li or Weiming if they knew where it was but then decided against it. Yao might have been alarmed if he knew that I was calling him with other Chinese around.

But then something hit me. I had no way of getting there. Petrolucci wanted to get back home to Francesca to make sure she was safe, and I didn't know Weiming well enough to ask him to continue the risky job of ferrying two foreigners around Guangzhou in the middle of a coup.

I ended the call wondering what to do. "OK, Richard?" Petrolucci asked.

"Well, yes and no," I replied. "The man is willing to see me right away, but I've no idea how to get there."

"No problem at all," he replied. "Just ride home with me, and Weiming will take you on from there."

Although that solved my problem, my relief was followed almost immediately by doubts about the advisability of putting this nice young man in continued danger. And I wasn't comfortable with the casual way Petrolucci had just made this decision for Weiming without even asking him. For my own peace of mind—because who knew how the evening might turn out—I had to make sure it was OK with Weiming.

Reaching over and tapping Weiming on the shoulder, I explained briefly what Petrolucci had just proposed and what I needed to do after we'd dropped him off at home.

"I want you to know that this could get very dangerous. I don't want you to do this just because your teacher says so. Please decide for yourself whether you really want to put yourself in danger," I said, wondering as I spoke what I would do if he took the out I was giving him.

But Weiming answered with an intensity that surprised me.

"The Triads have already destroyed my life. I will not let them destroy my country too. I will go with you, no matter what," he said, and gave me a hard look in the rearview mirror.

Well, that was pretty clear, I thought, and turned to McHale. "Look, I'm sorry, but this contact I am going to see would freak out if you showed up to meet him and he found out who you are. Do you mind if we drop you and Sister Li off back at Brother Li's house?"

"Let me get this right. You have a contact with the Waiban of the Guang-zhou PSB, and in the middle of a coup you are willing to trust him?"

"Have you got a better idea?" I asked.

"No," he said, "but let me try Nick Ehrenfold again."

This time he got through. "Nick," he said, "I'm the middle-aged guy who was at your birthday party earlier this week, you know, your dad's friend? I can't say my name, but your dad will know who I am. I have a very important message for him. Do you think you can remember to tell him?"

McHale was obviously satisfied with the response and said very carefully into the phone, "'Phoenix Three, repeat Phoenix Three tonight, I'm OK. How exit? Use Nick's phone.'" Then, like a first-grade teacher patiently coaching a student to spell out the words on the blackboard, McHale repeated the message with, I thought, almost touching gentleness after his snarling response to me a few minutes earlier. He said, "Please repeat after me, 'Phoenix Three tonight. I'm OK. How exit? Use Nick's phone.'" McHale had to repeat it twice before the bewildered teenager was word-perfect. But he got it, and I marveled at the bizarre telegraphese these spooks used. What really intrigued me was that Ehrenfold not only knew about McHale's Langley credentials but also was apprised of the specific information McHale was trying to collect.

We repeated what had become a pattern of Weiming's drop-offs at all the addresses we had approached since I had first gotten into the little Toyota with Petrolucci. The car stopped a few blocks away, and Sister Li got out alone first, looked around carefully, and then motioned to McHale, who then exited the car and briskly followed her to Brother Li's safe house. We waited until we could see that they were safely inside, rather like dropping off a date in a risky neighborhood, then drove back to Petrolucci's apartment near the university.

"Don't get out, Richard. But I'll keep my mobile on and with me at all times in case you need me again."

"Thanks for everything, Giuseppe. You were a lifesaver."

"Just tell Burton he owes us dinner at the Essex House in New York when we get back there, OK?"

"What's the Essex House?" I asked innocently. Petrolucci's eyes twinkled as he replied. "Alain Ducasse at the Essex House is probably just the most expensive restaurant in New York City, easily two hundred dollars a head with beverages, and it's American food prepared the French way. Francesca adores it. Talk to you later."

"Right." I'd been to Manhattan plenty of times, but neither Burt nor anyone else at *Epoch* had ever even mentioned the Essex House to me, much less taken me there. I thought I was this savvy foreign correspondent, but I'd never even heard of New York's swankiest restaurant.

But there was no time to waste. As I watched Petrolucci walk through the front door of his apartment building, I noticed Weiming look in the car's rearview mirror and suddenly freeze. "Tang xia! (Lie down!)" he hissed urgently. I dropped instantly to the floor of the car. I heard a truck rumbling up from behind, and my heart skipped a beat as it slowed down to pass us at a crawl. Weiming very cleverly and quickly turned on the car radio to the basketball game, rolled down the driver-side window, and turned up the volume. As the truck, full of heavily armed soldiers, pulled alongside, he grinned at the driver and gave a thumbs up. Of course, I didn't see this, but he told me about it later. I heard the driver shout, "Shei defen gao? (Who's leading?)," and I heard Weiming shout back, "Women (We are)."

"Tai hao! (Great!)," the driver shouted back and picked up speed with his load of troops. I wondered where they were going. I got up and put the question to Weiming. "Oh, probably to one of the hotels," he said knowingly. "They don't want foreigners interfering with things. They won't hurt them in any way, but they'll stop them leaving the hotel for a day or two." I suppose growing up with a cop for a dad he knew about these things.

Now that it was just the two of us in the car, I had a chance to get my first good look at Weiming. Although he couldn't have been more than twenty-two or so, he had a maturity about him that is rare among young Chinese, who for the most part look and act younger than their American contemporaries. He had a square face and a firm set to his mouth. He looked to be of average height but was stockier and broader in the shoulders than the typical Chinese man, and I suspected that he was among the small but growing number of young urban Chinese who had discovered the benefits of the gym.

Weiming didn't say anything as we continued our journey, but I could tell he was relieved when I decided to resume my position on the floor of the Toyota and stayed there all the way to Yao's apartment. I could hear many heavy vehicles on the road, and I asked Weiming to give me a running commentary of what he was seeing. It turned out, he was surprisingly good at it, which made me think that he had the makings of a good reporter. "Three trucks parked on the left with soldiers," he would say, or "two tanks at the intersection ahead," or "soldiers setting up machine-gun positions in the lobby of that bank building on the corner." The plotters had timed the coup well. In addition to the basketball game keeping many Guangzhou citizens indoors glued to their TVs, it was a weeknight and not many people were out.

Yao's apartment block was in the Dongshan section of Guangzhou, away from the heart of the city and, therefore, less likely to have patrols coming through. Once more, Weiming stopped the car a few blocks away. As I got out, he reached under his seat and pulled out a large straw hat folded tightly, a cotton surgical mask, and a pair of dark glasses. Turns out that when Petrolucci asked him to help drive some fugitive foreigners around, he had anticipated that a disguise might be needed at some point. I was struck again that Weiming was unlike any other Chinese of his age I'd ever met: confident, quick-thinking, and able to take the initiative.

When I asked him about the suitability of the surgical mask as a disguise, he joked, "SARS. You never know," a reference to the sometimes deadly respiratory illness—Severe Acute Respiratory Syndrome—that almost shut China down in 2003. Thus "disguised"—surgical mask, straw hat, and dark glasses—I walked as inconspicuously as I could to Yao's apartment. Just as I was about to enter the building, I noticed that Weiming had driven the car closer and parked where he could keep an eye on the main door. Boy, he was sharp, just as Petrolucci had said.

Yao's apartment was on the eighth floor; and, to my relief, there was no one in the entryway when I entered, so I was able to quickly locate the stairs and start climbing. The elevators in the older, government-supplied apartment buildings like Yao's were always manned, in part because they were so unreliable that it was safer to have a person on hand who knew how to run them. But it was also a way of trying to achieve full employment in a nation with a huge surplus of workers.

I knew that if I rode up to the eighth floor in the elevator, it would be eight floors of being the subject of scrutiny by the bored elevator operator.

Not only would she (the elevator operators were always women) quickly see through the ridiculous disguise; she'd be able to give anyone who might later question her a full description of my appearance as well as exactly which floor I got off at. Knowing that, anyone would be able to quickly figure out whom I was going to see. I had learned long ago that if I wanted to visit someone surreptitiously in China, the elevators were to be avoided.

To my surprise, Yao was in the hallway outside his apartment waiting for me. He was smoking a cigarette and watching the elevator doors impassively. When he saw me emerge from the stairway, he nodded approvingly.

"Lai, lai, lai (Come, come, come)," he said, his tone both friendly and insistent as he shook my hand firmly and led me toward his apartment. I was even more surprised when we entered to find a woman in the living room, holding an infant. "My wife," was all he said in introducing her. She was younger than Yao. I wondered if he had married late, or if this was a second marriage. If the former, it was likely due to the years of his youth lost to the chaos of the 1966–1976 Cultural Revolution. If the latter, his first marriage could have fallen victim to the changing social patterns that were making divorce almost as common in Chinese cities as in Western societies.

Yao leaned down to stroke the baby under the chin, saying with a broad, proud smile, "My son." This set me a little at ease. If the entire setup, from the meeting at Chek Lap Kok airport to the business card exchange on the plane to the suggestion that we meet again, had all been a trap, I didn't think Yao would have let his wife and son stick around after my phone call earlier in the evening.

Yao motioned for me to sit down in one of two armchairs in the small living room. I noticed right away that the apartment had far more books than would be usual in the home of a typical government official, and there were Chinese newspapers and magazines scattered around. I even saw a recent issue of *The Economist* on a side table.

He didn't waste any time getting to the point. "Your Mandarin is very good, so we'll speak in my language," he said in Mandarin. "I can read English but don't speak it very well." He continued to smoke as we talked, holding the cigarette between his index and second finger and keeping it pointed upward in a strangely elegant manner. His gold tooth, which was the first thing I'd noticed about him at Chek Lap Kok airport, glinted as he spoke.

"You will want to know why I, an official of the Public Security Bureau, made contact with you, a foreigner. I must tell you, I didn't know you were a journalist when I first approached you, and if I had known then what I know about you now, I might not have talked to you. But I needed to talk to an American, and I could tell from your clothes and the way you were standing that you probably were an American, so I took a chance."

I interrupted him. "From the way I was standing? What do you mean by that?"

"Haven't you noticed? Americans, especially the younger ones, and also the taller ones like you, tend to slouch more than Europeans when they are standing."

"OK," I said unconvinced. I'd never heard that from anyone before, not even in Europe.

"I hope that you are not too late in contacting me. You see, a very serious political event has just begun this evening in Guangzhou. There are elements of the People's Liberation Army, along with the Triad organized crime group under the command of a dangerous gang leader, who are organizing a coup first to overthrow the municipal and provincial government, and then to spread the plot, if they can, to Beijing. I have known a little of what they were planning to do for several weeks, through a friend I have in another branch of the Public Security Bureau. We have been very close friends since middle school, and we agree very much on political matters.

"We both strongly supported China's opening to the outside world," he went on, "joining the WTO"—and here, instead of the long, cumbersome name in Chinese, Yao, like almost all Chinese, used the simpler English letters—"and working for a peaceful resolution of the Taiwan problem. But there were many around us who want China to take a much stronger line and who actually want the People's Liberation Army to threaten Taiwan with direct attack as soon as China is in a position to prevail.

"My friend told me about close contacts that have been developing over several months between some of the army unit commanders in the Guangzhou Military Region and the organized crime forces in this city, the Triads. Of course, the government has known for a long time that the PLA is riddled with corruption, but we assumed that most of the time it had no political significance, that it was merely a matter of criminal activity. Obviously, that has changed completely.

"My friend—I cannot tell you his name, for obvious reasons—informed me about two weeks ago that a meeting had been held the night before at a resort complex outside of Guangzhou, attended by several officers of the Guangzhou Military Region of the rank of colonel, and even with one general present, and the organized crime leader Dong Zhiqiang"—he used the Mandarin name for Tung Chi-keung—"and several of his associates. They were deciding whether they could marshal sufficient forces to upset the political structure of the province and eventually all of China. Many of those present had been influenced by Great Master Wu and other Qigong masters and were already very eager to make a move. Do you know what happened in Yuexiu Park this evening?"

"I was there."

"You were at the Zhenhai Tower?"

"Yes."

"How is that possible?" Yao said, flicking ash into an ashtray. "No foreigner was permitted to approach that part of the park, and all foreigners in the park earlier this evening were escorted out. Even overseas Chinese or Chinese with foreign passports were stopped."

"Well, you might say I was a coerced guest," I said. "I had been invited by Dong to a dinner at an expensive restaurant on Er Sha Island. During the dinner, I was told that they had decided to make me the official foreign eyewitness to a major event in Chinese history. I wasn't given the choice. They told me they had decided on this, and just to impress upon me the seriousness of the job, they murdered right in front of me two men they said were working for foreign forces." Even as I said it, I still couldn't believe that I had actually watched this happen.

Yao's wife, who had disappeared with the infant after we were introduced, now brought two mugs of Chinese tea, each with a traditional porcelain lid. After the rushing around of the previous two hours, it was a relief to be sitting down with something to drink. I was glad, though, that she was not in the room when I had mentioned the Ming Garden murders.

Yao looked at me with an expression of disbelief and astonishment. But his police mind was quick to follow up on what I had said. "Then how did you get away?" he asked.

"I had another foreign friend whom I managed to call surreptitiously from a bathroom in the restaurant when we were still there. I told him I needed some diversion in the park so I could escape from the plotters."

"Yes, there certainly was a diversion. In fact, after some firecrackers went off in the middle of Great Master Wu's Qigong performance, there was some real shooting in the park. Did you see that?"

"No, I was too busy running away."

"That diversion may have been decisive in slowing down the coup. We just don't know yet. There were some regular Public Security Bureau officers in the park who were not aware of the political developments planned for tonight. They were just doing their normal job of keeping an eye on the crowd. They were as surprised as Dong's men were by the unexpected firecrackers and ran toward the sound to see what was happening. One of them drew his pistol because he thought someone might have a gun.

"Rare though that is in China, it does happen now more often than we like to admit. But Dong's men, who hadn't anticipated either the unplanned fireworks or the presence of uniformed Public Security Bureau personnel with guns, panicked in the noisy confusion and started shooting at the PSB. They must have thought that other Public Security forces were interfering with their coup plans. About five PSB officers are now dead and seven civilians, some of them Triads."

"And the PLA units you mentioned? Have they been deployed yet?"

"Yes. Several companies of soldiers have been sent around the city to secure government buildings and keep foreigners confined to their hotels. But to estimate the extent of their planning, I need to know if there were any PLA officers at dinner in the restaurant."

"One officer, a Colonel Su."

Yao sucked his lips in as though he had just heard disturbing news.

"Is that bad?" I asked.

"Su," Yao replied, "is one of the most talented and able commanders in the entire PLA. He speaks perfect English"—Su hadn't let on at the restaurant—"and he even accompanied China's minister of defense once on a trip to the United States, where he was hosted by several of your elite military units. If anyone can persuade units in other military regions to join the plot, Su can."

"I just have to ask you: Why do you want to tell me, a foreigner, even worse, an American, all of this?"

Yao now smiled broadly. "Because when the matter involves a possible war in East Asia, a war of any kind, moderate and intelligent and wise people are all on the same side. Any new war in Asia would kill hundreds of thousands, perhaps millions of people. I've studied America quite a lot. As I said, I can read English and because of my PSB clearance I can subscribe to *The Economist*. I have also learned a lot about America from a Chinese-language magazine that the U.S. embassy puts out and sends free to select readers. A cousin of mine in Beijing sends it to me when he's finished reading it. It is called *Jiaoliu*, which means 'exchange.'" He gave the translation in English, then resumed in Mandarin.

"Even though it comes from the embassy, it is not government propaganda but just gives interesting articles about many aspects of American life. I have the impression that ordinary Americans do not like war and that public opinion quickly turns against any war that the U.S. government starts but which ordinary people think is unjust. It is absolutely vital that your government knows that any military movements taking place in Guangzhou—which your satellites and electronic surveillance will certainly detect—are not happening because the government in Beijing is behind them.

"If Beijing is unable to suppress this coup quickly, then other military regions may join and launch an attack against Taiwan on their own initiative. But even if the other military regions don't actually launch an attack, their military movements will be detected by your government, which may then launch a preemptive attack on China to forestall an attack across the Taiwan Straits. If that were to happen, there would be a terrible war between our two countries. By the way," he added as though suddenly struck by the thought, "why were you coming to Guangzhou earlier this week?"

I had wondered from the moment I arrived whether he would ask this question, and I had not really known until now how I would reply. But Yao had made himself vulnerable to me, and I didn't have any reason to hold back the information about McHale.

"There's an American businessman who disappeared in Guangzhou a few days ago. He had been investigating the Triads. My superiors in New York asked me to try to find him."

"Yes, McHale," Yao said, without any show of surprise, using what I presumed was McHale's Chinese name: Mai ke hei er.

"You know him?" I said in amazement.

"Oh yes, we know a lot about McHale. We've been watching him for years, whenever he comes into China—which I must say is quite a lot. The Ministry of State Security, which guards against foreign espionage, has him under surveillance almost constantly. The PSB only deals with domestic crime, as I am sure you know. But because McHale was poking around the Triads in Guangzhou, I heard about him."

"Did you know he had disappeared?" I asked.

"Yes, and it took us by surprise. I heard from someone at State Security that they had lost him in one part of the city and that he seemed to have disappeared. Do you know where he is?"

"Yes. I—"

I stopped. We were wary new friends, each circling the other, wondering how much sensitive information it was safe to reveal to the other. Yao watched me pause in mid-sentence, and he half smiled, exposing the gold tooth.

"Well, I can see that you don't want to tell me where he is now, or anything about the place he is hiding. But we're strange allies in a scene that neither of us could have previously imagined; I, the Chinese policeman, and you, the American journalist. How interesting." He snuffed out the cigarette now because it had burned down almost to his fingers. We both looked at each other as the idea sunk in.

But I wanted to break away from this awkward impasse that threatened to sabotage any chance of getting me and McHale out of Guangzhou, and as it was becoming increasingly obvious, Yao as well.

"Are your mobile phone and home phone tapped?" I asked.

"I'm pretty sure my home phone is monitored. If you need to call locally, you can use my wife's mobile phone. But if you call overseas on it your conversation will be listened to and the mobile phone location may be traced."

"What about pay phones?"

"The ones in the hotels foreigners stay at will be monitored, but the ones local Chinese use may be OK. Still, it's a risk."

"Well, I'll have to take that risk. It may be the only chance we have of contacting certain people."

I thought back to McHale's cryptic message to Ehrenfold, the consul-general, in the car. I wondered how much information had been contained in the words *Phoenix Three*. It wasn't clear to me that Yao knew more about the situation in Guangzhou than McHale did. On the other hand, Yao was an inside source on the situation and, therefore, a far more valuable witness than either me or McHale to what was happening in Guangzhou.

I was trying to sift through all the massive amounts of information I had absorbed in the last few hours, but Yao brought me back to the present with a jarring piece of new information. "You probably know that Great Master Wu has been speaking out very strongly against foreigners and foreign influences on China and about China's humiliations in the nineteenth century. I got a call half an hour ago, before you arrived, that two foreigners, both Americans, had been attacked and killed on Jiefang Beilu, which as you know runs down the side of Yuexiu Park, hacked to death. Nobody knows yet whether it was the work of Triads or just of people stirred into madness by the rhetoric of Wu. Unless we can stop the situation from deteriorating very soon, it will get out of hand and terrible things will happen."

Two foreigners, both Americans, killed just outside Yuexiu Park? I hoped fervently that it was not Jake and Jennifer, caught up in a mob after they were turned away from the park gate by Tung's men. I asked Yao for more details, but he had no additional information, not even whether the victims had been a man and a woman.

I followed up with another question.

"Here's something I just don't understand. Why would anyone organize a public meeting in a park at the start of a military coup? Coups are usually organized in great secrecy and then carried out in the wee hours of the morning."

"You don't understand the role that Great Master Wu has played in preparing this," Yao said. "He's gotten many of the senior staff officers of the military region mesmerized by the possibilities of Qigong both for providing a superb mental and physical training for ordinary soldiers, and for mobilizing anti-foreign sentiment. Wu needed to spread his message in a public setting, even a relatively small one like the Zhenhai Tower. As I just told you, some of the spectators—I assume they had been to the performance—digested the message altogether too well, and now two Americans are dead as a result. The military side of the coup has been organized independently of Wu's actions, but Wu has provided a cloak of confusion and fear."

"I'll say," I replied grimly.

Yao's cell phone, sitting on one of the side tables, interrupted us, and he answered it immediately. He listened, then said "Shi, shi (Yes, yes)" to the unknown caller and hung up. "Things are now moving very fast," he said. "The rebel military forces have already seized control of the TV and radio stations and are putting out announcements telling people what to do. They are telling ordinary citizens to apprehend any foreigners they see in the street. Unless we can stop the developing situation very soon, it may get completely out of hand. Then China will have another Boxer Rebellion on its hands, far more serious than the one a century ago because there are far more foreigners in China now and because the international stakes are much higher. A century ago, eight foreign armies were able to force their way into China, rescue the foreigners, suppress the Boxers, and restore order in the country. But today, if a foreign country even thought about attacking China, it might lead to a world war."

"Then we must move very quickly," I said. "Can you take me to a pay phone on the street whose calls are probably not monitored?"

"Yes, but if it's right on the street you'll be spotted immediately and arrested—or worse." He paused, pursed his lips in thought, then said, "But I know of a phone three blocks away in an alley that's pretty deserted. If you wear that disguise again, you may be all right. I'll come with you and act as scout in case any patrols come by."

"Fine," I said, "but what should I do about the Chinese who is driving me? He's on our side, by the way."

"Where is he now?"

"Down the block."

"I'll go out and talk to him."

"No, don't do that. He doesn't know you, and if he sees you coming, he'll think they've caught me and that you're coming for him too. Let's do this: He'll see me when we come out of the entrance to your apartment building together, and I'll give him a hand signal that I'm OK and that he should wait for me."

As we left the building, I looked at Weiming in the car down the street. Fortunately, he was paying attention and acknowledged my hand signal that things were OK. Yao appeared to be paying no attention to this. Only a few people were out on the street, which made it a little easier to get to the pay phone without being spotted. But there seemed to be plenty of police cars about, and occasionally a truck full of soldiers roared by. I wore my ridiculous disguise of dark glasses, straw hat, and surgical mask, grateful for the SARS epidemic of a few years ago. It provided a plausible reason for wearing a surgical mask, and it deterred people from being curious enough to come close to me.

The alley where the pay phone was located was deserted, which made phoning easier. Yao stood about ten yards away, where the alley opened up onto the main street.

I used the China phone card I always carried in my wallet. They were handy for those reporting situations where I could not use my cell phone, and I'd found that calls overseas were not prohibitively expensive when using these cards. They generally came in small denominations—fifty yuan or one hundred yuan (about six dollars or twelve dollars)—so I always had several on me.

Burt, thank God, was in his office and not at one of those interminable editorial meetings—which I knew he detested—that Reddaway liked to call without notice The meetings ostensibly were to announce some late-breaking cover story, but I always thought they were just Reddaway's way of throwing his weight around and showing who was in charge.

"Burt, it's Rick here, and I'm in Guangzhou with very little time to talk because things are moving fast."

"Yes, I've seen on CNN that something very strange is happening there," Lash said. "All the foreigners have been confined to their hotels, or something."

"It's not just strange; it's downright dangerous. There's a coup going on in Guangzhou, and they're picking up foreigners on the street on sight, sometimes doing worse to them. Two Americans have been killed already. The good news is, I've found Chuck, and he's safe right now. But I've got to get him out of China as soon as I can. You're right about who he works for, by the way. So now we have to contact his employers and see if they'll guarantee defector status for a key Chinese who's on our side in all this. If he gets out to Hong Kong, we need Langley's people there to get him out without the Hong Kong authorities knowing."

"Richard, look, I can see that it's really tense there, but I can't give you any guarantees on the phone about anyone without talking to them. What do you want me to say?"

"The man's name is Yao Fanmei, and he works for the foreign affairs department of the Public Security Bureau. If he stays in China, his life won't be worth a fortune cookie."

"Yes, I understand. But you say there's a coup. What are they trying to do?"

"They're trying to take over Guangzhou, draw in other military regions of China, and start a war with Taiwan in order to provoke the Americans."

"Why do they want a war with us right now?"

"I can only assume they think that we are so thinly stretched around the world that it gives them an advantage in some regional contexts." I was surprised at myself for managing to sound so articulate in the midst of all the pressure.

There was a pause for several seconds, and I thought the line had gone bad.

"Burt, are you still there?"

"Yes, I'm here. Are you sure of this, I mean really sure?"

"I was at a dinner tonight—an invitation you can't refuse, if you know what I mean—with some of the main planners of the coup. I got away from them, but if they knew where I was now and who I was talking to, they'd kill me on sight."

"But you're safe now?"

Sometimes Burt could be almost bovinely slow in the uptake. His mind was so methodical and thorough he always wanted to be sure that all alternative explanations for why things were the way they were had been eliminated before accepting the obvious. How did he think I was calling him from amid all this mayhem unless I was "safe"? But even though I was safe now, in a minute's time I might not be.

"Yes, I'm safe for the moment, Burt, but none of us will be safe, you won't be safe, unless the U.S. government understands that any provocative military moves that look as though China is planning on using military force against Taiwan in the next few days are not—repeat not—the result of Chinese national policy."

"Well, an attack is an attack, no matter who ordered it."

This was infuriating. He was not getting it.

"Yes," I said, trying hard not to let any irritation enter my voice, "but there are lots of things that happen before an attack actually starts that make it look as if an attack is imminent. Weapons, troops, equipment—it all starts to assemble. What the White House has got to know is that what's going on here has not been ordered up by Beijing. On the other hand, it's real. The troops and the equipment are real. These guys really do want to start a war over Taiwan, but Beijing doesn't want that at all. Beijing will move fast to smash this coup, if it can, because it doesn't want to go to war with the U.S. right now. Maybe some nuts in Beijing want that, but the leadership doesn't."

"And Burt, this guy here in Guangzhou, Yao, he wants to tell the Americans this and he's with me right now."

"Can I talk to him?"

"No, he doesn't speak English." I was glad I could sweep that idea right off the table. Burt would probably be hiring Yao as our Guangzhou stringer if I let him.

"Burt, I've got to get him out of China, but the Langley boys are going to have to spirit him out of Hong Kong very quickly before anyone knows he's there. Same for Chuck. I'm going to have to try to call you or get a message to you one more time and tell you how and where we're going to arrive in Hong Kong. But you can bet it won't be at the Hong Kong railroad station or the international airport. Look, I never intended to get into U.S.

intelligence operations when I started this story, and I know perfectly well
what you think about that sort of thing." (Lasch had sent a "personal and
confidential" memorandum to every *Epoch* foreign correspondent warning them that any work whatever conducted on behalf of any intelligence
organization, including U.S. intelligence, would be grounds for instant dis-
missal. We'd all been grateful that he'd done this because, in many dangerous places, our lives were worth nothing if the locals thought that we had
any connection at all with the CIA. We all made a point of telling anyone
who would listen about the memo.)

"You've got to do this, Burt," I continued, "not just because it's a matter of life and death for Chuck and me, and for Yao, but because it may be
a matter of war and peace between China and the U.S." I could imagine
Lasch licking his upper lip nervously as I said this.

"Look, Richard, if it's a matter of life and death, or war and peace for that
matter, I'm certainly with you. Well, I guess that's another story Reddaway
has lost," he said, and I could hear his guffaws above the street noise. "I'll keep
my cell phone on and with me at all times. You call me as soon as you know
your next move. I'll get working on things on this end. Katie, Katie," I heard
him shouting through the door to the reception area, "get me the Washington Bureau! Richard, good job, good job. Take care, now. Good-bye."

"Bye Burt." Out of the corner of my eye, I had noticed Yao looking
alternately up the street and back at me on the phone, and pointing at his
watch. I made a sympathetic face back at him, but I wasn't finished. All of
a sudden, I wanted desperately to talk to Trish. I really needed some emotional support. I called her on her Philippine cell phone, which I thought
might be faster than going through the switchboard at her hotel. I hoped
this time I'd actually get through to her and not get transferred to the voice
mail again. Miraculously, she answered!

But I also heard boisterous church singing in the background. I felt like
groaning. "Trish, it's Richard, and I'm in Guangzhou. Have you heard about
the coup yet?"

"I'm sorry, Rick, I can't hear you. Could you call back in five minutes?
We're in the middle of a prayer meeting."

At that moment, I felt like throwing Clarissa's large Bible at her. Here I
was, her boyfriend—at least that's what I had been a week ago—in mortal
danger, and all she could do was tell me she was in a prayer meeting.

I spat out an expletive. "No, I can't call back in five minutes." Even as I
said it I knew I was being brutally harsh. "I'm on the run in China, there's

a coup going on, and I may have to go into hiding any moment. Bye Trish. Tell Clarissa to pray for me."

I hung up in haste as Yao came running toward me, waving his hands and shouting at me to get off the phone. "Lie down on your stomach right away and pretend you're drunk!" he ordered, "There's a patrol coming!" I did as I was told and hit the ground fast and hard, twisting myself around as I went down so that I was face down. In a second, Yao was practically on top of me, playing the role of the solicitous friend of a fallen drunkard.

It wasn't exactly a convincing scenario. Chinese aren't given to drunkenness the way some other ethnic groups are, and even when they are they usually don't make a public spectacle of themselves. If this had been New York or Tokyo, the scene wouldn't have elicited a second look. But this was China, and a coup was taking place. I heard the Chinese sergeant wheel his marching troops right into the alley and order them to halt a few feet away. "What's wrong with this man?" the sergeant barked.

Yao's answer astonished me. He said nothing about drunkenness. "I am so sorry, sergeant," Yao said, "You see, my cousin has the AIDS virus. He was visiting his family in the countryside and was in a car accident. The hospital gave him a blood transfusion and the blood was contaminated. Now he's weak and loses his balance easily. He doesn't usually fall down completely, but he's been very tired recently so I am letting him rest for a little before getting him up. Thank you so much for offering to help"—the sergeant hadn't done anything of the sort—"and thank you for showing such concern."

I'd have given anything at that moment to have seen the sergeant's face, but it was easy to imagine it. "OK (Hao ba)," I heard him saying. "If you don't need any medical assistance and you're sure he's all right, we'll keep moving. Squad! About face! March!"

The entire squad left the alley immediately, and I was sure they wouldn't come back. Just the fear of being near anyone with AIDS had terrified the sergeant into backing out and leaving us alone. I was impressed by Yao's quick thinking and inventiveness. Few Chinese have accurate knowledge about AIDS, but almost all are terrified of it, much of their fear grounded in ignorance. The mere mention of it had frightened off a military patrol.

"What now?" I asked, scrambling to my feet as soon as it was clear the patrol had left and adjusting the straw hat, dark glasses, and surgical mask as I did so. Yao looked at me as if sizing up a recently arrested suspect and burst out laughing. "Ai Erdun," he said through his laughter, "you may be able to appear drunk or even on occasion to be suffering from AIDS, but you'll never fool a Chinese into thinking you're Chinese."

"I know that," I said, relieved that he saw some humor in it all, "but it's comedy central or the jailhouse at this hour."

He didn't respond to my attempt at a joke, which admittedly did sound a little strange in Chinese. He was obviously thinking hard about what to do next. He took a small notebook out of his pocket and, with what seemed to me to be painstaking slowness, began to flip through it, reading the pages by the weak light from a building halfway down the alley. This time I was the scout, and though I didn't dare show my face on the street, from a vantage point just inside the alley I could look up and down the street with my face still in the shadows. Between keeping watch on the passing traffic, I looked back at Yao a few times, wondering what he was doing and why it was taking him so long.

Finally, he approached me looking confident. "Ai Erdun," he said, "I think I can find a way to get you and your friend out of China. But to do so, I must be sure that the Americans will take care of me if I come out too. Can you promise me that?"

Boy, he had me on that one. I knew that Lasch would pull every string among his Washington contacts to ensure that the White House and the CIA understood what was afoot in China. I also knew that the CIA could occasionally be unbelievably bureaucratic and unimaginative. And for all I knew there might be powerful diplomatic reasons why it might cause some kind of major crisis in U.S.–China relations to offer political asylum to a Chinese policeman at a time of major unrest in China. A panicky thought flashed through my mind that some junior bureaucrat in CIA headquarters in Virginia might insist that Yao go to the U.S. consulate for an interview before being granted political asylum. But in almost the same instant, I realized that McHale was my trump card: no asylum for Yao, no exit strategy for McHale. And McHale was one of their boys, thank goodness.

"Yes," I said, looking steadily at Yao.

"All right," he said, "now I must make some phone calls. Please keep a lookout for me."

I did, and the long minutes that Yao spent making his calls were among the most agonizing of my life. I didn't know who he was talking to, but I knew that he was the only Chinese in Guangzhou right now whom I could trust and who offered me and McHale any hope of getting out of China.

On the street, traffic had become lighter, but there seemed to be more military vehicles.

Finally, Yao hung up the phone and put his notebook away. Walking slowly toward me, he said carefully, "What I have prepared will be a very risky course of action. But speaking frankly, it represents the only chance you, McHale, and I have of staying out of the hands of the Triads and the PLA, and possibly even staying alive in the next twenty-four hours. Are you ready?"

"What choice do I have?" I answered.

"All right, then, let's go to your friend with the car."

We walked back briskly to where Weiming was still waiting patiently in the Toyota. A bright full moon had already climbed high in the night sky, and its milky light was splashing on to the façade of the older buildings of Guangzhou. It was close to 11:00 p.m.

Chapter Eleven

Weiming, the poor guy, had fallen asleep draped over the steering wheel, exhausted by the hours of driving around, the excitement and the tension, and the long waits each time I disappeared. He was lucky he hadn't been spotted and questioned by a passing foot patrol or patrol car.

I tapped as gently as I could on the driver side window, but he still awoke with a frightened start until he realized it was me. He hit the power locks to unlock the doors, which he had wisely kept locked, and I introduced him to Yao. "My friend," was all I said as I took up my accustomed position in the backseat.

Yao got in the front, then turned to me. "First, we have to pick up your American friend," he said. "There is absolutely no time to lose because I have learned that by dawn all the waterways leading into Guangzhou will be patrolled by forces loyal to the coup planners. And even within Guangzhou city proper, it is going to be very risky. They have started putting checkpoints up on some of the main roads, not the elevated expressways though, just the street level roads. We will have to think very carefully about how to get to wherever it is your American friend is.

"But I do have some good news too. I called two people in Beijing whom I trust completely, and who trust me. Both have friends very high in the leadership, one even in the Politburo, and both will immediately alert the national leadership about what is going on here. Of course, Beijing was aware that something strange was going on here, but what they didn't know was the full extent of the plan to trigger actual war across the Taiwan Strait as soon as possible. But if we are going to escape at all, we will have to be extremely careful."

Yao now turned to Weiming and spoke in Cantonese, and it was clear that they were figuring out between them how to get to Brother Li's house. At one point, they seemed almost to be arguing. "No, no," I understood Yao to be saying, "the elevated roads will be clear because they assume that all drivers eventually have to come down to street level and can be checked once they've come off the expressway."

"Are you sure of this?" Weiming said with some skepticism in his voice. I was a little surprised. Normally a Chinese as young as he wouldn't stand up to or question someone clearly his elder, and a senior PSB officer to boot. Unquestioning obedience is the traditionally correct and accepted— as well as expected—response. My estimation of this young man went up yet another notch.

"I took part in simulated emergency planning to prepare for civil un- rest and a national emergency, and I know what the plans are," Yao said a bit testily. He'd noticed Weiming's attitude, too, and his reaction was quite different from mine. Weiming just grunted lightly, apparently not entirely convinced.

Nonetheless, the two quickly agreed on what they thought would be the best way to get to Brother Li's house while avoiding any possible checkpoints. The route took longer on the elevated expressways than if we had gone directly, and for awhile we seemed to be driving around in the opposite direction from where I thought we needed to be going. As we drove carefully along the elevated expressways, trying to go neither too fast nor too slow, we caught sight of checkpoints being set up on the streets below and traffic halted as troops checked passengers in the vehicles. Tanks had been deployed at key intersections, and at several places I noticed that machine-gun nests had been set up. I had also never seen so many Chinese national flags on display. They seemed to be mimicking American displays of patriotism.

But we made it to the drop-off point two blocks away from the safe house without incident, and this time I was the one getting out, donning my ridiculous surgical mask, dark glasses, and hat. Before I rang the bell, I had the presence of mind to take off the mask and dark glasses so I would be recognized and not taken for a stranger. This time, it was Brother Li himself who answered the door, with a very fidgeting and worried-looking McHale directly behind him.

I had planned to greet Brother Li very briefly, thank him for sheltering McHale, and then hurry Chuck out to the car. But Brother Li had other ideas. "Would you please come in for a few minutes? I need to tell you some things about Great Master Wu," he said, drawing me by the arm into a reception room off the vestibule, "about Qi, and about Qigong."

He motioned us to sit down on the simple rattan chairs as he closed the door, then sat down himself. Perched on the edge of his seat, his whole body conveying earnestness, Brother Li continued: "You may not think this is very important because a coup is taking place right now in Guangzhou, and you are anxious to leave. But we think there are spiritual forces involved in this. I don't know exactly what you believe. You are not a brother, but you are trusted by brothers in Hong Kong whom we trust. This is what we think: we are totally against Qigong. We have had many people become believers because they have dabbled with Qigong and it made them very confused. We even heard of one Beida student whose mind had for awhile become controlled at a distance by a Qigong master practicing external Qi. We think there are occult forces involved."

"Occult forces? What do you mean by occult forces?" I asked. I was torn between the need to get this conversation over with as quickly as possible and get moving, and the intriguing turn it had taken, and the desire to figure out what he was talking about.

"Qigong is derived from the ancient Chinese traditions of shamanism. Shamans invoke demons to come and possess them. Today, in some Daoist temples, the same thing happens. The Daoist believers ask the local gods of the temple to possess them personally. You know, it's a form of idol worship." Now he'd gotten my attention. This is what McHale had told Lasch in their enigmatic conversation the last time the two had talked. I glanced at McHale. His face was registering all this, but he didn't comment on how closely Brother Li had confirmed his own judgments to Lasch.

"Idol worship?" I said. "That sounds pretty strange."

"Strange and evil," Brother Li said, emphatically emphasizing "evil." "We are sure that it is evil. Look, I won't go into all the spiritual reasons or what the Bible says. I don't think you would understand or agree." Well, he had that right, I thought. "But, if nothing else, just look at what Wu is preaching. First, he wants to throw out all the foreigners. Next, he wants to overthrow the government in Beijing. Then he wants to attack Taiwan. That will mean war and thousands, perhaps millions, of Chinese on both sides of the Taiwan Straits will lose their lives."

"Well, I understand that," I interrupted, "but what do these Qigong people mean when they talk about China recovering her Qi? What is China's Qi?"

"I believe China's Qi is the Qi—the breath of God—that is in *sheng ling*"—he used the Chinese term for Holy Spirit—"and I believe China will never play her true role in the destiny of mankind until she submits to God and takes on God's Qi, which is the Holy Spirit."

This was all getting way beyond me: China's Qi, God's Qi, and now the Holy Spirit too? I didn't know what to make of all this, and out of the corner of my eye could see McHale worriedly looking at his watch.

"All right," I said, "I'm not sure I understand what you are saying, but I'm sorry, I really don't think we have time to talk more about this. What do you want us to tell Brother David if—no, when—we get back?" I was amazed that in all the excitement of the evening I managed to remember Herman Fielding's code name right.

"Oh, you will get back," Brother Li said confidently, nodding his head for emphasis. "Just tell them to keep on praying for us."

"Of course. But how are you so sure we'll get back OK?"

Brother Li smiled ever so slightly. "I just know," he said.

Turning to McHale with an apologetic look, he said, "I am sorry to keep you just these five minutes, but I think in the future you will understand." He looked long and hard at me, and said slowly, "I know Ai Erdun will."

I had no idea what he meant, but there was no time to ask. I shook Brother Li's hand warmly, but to my surprise, he wanted to hug me—virtually unheard of for a Chinese man. But with everything he'd done for us, I wasn't about to refuse. So, somewhat embarrassed, I embraced him awkwardly. Then, after putting my head out the front door a fraction to make sure no one was observing us, I quickly led the way to Weiming's car, with McHale following.

As soon as we'd climbed into the backseat, Yao briskly took charge again. "Take Zhongshan Avenue West toward the Nanhai Temple. Before it reaches Nanhai, the name changes to Huangpu Road East," he told Weiming. "If you see any checkpoints ahead, let me know immediately."

I looked at McHale, who appeared as exhausted as I was beginning to feel. It was approaching midnight, and we had to somehow clear the city by daylight if we were to have any chance of getting out of China safely. McHale leaned over the front seat and, in surprisingly poor Mandarin, tried to elicit from Yao the plan for getting us out of China, but all Yao would say was, "Everything's arranged. You will see." Eventually, McHale gave up and seemed to subside into the backseat. Soon, he and I had both dozed off as Weiming drove the eighteen miles to Nanhai.

Less than half an hour later, I woke with a start. Yao was jabbing me and McHale.

"What's happening?" I asked blearily.

"Road block ahead," he answered. "You two will have to get into the trunk."

"What?" I said. "Are you crazy? We can't both fit in there!"

"You're just going to have to," Yao said grimly. "It's the only chance you have. If they see a foreigner in the car, we will all be arrested. Quickly now. Weiming is going to pull into a spot just up ahead where we will be out of sight of the roadblock. As soon as we stop, both of you get in the trunk!" he ordered, then softened and added, "We'll let you out as soon as it is safe."

McHale surprised me by raising no objection to this, his earlier feistiness perhaps tamed by the long night's tensions. At a bend in the road, Weiming pulled the car off the shoulder so that we were out of the line of sight of the roadblock looming about three hundred yards ahead. There was a bus ahead of us, and the time it would take to inspect the IDs of all the passengers might be just enough time for us to get into the trunk.

Weiming pulled the lever next to the driver's seat to unlatch the trunk, then leaped out of the car to make sure we got in it as quickly as possible. A quick—and rather obvious—question rose in my mind that I put to Yao immediately. "What happens if they want to inspect the trunk?" I said.

"They won't," Yao briskly replied. "They're looking for people not bombs. I'll sit in the backseat now so that it looks like Weiming is my driver. I think my PSB pass will get us through."

McHale and I climbed in and arranged ourselves as comfortably as we could, considering that he must have weighed two hundred pounds though he was shorter than me by several inches. The small Toyota had a surprisingly roomy trunk for a car of its size, but still I silently cursed Chuck's heft and my height as we somehow folded ourselves almost double. Without a word, Weiming slammed the trunk shut. My head must have been raised a little too high because the lid came down hard on my temple. Then the Toyota almost screeched as it lurched forward.

I mustered up the wit to say to McHale in a stage whisper, "This is about as close to the CIA as I ever want to get." He chuckled and that helped lower the tension, though it did nothing to lessen the throbbing in my head from being hit by the lid of the trunk and the sharp pains that were shooting up my back from our cramped and unnatural contortion. I wondered, in a curiously detached way, how long the air would last.

The Toyota was at the checkpoint in less than a minute. I heard Yao present his ID first, from the backseat. Then Weiming, too, offered up his ID and driver's license. There was the sound of a brief conversation between Yao and one of the soldiers, some laughter, and we were off again.

After what seemed an eternity, but probably was less than a few minutes, the car pulled off the road again and the trunk popped open, a worried-looking Weiming staring down at us. With considerable pain as my joints untangled themselves, I slowly got out of the trunk, helped by Weiming. Yao extended his arm to McHale.

"What happened back there?" I asked as we got back in the car.

"It was very easy," Yao replied. "As soon as they saw my PSB pass, they let me through. I told them I was traveling to see my mother who had suddenly gotten sick earlier in the evening. They believed me."

Shaken, and still in some pain from being in the trunk, McHale and I were both now wide awake. We still didn't know where Yao intended to take us.

As though he had been reading my mind, Yao now turned around in his front seat and looked at both of us.

"We are going to a place beyond the Nanhai Temple, right at the edge of the Pearl River. There a boat will pick us up and take us into Hong Kong waters. Of course, Hong Kong is now under Chinese control, so we won't automatically be safe once we get there. But I think the Hong Kong Special Administrative Region will not throw its hand in with Guangzhou and will await orders from the central authorities in Beijing. Mr. McHale," he said, looking straight at Chuck, "I have fulfilled my end of the bargain by helping you leave China. Now do I have your assurance that you will take care of me in Hong Kong?"

"As soon as we are in Hong Kong waters, I will set things in motion to get you to the United States. We won't let you down," McHale said confidently.

He said it as though it was a done deal, but I wasn't so sure. To get Yao out of Hong Kong would require immense expenditure of resources by the U.S. government and would almost certainly involve the U.S. Navy. Washington might be willing to do that for Chuck McHale, who was one of their own. But for a completely unknown Chinese police officer who was coming in from the cold? Maybe it was my natural skepticism, enhanced by years as a hack, but it just didn't seem likely to me.

We drove on for perhaps another half hour and passed on our right the Nanhai Temple, the only surviving temple to the God of the Sea in China.

Initially built in the sixth century and still covering 323,000 square feet today, it looked out over the approach to Guangzhou from the ocean. In ancient times, sailors came to the temple to pray for a safe and smooth trip before setting out to sea, and I now wondered idly if we wouldn't benefit from a stop there ourselves.

But it was during the Sui dynasty, a few hundred years later, that Nanhai was at its most glorious, the Sunbathing Pavilion being one of the most favored places in China from which to view the sunset. During the Tang dynasty, Guangzhou had enjoyed a thriving trade with the other side of the Indian Ocean, and both Chinese and foreign ships had sailed back and forth over what was sometimes described as the "marine Silk Road." Guangzhou in the eighth century had even had a foreign quarter with as many as 120,000 Arabs living in it.

Not long after we passed the temple, we turned off the main road and drove down a roughly surfaced side road to what I guessed must have been the bank of the Pearl River, but in the inky darkness, I couldn't see a thing.

We stopped, and for a moment nobody moved or said anything. Then Yao turned around again. "We now have another stage in the journey, perhaps not as dangerous as the one just now by road but still risky. We are going to board a high-speed boat and head toward Hong Kong, but when we arrive there it will once again be very dangerous. You, Mr. McHale, and Ireton, may be all right if the Hong Kong authorities come across us, but I will be in great danger. I am relying on you, Mr. McHale, to ensure our safe passage out of Hong Kong."

I gulped once again on hearing this. I knew that McHale couldn't possibly have had time to plan for, much less arrange, any Hong Kong logistics, and we might be less than three hours away from Hong Kong landfall once we got on whatever conveyance Yao had arranged.

McHale, however, seemed to be unaffected by any similar worries. "Mei wenti (No problem)," he said, as though he'd done this a hundred times.

We were still in the car mulling over the next stage of the trip when a figure came toward us out of the darkness of some trees. We all saw him at the same moment, and I looked questioningly at Yao.

"Lao Zhao (Old Zhao)," he said, using the typical greeting for an older person who is both respectful and affectionate. Then to us he said, "He is our guide for the next part of the trip."

We got out of the car and stood up to stretch ourselves. Weiming found two plastic bottles of water that had been in the trunk all this time, and we passed them around, each taking a few gulps. Zhao—we never did learn his given name—was a larger-than-average Cantonese who I judged to be in his sixties. His hair was short, almost crew cut, and was salt-and-pepper all the way through. He was wearing jeans, hiking boots, and a nylon windbreaker over a very worn-looking Adidas T-shirt.

Weiming now looked at me and, for the first time in hours, actually cracked a smile. "I think my job is over now," he said. "I will go back to Guangzhou and tell Giuseppe everything that happened. Do you expect ever to come back to Guangzhou?"

"No doubt about it," I said, "as soon as all this stuff calms down. I actually like the city. Thank you, Weiming. I don't think we will ever be able to repay you for everything you have done."

"Oh yes, you will," he said with a serious look now. "I plan to go to America to study, and I will need your help getting a visa." At this, he looked meaningfully at McHale.

Chuck reached out his hand immediately and said, "Weiming, if I have to sit on the desk of the consular officer in Guangzhou who handles your case, I will see that you get that visa."

Weiming laughed, shook hands in turn with McHale, Yao, and me, then without further comment, he got into the Toyota, backed into a three-point turn, and headed back up the dirt road. I was a little sad to see him go. He had impressed me with his cool head and rare maturity, and, of course, I now owed him a huge debt. I didn't know how I would ever repay him, but I sincerely hoped this was not the last I would see of him.

I turned my attention now to Zhao, who had been hanging back while all this was happening, engrossed in picking his teeth with a toothpick. He looked as weather-beaten and tanned as any man I had ever seen. But it was his mouth in particular that struck me. His teeth were yellowed and ill-formed, almost grotesquely, and when he spoke, he revealed gums that were an unhealthy bright pink. I suspected that he had never been to a dentist his whole life, and I remembered that Chairman Mao's teeth had been similarly yellowed because, according to his doctor, he believed that he could do without toothpaste if he swilled his mouth out with tea after eating.

"Hao le ma? (Ready?)" Zhao asked in Mandarin but with a heavy Cantonese accent.

"Hao le (Yes)," Yao said for all of us.

"Zouba! (Let's go!)" he said, and without waiting for acknowledgment, turned and headed toward the trees. I had seen no sign of the river, even though I assumed it must be nearby. The dirt road had ended at a tennis-court-sized open area with crumbling brick walls on three sides. It reeked of urine—not the kind of place you'd choose for a picnic.

We walked single file on a narrow path through thickly clustered trees, stepping over what seemed like Banyan tree roots. At one point, I heard a hasty rustling quite close to me on the left and wondered if we had unwittingly disturbed a wild pig, dog, or maybe a large rat. I didn't ask.

A few minutes later, we found ourselves on the bank of a small creek, barely wide enough for a launch to navigate and too narrow for anything but a rowboat to turn around in. A low, dark shape, about forty feet long, loomed in the dark. This, apparently, was our next mode of transport.

As we approached, another man appeared out of the gloom. "This is Wang," Zhao said simply, and the three of us said, "Ni hao (hello)" almost in unison.

Zhao produced a powerful flashlight from a holster clipped to the back of his jeans that had escaped my notice. He switched it on and illuminated the launch. Wang and Zhao quickly set about preparing the craft, removing a protective tarpaulin that had also concealed the boat from anyone who was not looking straight at it. My reporting instincts were instantly aroused by all of this. I wanted to know who owned the boat, how often it was used, what it was generally used for, where it usually went. But I thought better of asking any questions right now. I knew Yao would be annoyed, and I didn't want to delay our departure by a minute.

Zhao and Wang wordlessly worked together in a practiced choreography without a single wasted movement. Just three minutes later, they were brusquely motioning the three of us toward a cockpit featuring a three-seat bench of artificial leather and a passenger area behind with two seats, each also for three people. McHale was first to board, showing a surprising agility for someone of his size. Then Yao got in, and I followed. All three of us sat in the passenger area.

As I followed the passing beam of Zhao's flashlight to look around, I saw that behind the passenger area was a much larger open area capable of holding substantially sized cargo. "What do you usually transport in this?" I asked Zhao as he prepared to cast off.

"Oh, Mercedes, Jaguars. We even brought out a Ferrari once."

So . . . they were car smugglers. Well, they weren't the only ones. For years, thieves have been stealing luxury vehicles in Hong Kong and transporting them to Guangdong and other coastal provinces for sale, often enough to the PLA or the PSB. I remembered a story about a woman who left the Hong Kong Country Club after a tennis game, found her car missing, called up the cell phone installed in the car, and heard the insolent voice of the thief telling her, "Yes, we have your car and we are taking it to China." In the 1990s, when the activity was at its height, a smuggler pocketed $2,500 to more than $12,000 per vehicle and could turn around one hundred vehicles a month. When China's leadership launched a big anti-smuggling campaign in the mid-1990s, they estimated that the value of all goods—not just cars, but electronics, cigarettes, even imported beer and plastic to make garden chairs—smuggled into China totaled more than $1 billion every year.

Well, Yao's knowledge of the criminal world of Guangzhou had now come to good use, I thought.

With Zhao fending us off the narrow banks of the creek with a pole and Wang at the steering wheel and throttle of the launch, we backed slowly out of our hiding place. It took us several minutes of this slow backward progress before the creek suddenly ended and we found ourselves on a broad stretch of the Pearl River. Now Wang turned us around so that we were headed out toward the main channel. We drifted downstream within about fifty yards of the shore with the engine idling for several minutes while Zhao talked into a mobile phone.

Yao saw me watching all this very intently and explained. "These men are car smugglers," he said. "They've each spent time in jail more than once. But I helped them out once when I was a junior officer in Foshan County, not yet in the foreign affairs section. They were in court on a charge of an unpaid truck license—the authorities didn't know they had a boat as well or they would have confiscated it. I would guess at this moment that Zhao is calling someone further downstream to find out who's on the river."

I nodded. I knew from experience that it was *guanxi* that oiled the mechanisms of nearly all relationships in China; someone did you a favor and you did them one in return. Nothing was ever written down, and nothing ever needed to be said. But everyone understood the way this centuries-old exchange worked. So when Yao had called Zhao and Wang, as I guessed, from the alley by Yao's apartment earlier in the evening, they had understood that it was payback time for them.

I pressed a button on my digital watch, and it lit up to reveal the time: close to 1:00 a.m. It would start to get light in four hours, and we needed to be well into Hong Kong waters by then.

With a roar and a lurch that pinned all three of us briefly to our seats, the launch took off without warning. It accelerated until it was traveling close to fifty miles per hour, by my estimate. At first, I was exhilarated; surely no PLA patrol boat could catch us going at this speed. But then I realized that a patrol boat that saw us zooming past didn't need to catch us. It could rake us with fifty-millimeter machine-gun fire, which would either blow us out of the water or send us quickly to the bottom. What an inglorious end that would be to a promising journalistic career, to be riddled with machine-gun bullets on China's Pearl River on the way to Hong Kong in the company of a CIA agent and a defecting PSB officer.

After a few minutes at this breakneck speed, I realized something else: we seemed to have the river pretty much to ourselves, at least so far. In the distance were one or two slow-moving freighters, probably bound for Guangzhou. Relaxing a little, I turned to Yao, my reporter's curiosity surfacing again. "Don't these boats ever attract attention from naval patrol boats?" I asked.

"Very seldom," he said. "Zhao's never been shot at, but a few times he's had to make the launch go at its highest possible speed to escape interception."

"And what's the fastest it can go?" I asked.

"I don't know. Let me ask Zhao."

He shouted the question in Cantonese toward the cockpit. Zhao grinned for the first time and shouted back over the noise of engine, "Maybe one hundred kilometers an hour." So my estimate of fifty miles per hour—about eighty kilometers per hour—had not been far off the mark.

My attention was now caught by what looked to be a Chinese patrol boat moving in a direction that would have directly crossed paths with us. I nudged Yao and pointed. He in turn shouted again at Zhao and pointed at it as well. Zhao turned his face toward us and flashed his yellow-tooth smile once more. He said something in Cantonese, which I didn't catch. "He says, 'The patrols are all taken care of this month,'" Yao said.

"Meaning they're paid off?" I asked, knowing I sounded naïve as I said it.

"Yes," he said simply.

Soon, the noise of the two outboards became a monotonous backdrop to the regular thump-thump of the launch rising with the slight swell and falling onto the surprisingly calm surface of the Pearl River estuary. Being out on the open water in the middle of the night and at the speeds we were traveling, I was soon chilled by the wind and the spray. I looked enviously at Zhao's windbreaker, wishing I had something more substantial than my tropical suit, which apart from providing no warmth whatsoever was looking rather rumpled now.

We soon passed the Humen Fort, a looming presence over the river, which meant we were only about forty-five miles from Hong Kong. The fort, the "Boca Tigris" (mouth of the Tiger), guarded the Pearl River approach to Guangzhou and had frequently been attacked by British naval forces throughout the nineteenth century from the Opium War onward. Now rapidly coming closer on the left was the Shenzhen airport. Zhao steered the launch farther out into the estuary as we approached so we would be less noticeable. Of course, we carried no lights, and the sight of an unlit craft tearing out of Chinese territorial waters in the early hours of the morning would certainly have aroused curiosity if anyone had been paying any attention. I wondered if the radar operators at Shenzhen had been paid off as well.

About ninety minutes had passed, and, though it was still dark, we had to make landfall and Zhao would have to be well on his way back before the first light of dawn. There was no time to waste.

I had not thought to ask Zhao where exactly he planned to take us until now. I turned to McHale, who had fallen asleep again, stretched out on the other three-person bench, his arms wrapped tightly around his chest in an attempt to stay warm. With the cold and the thumping and rollicking of the boat, I marveled that he could sleep at all; the man must have been thoroughly exhausted. Hating to do it, I nudged him awake. "Where on earth should Zhao drop us off in Hong Kong?" I asked him. For a moment, he looked as though he hadn't a clue where he was or what was going on. He blinked slowly a few times, then to my surprise said, "Lantau Island."

I wanted to know what Zhao himself had in mind and asked Yao to ask him in Cantonese. Zhao's response was the same, "Lantau."

"But that's where the airport is!" I protested to McHale.

"Chek Lap Kok, the airport, is on the north side of the island. Zhao will probably drop us off on the southern part of the western tip of Lantau."

"How do you know that?"

"I've lived in Hong Kong for many years, and I've been to most of the outlying islands in somebody or other's junk. Lantau is by far the largest of the Hong Kong islands and has the longest coastline. It makes a whole lot more sense to land us there than to fiddle around with some of the totally obscure islands farther out. After awhile, you get to think of these things, you know."

Well, I suppose you did if you were CIA. However, if you were a reporter using Hong Kong mainly as a base for traveling around Southeast Asia, you didn't think about those sorts of things much at all, and you had precious little time for the outings on private junks that Hong Kong expatriates had long been famous for.

"Try your mobile," McHale said.

I took the phone out of my pocket and, from force of habit, called the bureau in Hong Kong even though I was sure no one would be there now.

But I was wrong. Someone picked up.

"*Epoch*. Meitnic," he said.

"Jeez, Steve," I said, "what are you doing in the bureau at this hour of the night."

"Waiting for you to call, of course," he replied dryly, then more urgently, "Rick, where are you?"

"Well," I said, "I'm on a car smuggler's launch heading for Lantau Island."

"Are you OK?"

"Aside from having a gazillion-dollar Triad contract on my life and needing a shower and a bed, I'm fine."

"Is McHale with you?"

"Yeah. Has Lasch roped you into this too?"

"Has he? You'd think you were the last surviving Japanese soldier in the Philippines the way he's mobilized practically every single *Epoch* reporter in the world to keep a watch out for you. He's had Hensley fly in from Bangkok, and Morrow's landed in Beijing to see if they can do anything from that end. So what's the plan?"

"Steve, I don't know. Let me talk to McHale and see if he can think something up. I'll call you right back. Meanwhile, alert Lasch, would you, that we're close to home, and tell him to prepare to put a full-court press on Washington to facilitate our insertion back into the normal world. By the way, how's the coup going?"

"Looks like it's going to fizzle. Beijing mobilized its conventional forces with surprising speed, made a public announcement—not like the Foreign Ministry's usual sleepwalking speed, if you ask me—that any action taken against Taiwan would be contrary to government policy. They also seem to have gotten control of all the other military regions and forestalled any action by them sympathetic to the coup. There's reportedly an arc of pro-government troops positioned north and east of Guangzhou to prevent any Guangzhou breakout into the rest of China. Washington says it supports the central government in this one and will lend any help requested to restore central authority."

"Just so long as we are not talking about Taiwan," I said cynically.

"Right. Look, go have your parley with McHale and call me right back. Bye."

I repeated to McHale—and then to Yao in Mandarin—the news that Meitnic had given me about the coup. "Not surprised," he said. Yao just nodded.

"Well, what do we do now?" I asked McHale.

"We've got to get off Lantau as soon as possible after arriving there. There's a good possibility that Hong Kong government choppers will be flying over every part of the Hong Kong Special Administrative Region looking, not for us, but for rebels who might be trying to hightail it here. But that doesn't help us. I know it will sound crazy to you, but the only way we can reenter Hong Kong without alerting the whole SAR security system and Beijing as well is to enter the territory legally from the Philippines. And we've got to go through the motions of landing there legally too. But it's a lot easier to land there than to land here.

"Who do you know with a junk that can get to Lantau ASAP and take us on board?" he asked me. "At least that way we can be hidden in a safe place until everything else is in place to get us to the Philippines."

"Look," I shot back, incredulous that he seemed to think I hung around with the junk-owning crowd, "you've probably been on more junks around these parts than anyone. The only junk I've ever been on is Harry Wok's, and fat chance of getting that before dawn on a weekday."

McHale thought for a moment and then brightened up. "I know, the Sutherlands. He's an American banker who, I happen to know, is on vacation this week and is hanging around on his junk." Then, just as quickly, his face fell. "Problem is, I've no way of getting hold of him. I don't have any mobile phone number for him and, of course, there's no one at his office right now."

He fell silent again, apparently stumped. We looked at each other for a few minutes. Was this whole mad escapade going to fail for want of a phone number?

"Does he have kids who go to the Island School?" I asked tentatively.

"I think so. Why?"

"Because I've got the mobile of one of the teachers there whom I dated about six months ago. Fortunately, we parted on good terms, so I don't think she would hang up on me if I call her, even at this hour. It's possible she might be able to reach him. I'll give it a try."

I took out my PDA and looked up Christina Short. She was a twenty-something-year-old from Nebraska. I had been, to be honest, more attracted to her mind than the rest of her. But we'd gone to a couple concerts together at the Hong Kong Arts Festival, and though we'd never become an item, I liked her and I think she had a liking for me. I punched in her number.

It rang for what seemed like an eternity, and I thought the voice mail was about to kick in when she picked up.

"Yeah, what is it?" the barely conscious voice on the other end said.

"Christina, it's Richard Ireton. Look, I know this is an impossible hour to call. But it's really an emergency. I've got to locate—" I looked to McHale to supply the details, then I repeated them to her—"Mike Sutherland's family—I think he's a junior at your school. I thought you might have a mobile phone number for one of them. This isn't a joke. I actually do have a good reason for calling you in the middle of the night like this. I'll take you to the Mandarin Grill to tell you the whole story."

"Is that a promise, Rick?" She was waking up now.

"Yes it is. Do you have the number?"

"Just a minute, just a minute. I was totally asleep when you called." There was the sound of paper being shuffled around, purses being opened and rummaged through, and finally a triumphant cry.

"I've got it," she said. I'd taken out my notebook, and now I quickly scribbled the number down, repeated it to her to make sure I had it right, and thanked her.

"Rick, are you OK?" she said in a sort of dreamy voice.

"I am now that I know we can get off Lantau Island. Thanks, Christina."

I hung up and immediately called up the Sutherland boy. Once again, the phone seemed to ring forever.

"Yeah," he said in a slurred voice. "Who is this?"

I gave the phone to McHale, who handled the call perfectly. "Mike," he said, "I know it's a crazy hour to call, but this really is an emergency. It's Chuck McHale. I was out on your family boat three weeks ago. Can you give the phone to your dad?"

There was a silence as McHale listened to the boy's reply. "Yes, I know you'll have to wake him," he said patiently, "but when he hears what I've got to say he won't be mad at either you or me. Look, imagine you got a call in the middle of the night from a CIA officer who needed your dad's help to prevent the outbreak of World War III. Would that do it for you?"

With the phone still to his ear, McHale winked at me. It amazed me that this overweight, middle-aged, hard-boiled intelligence agent could actually be quite adept on the phone with teenagers. Finally, I saw him concentrate again.

"Roy," he said, "really sorry to pull this one on you, but it's actually a matter of national security for the United States."

Pause.

"No, I'm not kidding. Have you heard about the coup in China?"

Pause.

"In Guangzhou. It started a few hours ago, the local military trying to force the hand of Beijing against Taiwan. I'm told they may have the coup under control, but meanwhile I'm a fugitive from the mainland with an American reporter and a Chinese security officer with me. Someone who brought us this far is going to set us down on Lantau Island. Could you bring your junk around to pick us up as soon as possible? It will be increasingly risky during the day because of Hong Kong's patrols."

Pause.

"I'm guessing we'll need to be on your boat for only a few hours. I'll get the U.S. Navy to take us off your hands. We'll be on the southwestern tip of Lantau. If you approach the coast slowly, we'll spot you and come out of wherever we're hiding and get your attention."

Pause.

McHale now began to chuckle at something Sutherland was saying to him.

"Yeah, Roy, I promise to personally introduce you to the director of Central Intelligence in Langley, Virginia, when this thing is over and you are next in the States. . . . Hold on, I'll ask." McHale now turned to Yao. "How long do you think it will be before we make it to the southwestern tip of Lantau?" he asked.

Yao repeated the question to Zhao in Cantonese and translated back his reply into Mandarin.

"About another forty-five minutes," McHale said back into the phone. "Yes, we'll be there waiting, and our boat will be gone well before you get there. See you later. And, Roy, thanks."

I noticed that Yao was becoming more subdued as all this was going on. I suspected that he was sobered by the realization that at this point there was absolutely nothing over which he had any control. Even Zhao seemed to shrink a little, as though Hong Kong were still culturally alien to him, despite having traveled this smuggler's route probably hundreds of times. Wang, in the cockpit with him, never said a thing.

I asked for the phone back to call Meitnic again and tell him our plans. He was as chatty now as he had been a half hour earlier. "Steve, here's the plan," I said. "We're going to be dropped on Lantau Island, and"—I suddenly caught myself as it hit me that the phones in the *Epoch* bureau most certainly were tapped right now. "Well, forget Lantau," I said, furiously trying to backpedal, "somewhere in Hong Kong waters, and we'll be met by a friend. Look, I'll get word to you some other way. It's too risky to tell you on the phone right now. But tell Lasch we're all OK and we'll be in touch soon."

I hung up with a sinking feeling that I'd probably just given the whole game away by alerting the authorities to an illegal landing planned for Lantau. What an—

"You need to watch any calls to any American office in Hong Kong," Chuck said unnecessarily. "They are almost certain to be tapped right now. Here, if you don't mind, let me take over with my contacts."

McHale then embarked on what seemed like a blizzard of calls in Hong Kong. Sometimes his rapid, code-type talk seemed quite impenetrable. I caught a few "Phoenix Three" references in his conversation but there were other, obviously coded references that meant nothing to me at all. The gist of it, however, was becoming clear; he was asking the U.S. Navy to take us out of the Sutherlands' junk, transfer us on board a Seventh Fleet carrier, and then quite legally land us in the Philippines either on a carrier shuttle flight or through simple shore leave arrangements when the fleet anchored off Manila. At that point, Chuck and I could legally reenter Hong Kong and no one in the Special Administrative Region would know that we had illegally left China, illegally arrived in Hong Kong, and then illegally left Hong Kong as well. The question that bothered me was this: Was the CIA going to come through for Yao?

I sensed that Yao was becoming increasingly uneasy as McHale went to work on the details of the Hong Kong extraction. Chuck explained nothing to him as he made his flurry of phone calls.

Directly ahead us now, we could see the lights of the airport and aircraft taking off and landing. Chek Lap Kok had been built on one of the largest land reclamation projects anywhere in the world, literally thousands of tons of landfill dumped off Lantau in one of the deepest harbors in Asia. It was an artificial construction all right, but right now, with its familiar and orderly terminal buildings and hangars, it looked a lot more real than the launch we were riding in, thudding across Hong Kong's waters. We began to head further out to sea now as Lantau approached, anxious to stay clear of the coastline until we could actually land on the southwestern tip of the island. The water became rougher, and Zhao had to slow down considerably so the craft could ride the waves better.

I turned to Chuck again. "You know, Yao's really worried," I said. "Are you sure he's gonna be all right? I mean, have you got an absolute assurance he'll be given political asylum?"

"No I haven't! That's above my pay grade. The most I can do right now is to get the Navy to agree to take him aboard on a temporary basis, as though he had been rescued at sea."

"Chuck, we've got to do better than that for him. There's no way I'm going to allow myself to be rescued by the U.S. Navy if there's any doubt about his status."

"You mean, you're going to refuse to be rescued unless his situation is resolved?"

"In a word, yes."

"Rick, we're in the real world here. This isn't the time to be playing Mother Teresa or Joan of Arc."

"Nor is it the time to be playing Benedict Arnold."

"What do you expect me to do, call the White House and have a chat with the president?"

"If you could get through, yes."

We both fell silent as the launch, a lot slower now, headed around Lantau on its long, wide arc.

"Can I have my phone back?" I asked.

McHale looked at me as if I was going to push him overboard, but he handed it over. I looked at the battery level and groaned. It would probably close down in three or four minutes. Now we were really in a fix. I couldn't call the bureau for fear the line was bugged, and I couldn't be sure the phone would last long enough to cover an intelligent conversation with anyone else.

I suddenly realized there was one person I could call and would probably get through to—Trish. She might be our only hope.

I dialed the number, and she picked up after the third ring.

"Hello?" Just hearing her deep, low voice helped settle my nerves a bit.

"Trish, it's me, Richard. Look, I have very little time before my cell phone shuts down so I've got to be really quick. Trish, it's no longer life or death for me, but it might be for a Chinese man with us if we don't make arrangements for him to get asylum. We're about to be dropped off on Lantau Island by a boat that shouldn't be there at all. It's all totally illegal. Then we're going to be picked up by an expatriate junk and transferred to a U.S. Navy ship for passage to the Philippines.

"Trouble is, there's no guarantee the Chinese guy will get asylum in the U.S. If he doesn't and has to go back to China, they'll execute him for sure, simple as that. And the blood will be on our hands. I know this is all very sudden and I'm practically stampeding over my own words getting them out, but is there any possible way you could do something about this on the Philippine end? Let me give you two phone numbers. One's my boss in New York, Burt Lasch, and one's a mobile phone on the boat that's coming to pick us up." I gave her Lasch's number and Mike's and made her repeat them.

"Thank God you're safe, Rick. I was really worried about you after your last call. I told Clarissa, and she"—the phone went dead.

But at least Trish had two crucial phone numbers: Burt's and the Sutherlands' on the boat. Now everything was out of my hands too. McHale looked at me and I smiled wanly. Then I looked at Yao and smiled at him with what I hoped was a bit more confidence. To myself, I said, Somehow, this is all going to work out.

Chapter Twelve

The first light of dawn was slowly peeling the darkness away from the hillsides of Lantau as we rounded the most westerly tip of the island and searched for a point to take the launch in. In the darkness, we couldn't make out any beach, and I could tell that Zhao didn't like the looks of the rocks. One of the problems was finding a spot from which we could observe arriving boats but stay hidden. Hong Kong's helicopter fleet did a good job of patrolling all parts of the territory, and the last thing we needed now was a run-in with the Hong Kong police.

But the swell was light, and that, at least, made our landing less hazardous than it might have been. Eventually, after going back and forth twice and rather riskily shining his flashlight on the shoreline from about fifty yards away, Zhao was satisfied he could take us in. It was an extremely narrow patch of gravelly beach, barely wider than four launches abreast, but it was at the foot of a less steep slope of the shoreline than other parts. He slowed the boat down to a little above idling speed and nosed us in.

Wang was first off the bow with the bow line in hand, and he stood in shallow water holding the boat steady. Then Yao, McHale, and I, after thanking Zhao profusely and pumping his hands furiously, trying to express unspeakable gratitude, jumped off the bow, trying not to get our feet wet in the process. We all failed, of course, and splashed loudly as we landed. I could feel the seawater squelching around in my dress loafers.

Yao had huddled with Zhao for a few minutes before we came close in to the shore, and I assumed that he was going over any monetary arrangements that still needed fixing. Although Zhao had certainly paid back a great debt he owed Yao from Zhao's previous run-in with Chinese law, the payback was not going to be free; that much was understood. I hoped the

U.S. government was going to come through with money for this, but it didn't look at all clear at the moment.

Zhao didn't waste any time hanging around, and as soon as Wang was back on board, the launch was back out in deep water and roaring back toward the Pearl River estuary. Zhao was really gunning the two outboards now, no doubt worried about those dawn patrols he had been warned about. I was sorry to see him go. He was another Chinese who had risked his life for us and for our newfound Chinese ally, and my admiration for his courage knew no bounds—car smuggler or not.

The slope was less steep in this part of the island's corner coastline than in other places, and we were able to scramble up one hundred feet or so to some thick bushes. Getting ourselves hidden under them was difficult and painful; but after a few minutes' squirming and some muttered "ouchs" from each of us, we were safely underneath, invisible to all but a helicopter directly overhead. Inexplicably, Yao now started to cry, great dry, wracking sobs of remorse, grief, relief—we didn't know what. McHale and I looked at each other, unsure what to do and more than a little embarrassed. We decided it would be best to just let him get it out of his system. I figured if he wanted to tell us what was tearing him up, he would.

The sun was beginning to climb in the sky behind our shoulders and in the slopes of the shore way in the east. We were all as thirsty as camels coming out of China's Taklimakan desert, and I, for one, was getting hungry too. I hadn't eaten anything since the banquet, and a large part of that meal was on the cement floor of an execution chamber in the Ming Garden Restaurant back in Er Sha Island. That all seemed like half a lifetime ago now.

From our perch, we had a clear view of the waters off western Lantau, and unless Sutherland had completely misunderstood where to begin his search for us, I was confident that we would rendezvous successfully.

But McHale wasn't, and he began to look at his watch ever more frequently, getting increasingly and visibly irritated over the wait. Strange, I thought, what you learn about people's real character when they are under great stress.

I thought it might take his mind off of things in the present if I asked him how he had come to run into such trouble with the Triads in the first place. He seemed happy for the distraction.

"I'd been cultivating a friend in the general staff of the Guangzhou Military Region. He'd been unusually friendly with me at a reception Josh Ehrenfold organized at the consulate, and I assumed, as one always does in these situations, that he wanted help getting his kid to some college in the States. So I played along, and we met for lunch a couple of times. It was all very relaxed and friendly.

"Then one day he called up and said, kind of panicky, that he couldn't meet with me anymore, that he was sorry, but some really important things had come up.

"I knew right away that someone had been observing his contact with me and had cut him off. But I didn't know why. Then, in a casual conversation with Josh, I learned about the rising prominence of Great Master Wu and his Qigong adept followers. Josh told me that a number of senior officers had been turning down invitations to events at the consulate that they had previously attended with some eagerness. One of them had confided to him that Wu was beginning to influence the thinking of the general staff toward foreigners and that he suspected anyone who was thought to be getting too close to us would have his knuckles rapped.

"At that point, I began nosing around the Guangzhou Qigong Scientific Research Association and asking a few, you know, naïve questions. That's when I began to uncover these strange Triad connections because one of the research officials, almost casually, mentioned Tung's name, probably assuming it wouldn't mean anything to me. I'd been scheduled to meet with that official a second time, a day later, and he flatly told me that Tung's 'friends'—meaning the Triads, of course—had been watching my movements and didn't want him to have anything to do with me anymore.

"So I went to ground immediately, fortunately having made that all-important contact with Brother Li already. I knew that, with their almost ubiquitous presence around town, if any Triad member saw me on the street I would be a goner. Those guys can move so fast even the Russian Mafia could learn a thing or two from them."

He paused and looked at his watch again. It was well after 6:00 a.m., and there was still no sign of the Sutherland boat. Suddenly, a helicopter roared out of nowhere, low over the headland slope where we were hiding, and I could see the markings indicating it belonged to the Hong Kong Marine Police. I suspected they were going too fast to spot us unless they had known in advance where we would be. We watched it fly by us and away, and were relieved that it didn't come back for a second look. But it was a sobering reminder of the new danger we were in.

Hong Kong was a Special Administrative Region of the People's Republic of China, which meant Beijing still did not directly control many aspects of life here. But it certainly did keep firm control over any matters related to China's national security and sovereignty. Had they seen us, the police would have been polite and respectful, but they would probably have arrested us pending investigation, and they almost certainly would have returned Yao to China. I didn't want to contemplate what his fate would be if that happened.

Yao by now had stopped his crying and was subdued and seemed a bit embarrassed. But it was clear he wanted to talk.

"I am sorry that I lost control," he said, "but this is the most serious crisis I have ever faced in my life. I do not want to betray my country, which is what I will do if I come over to the U.S., if I defect. For you, it is nothing, a mere change of point of view perhaps, a new life in a new country, and one that is very accepting of outsiders. But for me, it will be the end of a patriotic journey, in many ways a disgraceful end. Of course, my higher patriotism is toward China's future, China's destiny, which would be ruined by an attack upon Taiwan at this moment"—I didn't like the "at this moment" phrase—"and I was, and am, prepared to cooperate with foreigners to prevent that from happening. But I want you to realize what a high price I am paying."

"We do, Yao, we do," said McHale, now adopting his best be-nice-to-American-teenagers tone. "It is not just the United States but the whole world that will come to appreciate the role you have played in staving off this disaster." He asked me to translate this to be sure Yao understood.

Yao brightened. "You mean not just the United States and China but the whole world will someday learn about this?"

"Yes," said McHale, though I could see the effort to be nice to Yao was causing him some strain.

Just then, Yao cried out, "There's the boat!" as a cruiser, a junk more Lake Tahoe in appearance—and as we were soon to discover, in amenities as well—than anything remotely Chinese, suddenly came into view from the left very close to shore. Sutherland had obviously taken the quickest route to Lantau, which was an approach from the south. After carefully extracting myself from the thorny bush and standing up to make sure there were no helicopters in the vicinity, I quickly took my rumpled and soiled jacket off and started waving it overhead.

Sutherland saw me immediately and cut the engine to idle. He must have looked over the narrow beach that we had landed on and decided against trying to ground the junk on it because it didn't come any closer to shore. But the junk had an inflatable dinghy on its broad main deck. I saw Sutherland and a scantily clad woman—later introduced to us as his wife Amanda—wrestle it into a position where it could be lowered over the side. The three of us scrambled down the slope to the beach.

The junk was idling now about twenty yards off the shore, close enough to talk to Roy Sutherland. "Wait until the dinghy gets to you and get into it as fast as you can," he said, rather redundantly, I thought. "Thanks, Roy. You've got your Langley meeting." Roy barely acknowledged this from McHale and concentrated on keeping the junk in place with forward and reverse thrusts of the engine.

The dinghy had a small outboard motor, and Mike, Roy's son, was manning it with a grin the size of the Great Plains. He obviously relished being part of an exciting international thriller. He brought the dinghy in rather skillfully to the beach and we scrambled in, but it was a tight fit, what with the three of us and with McHale's large size.

As the dinghy approached the junk, I noticed the helicopter again about a mile away. If it came in our direction, the pilot might observe the pick-up in progress. It had apparently taken a sweep of the end of Lantau in a northerly direction, after overflying our position at low level, and was headed back around the end of the island again. Now I could see that it would indeed pass directly overhead.

We all realized this at the same time and scrambled quickly off the dinghy and onto the junk, then hoisted it rapidly up on deck. Roy hustled the three of us below, out of sight. Amanda, in an unbelievably small hot-pink bikini, laid herself out on an air mattress close to the dinghy. Mike lay on his stomach on the deck as though catching the sun as well. Down below in the junk's cabin, we didn't even dare put our faces to the portholes, but we could hear the helicopter approach, circle us slowly and then, to our collective relief, fly off on its original route. We waited until it was barely audible before heading back on deck.

McHale and I realized immediately what we needed to do: get to a working cell phone. We approached Roy, and he started handing his over before we even said anything. As I had done previously, I deferred to McHale and watched him punch an eight-digit number; it was a local call. "Jack," I heard him say, "Is the Navy going to deliver?"

Pause.

"They're not?"

Pause.

"So this is what I get for thirty years of service to Uncle Sam. Here we have the man who almost single-handedly warned the governments of the United States of America and People's Republic of China what was coming down, possibly avoiding the outbreak of war, and the U.S. government is filling out forms in triplicate, not sure whether the guy should be let in! It makes me want to puke." Even Yao, listening to this, could grasp what was happening. Now he began to cry again, very quietly, this time no doubt contemplating his likely demise: kneeling, blindfolded, in a scrubby field outside a Chinese military base with the bullet of an AK-47 assault rifle about to enter the back of his head.

"What are they saying is the reason for not extracting Yao?" I asked.

"Langley has apparently decided that an extraction of a Chinese PSB official right in the middle of a coup d'état against the central government would make it seem we had had a hand in the whole thing. The White House has decided at this point it cannot afford to rub China's nose in it. They say we've got to find our own way to get Yao out although if he makes it to a third country they'll take him in then."

"Let me have the phone," I said, with a calm I did not feel. McHale apologized to whoever Jack was, said good-bye, hung up, and gave the phone to me. I called Trish, and she picked up immediately. She had either risen very early or had been up all night.

"Trish, it's me. Can you talk now?"

"Sure," she said. "Did you get my message?"

"What message?"

"I called the number you gave me of your friends on the junk, asking them to tell you to call as soon as you arrived."

"Well, we haven't had a chance to say two words to one another yet, but I'm here, safely on the Sutherland junk, and I'm calling you. Do you have any news?"

"Yes, Rick, some really good news for you. I think we can get you and your friends to the Philippines. If the Chinese man gets there, I'm quite certain they'll give him asylum, even if the U.S. doesn't. I called my dad to see if he knew of any way of getting you out, and he says his brother is actually in Hong Kong now, on a sailing yacht that's due to return to the Philippines in a couple of days. If you can get all three of you transferred from the junk you are on, you will be able to get out of Hong Kong without the U.S. Navy."

She paused. I was astonished. I knew that Trish was quick on her feet—

I had seen that at the reception in Manila—but I had no idea that she could pull something like this off.

"Rick, did you hear me?" she asked

"Yes, Trish, I'm just trying to take it all in. So you are saying we don't need a chopper, and we can make the transfer to another boat?"

"Yes, but you might have to stay with the Sutherlands another day. It'll take that long to alert my uncle to what's happening and for him to arrange the departure to Manila ahead of schedule. Also, we'll have to think up a place where you can make the transfer that's not in sight of any Hong Kong authorities. It can't be close to Lantau because the port authorities in Hong Kong would be very suspicious of a Philippine sailboat bound for Manila that initially headed in exactly the opposite direction. The yacht right now is in Aberdeen, on the south side of Hong Kong Island. You'll have to make arrangements with my uncle where the transfer will be."

For someone who had arrived in Hong Kong for the first time just a few days ago, Trish was now sounding like a long-time resident. Boy, she was a quick study. My admiration for her—already considerable—was growing by the minute. But I still had questions about this plan.

"But when we get to Manila, how will the authorities accept us as bona fide passengers and not strays that they've picked up en route? I'll bet the Manila port authorities will check the certification of the boat's Hong Kong outgoing manifest, and they won't find McHale's name or mine on the list."

"Yes they will. We're betting that in the confusion and drama of events in Guangzhou overnight the Guangzhou Public Security won't have gotten around to figuring out that you and McHale have already made it out of China. They won't have passed on to the Hong Kong authorities your names. But your names will be on my uncle's outgoing manifest, as crew. What you'll have to arrange is for you and McHale to show up in the Aberdeen Marina in a normal way, find the boat and the captain, and report yourselves as crew. The Chinese man will have to stay on your friends' junk until my uncle's boat is on its way to Manila. Then, to elude radar, he will not be able to be transferred directly from boat to boat on the open water. He'll have to be either in the water swimming or in a very low-radar-profile dinghy when my uncle's boat comes by. The transfer will also have to be made during daylight because I doubt whether the Hong Kong port authorities will let you depart their waters at night. Do you think you can do all this?"

My mind was reeling. Here I was thinking that McHale, Mr. Fixit CIA, would have everything tucked under his belt by now, but it turned out he had been upended by the Washington bureaucracy. But Trish—my sweet, amazingly talented Trish—whom I had quite cavalierly thought of as little more than someone glamorous to hang off my elbow in Hong Kong for a few days was turning into the real savior. I was stunned.

"Trish, what you have just said is simply amazing. I'm sure we can make it happen. I just have one question though: when we arrive in Manila on the yacht and our Chinese friend—his name is Yao, by the way—is there, I mean, what do we say to the Manila authorities?"

"You tell them the truth. You picked Yao up from a dinghy in the open sea outside Hong Kong. I know our government is corrupt and inefficient and many times gets things wrong, but I am quite certain they won't turn back a Chinese defector to the Philippines. Of course, if Yao wants to leave our country and go to America later on, or even if he wants to go back to China, that's his business. Don't worry, even if Uncle Sam won't take him in, he's safe with us."

I found myself suddenly getting choked up as I listened to all this. I now realized that I had been in torment over Yao's fate ever since it began to be clear that getting Yao into the U.S. was not a done deal at all. A few tears started down my cheeks, and I said, barely able to get the words out, "Trish, Trish, I can never, ever, thank you enough for what you have done. Ever. I am so sorry for how I've messed everything up between us. Will you forgive me?"

"Oh Rick, I've already forgiven you. After all, our friendship has only just begun."

"Trish," I said as a few more tears fell, "I love you."

"And I love you, Rick. See you in Manila. Bye."

"Bye."

I wondered who I could call to find out about the coup without having the call traced. Then I had an idea. I would call Meitnic at the Intercon. He might not be there, but his wife Mary surely would be; and she would certainly have been watching TV, keeping track of things.

It was still an unreasonably early hour to call, but as it happened, Meitnic, after getting my second call and communicating what was happening back to New York, had gone back to his hotel. He was wide awake, picked up the phone instantly, and I could hear the TV on in the background.

"Steve," I said, "I don't think they're bugging you there at the Intercon, and even if they are, so what?"

Meitnic broke in, "So you made it to the drop-off point, I take it?"

"Yes, everything's fine. Now tell me what's happening back in Guangzhou," I said, wanting to hear the news.

"Well, I think the coup's a non-starter right now. It seems the Beijing authorities were able to suppress the rebellion before it spread outside of Guangzhou. Hong Kong, of course, never joined in and would have done so only at gunpoint. But the Central Military Commission in Beijing realized within minutes that deployments in the Guangzhou Military Region were taking place that had not been authorized by the central government. Neighboring military regions were immediately ordered to send out forces to take up blocking positions, so that if Guangzhou rebel forces tried to move north by land, they could be stopped.

"Apparently, Guangzhou's dissident colonels hadn't done their homework very well," he continued. "There was only one unit in Fujian Province that was willing to go along with them, and that was apparently surrounded immediately and taken into custody. Then—you'll love this—the PLA dropped an entire airborne division on Guangzhou at dawn, maybe an hour ago. There's been a lot of fighting inside the city, but it's dying down. Great Master Wu was arrested soon after the drop. Tung Chi-keung apparently had arranged his own escape beforehand, and no one knows where he is at the moment. But he's a marked man, and everyone CNN talked to seemed to think he'd be caught pretty quickly.

"The bad news is that several more foreigners were attacked on the street in Guangzhou, and seven of them were murdered."

"Do you know their names?" I asked, in panic that something might have happened to the Petroluccis or the American businessmen, Josh Wilkins and Tom Sperapani. And of course, I was still wondering about the two Americans killed right outside Yuexiu Park and hoping that it wasn't Jake and Jennifer, the American teachers.

"No names yet. Oh, and I'm sure McHale will appreciate this piece of news. The president of the United States issued a statement expressing grief for the deaths of Americans in China and sympathy for their families, appreciation for the efforts of the government in Beijing to restore order in Guangzhou, and full support for the legitimate government in China at this time of instability in that country."

"Has anyone said when the coup will likely be completely crushed?" I asked.

"It's hard to say. Most of the experts CNN brought on thought it would be over by nightfall. Of course, there are bound to be some holdouts. But in essence, it's over."

"Thanks, Steve, thanks. I'll tell Chuck and Yao what's been happening and what the plan is. Bye."

McHale, who had been listening intently to my side of the phone conversation, was anxious to hear what had happened and what the next arrangements would be, and Yao had perked up too.

"First, the good news," I almost declaimed on the deck, providing my own consecutive translation into Mandarin for Yao's benefit. "We're going to get Yao political asylum in the Philippines. Second, more good news. The coup's been busted by a Beijing airborne drop in the city. Third, the bad news," and I smiled at Yao for effect, "to get Mr. Yao to the Philippines, we are going to have to put him in a dinghy for awhile outside Hong Kong territorial waters so he can be picked up by a yacht. Is that OK, Mr. Yao?"

"Yes, yes, of course it's OK," he said, his whole body sagging with relief.

But I had to remind myself that this was only the beginning of the end. We were still in considerable danger. McHale and I, if caught by the Hong Kong authorities, might be held for awhile but would be released quickly. Yao was still at great risk, not just until we were safely out of Hong Kong waters but until we actually got to Manila. On the ocean between Hong Kong and Manila, he would still be vulnerable. Of course there were pirates, but there were also Chinese naval ships that crossed the sea lanes with increasing frequency.

But for the moment one of the first priorities was for McHale and me to recharge our cell phones, and fortunately there were sockets on board the junk to do that. Then, we needed to slake our thirst with real water, and we downed the contents of the plastic bottles Amanda gave us. She had also not been idle while we were on the phone and had put together ham and tomato rolls which we devoured on deck.

I explained to Sutherland the plans that Trish had laid out for me on the phone, and he took it with remarkable grace. Here we were, turning his pleasant vacation cruise around Hong Kong waters into a risk-fraught adventure in international intrigue. Sure, he and his son had seemed to enjoy the excitement of "rescuing" us off Lantau just now, but that was minor compared with what we were now asking him to do. However, he was taking it all in stride, as though it were just a slight course change.

As we ate, I explained to Yao in detail what was happening, and the relief on his face was evident. I knew I would have to put Lasch in the picture, and, still on Sutherland's phone, I called him up in New York, found him at dinner with, of all people, Clifford Reddaway, and relayed to him the incredible events since our last phone conversation.

"Richard, I'll fly out to the Philippines the day after tomorrow and wait for your arrival. How long will it take you to get there? Five days? Keep me informed as you cross the South China Sea. Katie will know my whereabouts at all times."

Then, to my surprise, Reddaway came on the line and said, "Well, I guess other events have pushed our takeout on Americans overseas off the front burner, Rick. But I think you'll earn a good dinner when you're in town next time by telling us everything that happened. I'll give you back to Burt." As the phone was being handed back to Lasch, I made a mental note to demand that they take me to the Essex House.

"Richard," Burt went on, "you don't know how relieved I am that you're out of that cauldron. I realize it's still risky until you get to Manila, but I think you're through the worst of the danger. Good job," he said, and after exchanging good-byes, we hung up.

While we were still sailing around Lantau, McHale, Yao, and I all felt safe on deck as long as there were no helicopters overhead, but once the junk entered the thickly crowded water lanes of Victoria Harbour, we went below and again stayed away from the portholes. Of course, it would have been much simpler for McHale and me to disembark in Central and simply take a cab back to our respective homes. But we were nervous that we might be spotted and tip the wrong people off to our presence back in town.

At Shau Kei Wan, the marina was a jumble of private water transportation—everything from sampans that could be hired by the hour to more mysterious, larger Chinese-owned boats that Chinese and other foreigners often board for unnautical pleasures. It was much easier for McHale and me to slip off unnoticed in the throng and for Sutherland to take the junk immediately back out to open water. McHale and I didn't have to report to the Aberdeen Marina for another day, but we decided it would be better to get over there right away and be seen around the marina as genuine crew members than to show up just minutes before the yacht was due to leave.

I knew that Trish would have returned to Manila by the time we arrived in the Philippines, and I was desperate to see her before leaving Hong Kong. But McHale warned me about doing anything but returning to my apartment in Deepwater Bay to collect items necessary for the five-day sail and perhaps buying odds and ends at a drugstore. We were still not out of danger, he said, and we should be careful not to do anything that might alert the wrong eyes to the fact that we were back in town. "Trish will have to wait," he said, adding with a smile, "but it will be worth it."

I took a cab to my apartment overlooking the Deepwater Bay Club golf course and the South China Sea. On summer evenings, I loved watching the sun go down from the balcony, but today I knew I was up against time. Not only was there barely a moment to grab the things I would need for the ocean trip, but I also had to scribble a note for my maid Carmencita, telling her of my movements, and glance at the last few days' mail before racing out the door again. In fact, I had told the driver to wait, and the meter was clicking away steadily as I took the long ride back down in the elevator.

"Aberdeen," I said curtly and sat back to read the *South China Morning Post*. There was a reference to Great Master Wu's performance in Yuexiu Park, but of course nothing about the coup, which hadn't unfolded until after the paper had closed for the day.

I suddenly realized that though it might be inadvisable for me to show up in Trish's hotel, it would be very unlikely that anyone would follow her to Aberdeen, and certainly no one would know I was there.

I punched her mobile number on my cell phone, but I only got through to her voice mail. "Trish," I said in the message, "I'll be at the Aberdeen Marina late this morning and afternoon. But I suddenly just realized I don't know your uncle's name or the yacht. I'll look pretty foolish if I show up as a crewman at a yacht whose name and whose skipper I don't even know. Please call when you get this."

Actually, the situation I'd just described could be rather awkward. Granted, there might only be a couple of Manila-ported yachts in Hong Kong at the moment, but I still wished I knew the name of the one I was supposed to be crewing.

Almost immediately my cell phone rang and it was Trish. She had put her phone on vibrate mode during the morning training session and left the room to call me back as soon as she saw from the caller ID that it was me.

"Rick, the yacht is called *Esperanza*, and my uncle's name is Francesco

Miranda. He goes by the Americanized name Frank most of the time. Can I see you at all?"

"Can you?" I repeated her question. "That would be fabulous. I'm headed to the Aberdeen Marina right now. Can't wait to see you."

The cab had reached the bottom of Deepwater Bay Road by now and turned right to Aberdeen. I was grateful that the *Esperanza* hadn't docked at the Royal Hong Kong Yacht Club on the other side of the island, where everybody would be scrutinized. I wondered how McHale was doing, especially now that he had lost so much face because of the U.S. government's refusal to take Yao in. I assumed that Yao himself was safe enough with the Sutherlands.

When the taxi pulled up at the marina, I checked in and asked where the *Esperanza* and Francesco Miranda were. The Chinese clerk behind the counter grinned at me. "*Esperanza* very beautiful boat. Miranda must be very rich man." Well, that was a relief. At least we wouldn't be sailing a tin can across the South China Sea to Manila. "*Esperanza* over at far end of marina," he said. "She going soon, I think."

I walked the two hundred yards to the part of the marina he indicated and indeed saw a beautiful sight: a cruiser that must have been fifty feet at the waterline and probably needed a crew of twelve. I was glad I had sailing experience. I wondered about McHale.

A very fit-looking Filipino, elegantly dressed in white pants and a blue blazer, the traditional uniform of a yachtsman, was inspecting the edge of the forward deck as I approached. I introduced myself and he smiled broadly. "Aha, the Yankee friend of my niece who needs a free trip to Manila," he said with the unmistakable Filipino lilt. "I am Frank. Welcome to the *Esperanza*."

I followed Miranda on board and immediately appreciated what the Hong Kong clerk had said. The yacht was immaculate and luxuriously fitted out with equipment far grander than would normally be needed by grubby sailors. There were at least sixteen berths aboard, a fully equipped bathroom with an actual tub as well as a shower, and no fewer than two toilets. The galley area and the dining quarters were spacious and beautifully appointed.

"Have you ever sailed before, Rick?" Miranda asked.

"Yes. Actually, I love to sail and I've done quite a bit but never on anything as grand as this. I've taken a lot of Hobie cats out and sailed in much smaller cruisers on two-, three-day trips."

"So you know which end of a boat is which?" And he laughed as he put this question to me.

"Of course. And I'm game for more training too."

"Well, we have a very experienced crew, and I suspect you'll only have to do two night watches. So you can hang around the boat the rest of the time. We do need a bit of muscle when we're out of the harbor or about to make our landing, but you'll find it a piece of cake. What about your other passengers?"

"Well, the other American might have sailed some, but I doubt very much if the Chinese man we're going to pick up has any sailing experience at all. I think it will all be very new to him."

"Well, since he will technically be a rescued person, he won't be required to do anything. I just hope for his sake he's not sick as a dog. We can get some pretty rough passages out there, you know."

"If by being sick he avoids being shot, I think he'll consider it a bargain," I said. Miranda looked at me oddly for a moment but didn't question my comment and just went on with his tour of the boat.

McHale showed up about an hour later, by which time the other crew members had begun to trickle in by twos and threes. He looked much fresher than he had on the way out of China and seemed to have recovered his spirits somewhat.

Then, around five in the afternoon, Trish arrived. McHale immediately started in on me, thinking I'd ignored his warning, but I hastened to reassure him that I had gone nowhere except to my apartment and that it was inconceivable that anyone was keeping her under surveillance. He relaxed a little, then relaxed considerably more when I introduced Trish to him and she had a chance to work some of her magic on him.

She was wearing casual linen shorts and a matching yellow blouse, her hair caught up in a ponytail. I'd never seen her in casual wear before. She also had on some wonderful scent, too, which she hadn't worn before, or at least which I hadn't noticed.

We wandered off to the Marina Club coffee shop and found a table away from the other patrons. As we sat at a window table, well-built gweilos—perhaps Australians—were walking in and out of the coffee shop, occasionally casting a furtive glance at Trish. She didn't seem to notice them, but I sure did. The coffee shop décor was standard international marina, with plastic tables and chairs that were probably produced just across the

Hong Kong border in a Shenzhen sweat shop. The lighting was bright and unforgiving, hardly conducive to a romantic rendezvous.

But somehow that didn't matter now. It was obvious that Trish's feelings toward me had undergone a change since it had become clear that my life might actually be in danger. When we walked over from the yacht, she slipped her hand in mine. And now, sitting across from me, her face showed this change with an expression that was neither wary nor deliriously happy, just curiously open. We had already said, "I love you," which put our friendship on a different, deeper level. But I still had a needling feeling in the back of my mind that her newfound religiosity might be a barrier between us. She seemed to read my thoughts before I said anything.

"Rick, I know that we've had a disagreement about some things that are now very important to me," she said. "And I know that you are not where I am as far as how close we can become to each other, physically. But if you honor me where I am, I will honor you too. I don't know how close we will really become, but if you are willing to respect the values I bring to our getting to know each other, I promise I will never preach at you."

I could tell she was nervous because she lacked her usual eloquence, but she struggled on, fiddling with a matchbook from the table as she continued. "Clarissa, I know, would warn me against getting to know you in any romantic way because, she says, you are not a believer. But I really like you and respect you, and I want you to know I don't accept everything Clarissa says as wisdom from the pope."

"Well, as far as the pope is concerned, I don't think she does either," I said, and we both laughed. "All I ask is that you will let me . . . well . . . pay attention to you because that is what I want to do," I said, suddenly emboldened in my words.

"I like that expression, 'pay attention,'" she said, looking up shyly from playing with the matchbook as she said this. "It's a bit like the old-fashioned 'courtship,' and so much more pleasant than 'to date.'"

We ordered a simple afternoon tea and lingered over it, talking for nearly two hours into the evening. We didn't return to the subject of religion or physical closeness again, in part, I think, because we both felt that it was too awkward to say more. But we'd cleared the air about that, and now we were both strangely relaxed, despite the tense two days I had just gone through and the still-risky passage to Manila that lay ahead of Yao, McHale, and me. I couldn't put my finger on it, but in an inexplicable way,

Trish and I seemed to adjust without conscious effort to each other's mood. I had never had this experience with any other woman before, certainly not with Marcia.

We chatted idly, she telling me more about her remarkable upbringing at the hands of her brainy mother and of her very close relationships to all three sisters. It was as if the eccentricity of their childhood had brought them all closer together. We talked about birth order, with Trish being the eldest of her siblings and I the only son of my parents. We talked about books that had profoundly affected us growing up—in Trish's case James Baldwin, the African-American novelist, in my case Dostoyevsky. I couldn't get over the fact that I could talk to Trish about anything and she always seemed to have an intelligent response and insight, even if she was unfamiliar with the subject I brought up.

For her part, she said several times how much she enjoyed talking to a man on the same level. She told me that one of the things that had drawn her to me from the very beginning was that I had shown a genuine interest in what she was interested in, not just in what gave me a buzz. In a sense, we were trying to do in a few short hours what her visit to Hong Kong had originally been intended to do—get to know each other better. But with all that had happened, in another sense, we had already moved far beyond the "getting to know you" stage. We lingered for far longer than it took to drink our cups of tea as the sun set into the horizon of the South China Sea.

Too soon, the evening came to an end. Miranda wanted a crew meeting and sent a fellow crew member—fortunately not McHale—to summon me back to the yacht. I held Trish close but very gently before we parted. I wanted desperately to kiss her, but given what she'd said about physical closeness, I wasn't sure if I should. But strangely, it didn't matter all that much if I kissed her now or later. All I knew was that I just wanted to please her. Something about her manner had touched me in a way I hadn't expected—a new vulnerability, perhaps?—and I couldn't explain it.

We agreed to be in touch by mobile phone during the trip if there was any phone service out on the South China Sea. She told me she would be waiting on the docks at the Manila Yacht Club when I arrived.

Epilogue

The next six days were a blur. At our crew meeting, Miranda introduced McHale and me to all the crew, and then said that when we left port, he would have something special to say about the trip. Presumably, he was taking precautions against any crew member leaking news of our pick-up of Yao before it happened. The following day, after we were well out of the reach of shore, Miranda explained the plan to the crew. Without exception, they responded with enthusiasm, and when the time came, it was easier than I had anticipated.

For one thing, the weather was excellent: flat seas and a brilliant sky specked by small, puffy clouds. The weather, in fact, stayed surprisingly calm for the whole voyage. We picked Yao up on schedule within an hour of departing the Aberdeen Marina. He was in the same rubber dinghy that we'd used to get on the Sutherland's junk, and he said he had been bobbing around in it only for about fifteen minutes. That seemed to me like remarkably good timing in terms of the Sutherlands' dropping him off as well as Miranda timing our voyage to the designated spot. Both vessels were equipped with the newest Global Positioning Satellite systems that are accurate within twenty feet in telling a person his position on the earth's surface, and that no doubt helped considerably.

But poor Yao was seasick for most of his time aboard and spent much of the trip in his berth clutching a red plastic bucket. On the last day, he recovered sufficiently to come on deck and enjoy the fresh air a little. Since McHale and I were the only two members of the crew who spoke any Mandarin, he was left largely alone by the others though I was grateful that all of the men, about equally divided between Filipinos and foreigners (Brits, Australians, and Americans), treated him kindly.

But when we reached Manila and were standing in line to complete landing formalities, I got a real shock. There was a Chinese man waiting at the other side of the immigration barrier, looking decidedly mainland in his badly cut light gray suit among the Filipino men in their well-tailored barongs and batik shirts. He was in his thirties, and he didn't scowl or look hostile, but I froze almost immediately, certain he was from the Chinese embassy. Everything had gone so well so far; was it all going to be for naught? I pointed him out to McHale and Miranda, and we agreed that the three of us, along with four or five other crew members, would surround Yao as we exited the marine terminal just in case anything untoward had been planned for Yao by the embassy.

But it soon became clear that the mainlander intended no harm. He was smiling broadly, and as we hustled Yao out the door, he called out in Mandarin, "Yao Fanmei, Yao Fanmei, you don't have to worry. The government knows why you left China and is very grateful to you. The ambassador would like to see you." The man seemed friendly as he said this, but I didn't trust the Chinese authorities at all. After all, Yao had broken the Chinese law in several ways, not only in leaving China but also in helping foreigners to escape.

But there was another face there that I was thrilled to see—Trish. True to her word, she was waiting for me at the other side of immigration. I thought I'd never seen a more lovely sight in my life. She was in a short gauzy sheath of lemony yellow, and her face lit up in a huge smile when she caught sight of me. I couldn't get through the crowd fast enough to get to her. Dropping my bag, I took her in my arms, and when she reached around to embrace me as tightly as I was holding her, I wanted the moment never to end.

But almost immediately, her uncle was standing by our side, and she turned and gave him a big hug too. She was obviously one of Miranda's favorites, and he now teased, "Well, let me see now, do I approve of your new boyfriend? You know, I'd take him on as crew anytime." And he laughed loudly at the idea. Trish grinned and joined the group of Yao, McHale, and Miranda as we got into cars to leave the port.

Miranda continued to take care of us, putting us up in a large, comfortable guest house he owned in Manila's Forbes Park residential area. The house was as luxurious as the yacht had been. There were three guest rooms, and each was appointed like a hotel's presidential suite, with en-suite bathroom and Jacuzzi, and a king-size bed with multiple throw pillows. There were maids and houseboys galore, and it was obvious we would be well taken care of.

But I was concerned about Yao's security. If Chinese intelligence knew he had been on the yacht, they would surely know where to find him in Manila. Miranda had thought of this, too, and had hired a private security firm to guard the house. Yao had been admitted smoothly enough at the Manila marina by the Philippine port authorities, but because he carried no passport and anyway was considered a person of refugee status, he clearly could not go anywhere until we could be sure of his security in the country.

Lasch was in town, but had not been at dockside when we arrived. His assistant Katie reached me on my cell phone to tell me he had been summoned to talks with the Filipino foreign minister. Lasch showed up about an hour after we were comfortably settled into Miranda's guest house with some surprising news for Yao.

"Richard, can you please translate for Mr. Yao what the Philippine foreign minister told me this afternoon," Lasch said. "They are fully prepared to give him political asylum, and he can stay in the country as long as he wants. But the Foreign Ministry has heard from the Chinese ambassador that Mr. Yao is not regarded as a traitor for having left China without permission and will in fact be welcomed as a national hero if he returns. Could you translate all that?"

I did so, and Yao listened intently. Now it was his turn to ask questions of Lasch. "How do I know," he said, "that this is not just a trick to get me home where they will execute me? How does the Philippine Foreign Ministry know that the Chinese ambassador is telling the truth?"

"They don't," Lasch said after I had finished translating back into English for Yao. "But the Philippine foreign minister said that you could meet with the ambassador on Philippine government property whenever you want, with Filipino guards, so that you can make your own determination whether this offer is reliable or not."

"I see," said Yao. "May I think about it overnight?"

"Of course. Oh and, Richard, I have an offer I would like to make to you that you can also think about for a day or so but not any longer, mind you, because I have to get back to New York. The bureau chief's job in Jerusalem has just opened up. I think you've always wanted a bureau in a hot spot though, frankly, Hong Kong hasn't exactly been a rest home."

Jerusalem! My heart leapt. I don't know why but I had wanted that bureau more than anything else in *Epoch*'s system from the moment I was hired as a correspondent.

Trish heard all this and seemed to take Lasch's statement about the Jerusalem bureau with special interest. On the trip I had been too busy learning the ropes of the yacht, taking overnight watches, and talking to both Yao and McHale to give much conscious thought to her though she occupied a place in my mind and my heart framed forever by the conversation we had lingered over in Aberdeen.

I did not know what would become of us; I did not know whether the friendship, the mutual respect and admiration, and the tender concern that had all sprung into being in the course of the frenetic two days in Guangzhou and making my escape would translate into something more than an ephemeral moment, a sort of summer-camp romance. I needed to talk to her to see where she was now that Clarissa, and perhaps Clarissa's brand of religion, had taken a deep hold on the way she looked at life.

Lasch and McHale had decided to have dinner alone to catch up, and I was quite happy to let them go. There would be plenty of time for other dinners with Lasch. Already, the public affairs officer at the U.S. embassy in Manila was trying to line us up for dinners with the ambassador and senior political officers. The heads of the political sections at the Guangzhou and the Hong Kong consulates-general had flown out to meet me, and even Michael Young had come. I was in the position, strange to a hack, of being the center of media and diplomatic attention rather than the fly on the wall, a location I had always preferred.

I had already given Harry Wok's *Asian Reflections* a long exclusive phone interview about the Guangzhou coup. After all, it had been Harry who was responsible for hooking me up with Tung Chi-keung. He was entirely to "blame" for my harrowing insider's view of the entire coup attempt. His fiancé, Xialin, true to her parting words to me, said she was planning a hero's celebration for me when I got back to Hong Kong.

Now, during a brief lull in all the commotion, I took Trish by the hand and drew her away. We found a small flower garden behind the house, lush with well-cultivated plants, bushes, and trees. Manila's merciless afternoon sun had a difficult time penetrating the jungle-like profusion, and it was surprisingly cool and quiet except for a rich symphony of bird calls. I hadn't known there was a place like this within the boundaries of greater Metro Manila.

Sitting on a low stone bench, we faced each other gently, I still holding her left hand with my right.

"Trish," I said. "Rick," she said, at almost exactly the same moment. We burst out laughing and that seemed to cut the awkwardness. "You go first," I said.

"Well, that's a good sign. Seems we're on the same wave length. All I wanted to say was, I am so glad you are safe, that you got out of China. In so many ways, the trip to visit you in Hong Kong wasn't what I had expected. I have to tell you that I am in some ways a different person since meeting Clarissa, but in some ways I'm still the same person you met at that reception here in Manila two months ago. When we had that misunderstanding in Hong Kong, I realized later that you didn't mean anything by it. You just hadn't had time to hear me out." She stopped and looked at me with the most tender expression I had ever seen on a woman's face.

"Trish, I'm sorry again about that night at the Captain's Bar. I was just doing what seemed right, what felt right, at the time. It was the only way I knew to try to show you how I felt about you. And you know that that's the way it is usually done in the world today. But I understand that some things changed for you after you met Clarissa. I do not know what part of Clarissa's faith you are now sharing, but I am willing to listen. I may not understand everything, and, I have to be honest, I may not agree with everything. But I just want you to know that I really like you." I paused, swallowed hard. "No, I love you."

Neither one of us said anything for a long time. There were thoughts that we still couldn't—didn't know how to—articulate, but there was no tension, no embarrassment in the silence. It was OK to just be with each other. Then, without either of us saying a word, we leaned toward each other, and I kissed her gently but lengthily. Then she spoke again. "And I love you, too, Rick."

The next day, Yao and I were both lost in our separate thoughts all morning. Trish had had to go back to work and was not around. I found myself almost floating on an intoxication of affection, of longing, and, yes, of respect for her. But by noon, when I had to leave for a press conference on the Guangzhou coup and our escape—the hack turned into the target of other hacks—Yao had decided he would go to meet with the Chinese ambassador. We said our good-byes at the front door of the guest house, and he pumped my hand as though he would never see me again.

"Thank you, Ai Erdun, thank you. Mr. McHale did his best to bring me to the U.S. on an asylum ticket, but you actually succeeded in bringing me safely to Manila. And now, thanks to the time Beijing has had to reflect on things, I am getting the chance to return to my motherland. I know that you think it is a dictatorial and brutal regime, but it is the regime of my homeland, and I think at some point in the future, it will change. Thank you, Ai Erdun, again, thank you."

"It's been both a privilege and an honor to know you, Yao," I replied. "I respect your decision to return to China though it isn't what I would do. But if you do go back and if you later have a chance to travel outside of China again, in a normal way"—Yao grinned at this—"come and be my guest in Jerusalem."

A car and driver had arrived to take me to the Manila Hotel, where the press conference, expected to draw a huge crowd, was to be held. As the driver closed the passenger door behind me, I saw Yao saying something in Chinese that I couldn't quite hear. I rolled down the window and asked him to speak louder. But when he repeated himself, it was in clear though heavily accented English. As the limousine began to pull away, he said, "Next year in Jerusalem."

Author's Notes

Q*i* is a work of fiction but not a figment of my imagination. Many of the events, scenes, and characters are based on or inspired by real events, places, and people. Some readers may find it interesting to know which elements of *Qi* are factually based.

My experience with Qi and Qigong goes back to a reporting visit to China in 1993, and a meeting with some Chinese scholars who had been overseas in Europe and the United States. One of those present was a Qigong adept who first acquainted me with it. My interest piqued; I read several books and also talked to Chinese and foreigners who had experienced Qigong from the outside. From them come the descriptions of the manifestations of "external Qi" and reports of Qigong gaining popularity among the Chinese military. The experience of *Epoch* foreign editor Burton Lasch in encountering a New York cab driver who had received paranormal weapons training while in the Soviet army is an experience I myself had in the 1980s.

Chen Yuxian, the follower of Great Master Wu who was seated next to Richard Ireton at the Chinese banquet, is modeled on the Qigong adept I met in Beijing in 1993. The description of the Qigong show in chapter 3 is identical to a demonstration I personally witnessed of monks from the Shaolin Temple displaying their Qigong skills in a Hong Kong auditorium in 2000 or 2001. The conversation with the American English teachers in chapter 7, where they reported feeling "opposition" when they prayed after the visit of a Qigong group to their school, is based on accounts related to me by several Christian missionaries working in China about sensing "spiritual opposition" whenever Qigong practitioners are in the vicinity.

From Christian missionaries and in my own reporting for one of my nonfiction works, *Jesus in Beijing: How Christianity Is Transforming China and Changing the Global Balance of Power,* I can attest to the existence of safe houses in Guangzhou operated by Chinese Christians for pastors and teachers from house church communities in the Chinese countryside as described in chapters 9 and 10.

My own reporting, this time in the Philippines in the 1970s, is also the source of the accounts of the faith healing phenomenon among Catholics in the Philippines, as told in chapters 2 and 5.

Almost all the well-known places in Hong Kong and Guangzhou and references to places in Beijing that appear in *Qi* are actual places. For instance, the descriptions of Hong Kong's Intercontinental, Mandarin, and Peninsula hotels and its old and new airports, of Guangzhou's two train stations and Shamian and Er Sha islands, and also of Beijing's Zhongnanhai leadership compound and Beijing (Peking) University's Weiming Lake, are all true and accurate.

The Golden Panda Hotel is a fictitious name, but it is loosely modeled on the White Swan Hotel in Guangzhou. It is a well-known and popular landmark of the city and is indeed right next door to the U.S. consulate that handles all the baby adoptions in China. The Ming Garden Restaurant is loosely modeled on a real Er Sha Island restaurant, every bit as ostentatious as the Ming Garden, called the New Lychee, at which I dined in 2000.

Details such as the dishes at the banquet hosted by Triad boss Tung Chi-keung were gleaned from actual menus from some of Hong Kong and Guangzhou's top restaurants and from local contacts. There are many variations of the three penis soup served in restaurants in South China and Taiwan. The most popular animals are the dog, bull, tiger, deer, ram, and donkey.

The details about the CJ750 Changjiang motorcycle and sidecar came from sources in Beijing who know of American owners of these vintage bikes and from Web sites such as http://www.changjiangunlimited.com/Beijing2004.htm that reflect a large community of Chinese and foreign owners of these classic motorcycles. I've taken some liberty in placing one of these bikes in Guangzhou although locals there say they are not commonly seen.

As for the characters, *Epoch*'s foreign editor Burton Lasch is very loosely modeled on *Time Magazine*'s chief of correspondents Murray J. Gart, to whom this novel is dedicated. Other characters connected to *Epoch* are loosely based on personalities who worked for *Time* in the 1970s.

The character of Father Radim Malek in chapter 5 is loosely modeled on an outstanding Jesuit China-watcher resident in Hong Kong for most of the second half of the twentieth century. Father Laszlo Ladany (1914–1990) founded *China News Analysis* in 1953 and relinquished editorial control of it only in 1980. He was one of the outstanding minds observing China during the 1960s and 1970s, and an infallibly gracious human being.

Hong Kong newspaper publisher Harry Wok in chapter 6 is inspired by (and not modeled on) the brilliant and bold journalistic entrepreneur Jimmy Lai, whose *Apple Daily* newspaper, raucously independent of political correctness, was courageously founded by him in 1996, only months before the resumption by China of sovereignty over Hong Kong.

Finally, an excellent account of the Triads' historical connection with secret societies can be found in Martin Booth's *The Dragon Syndicates* (London: Carroll and Graf, 2001).

David Aikman, Virginia, June 2005